# RALPH WALDO EMERSON

**Ralph Waldo Emerson.**
Reproduced from the Collections of the Library of Congress.

# RALPH WALDO EMERSON

## Preacher and Lecturer

Lloyd Rohler

Foreword by Bernard K. Duffy

Great American Orators, Number 21
*Bernard K. Duffy and Halford R. Ryan,*
*Series Advisers*

**GREENWOOD PRESS**
Westport, Connecticut • London

**Library of Congress Cataloging-in-Publication Data**

Rohler, Lloyd Earl.
Ralph Waldo Emerson : preacher and lecturer / Lioyd Rohler ; foreword by Bernard K. Duffy.
p. cm.—(Great American orators, ISSN 0898–8277 ; no. 21)
Includes bibliographical references (p. ) and index.
ISBN 0–313–26328–0 (alk. paper)
1. Emerson, Ralph Waldo, 1803–1882—Knowledge and learning. 2. Speeches, addresses, etc., American—History and criticism. 3. Sermons, American—History and criticism. 4. Speeches, addresses, etc., American. 5. Sermons, American. I. Title. II. Series.
PS1638.R55 1995
815′.3—dc20 95–2105

British Library Cataloguing in Publication Data is available.



Library of Congress Catalog Card Number: 95–2105
ISBN: 0–313–26328–0
ISSN: 0898–8277

First published in 1995

Greenwood Press, 88 Post Road West, Westport, CT 06881
An imprint of Greenwood Publishing Group, Inc.

Printed in the United States of America

The paper used in this book complies with the Permanent Paper Standard issued by the National Information Standards Organization (Z39.48–1984).

10 9 8 7 6 5 4 3 2 1

## Copyright Acknowledgments

The author and publisher gratefully acknowledge the following for permission to quote from and/or publish Emerson's texts:

Leslie A. Morris, Curator of Manuscripts at the Houghton Library, for her help in obtaining permission from the Ralph Waldo Emerson Memorial Associaton for the publication of the following texts: Sermon number 1, "Pray Without Ceasing"; Sermon number 39, "Summer"; Sermon number 164, "The Genuine Man"; "The American Scholar"; "The Young American"; the lecture "Manners" first given in 1837; the lecture "Eloquence" first given in 1847; Speech of Welcome at Manchester, England, Nov. 18, 1845; "Robert Burns"; and "The Fugitive Slave Law," March 7, 1854. Reprinted by permission of the Ralph Waldo Emerson Memorial Association and of Houghton Library, Harvard University.

Reprinted from *The Complete Sermons of Ralph Waldo Emerson, Volume 1,* edited by Albert J. von Frank, with an Introduction by David M. Robinson, by permission of the University of Missouri Press. Copyright © 1989 by the Curators of the University of Missouri.

Reprinted from *The Complete Sermons of Ralph Waldo Emerson, Volume 4,* edited by Wesley T. Mott; Albert J. von Frank, chief editor, by permission of the University of Missouri Press. Copyright © 1992 by the Curators of the University of Missouri.

Reprinted by permission of the publishers from *The Collected Works of Ralph Waldo Emerson,* edited by Alfred R. Ferguson and Jean Ferguson Carr, Cambridge, Mass.: The Belknap Press of Harvard University Press, Copyright © 1971 by the President and Fellows of Harvard College.

Reprinted by permission of the publishers from *The Early Lectures of Ralph Waldo Emerson,* edited by Stephen E. Whicher, Robert E. Spiller, and Wallace E. Williams, Cambridge, Mass.: The Belknap Press of Harvard University Press, Copyright © 1959, 1964, 1972 by the President and Fellows of Harvard College.

Reprinted by permission of the publishers from *The Journals and Miscellaneous Notebooks of Ralph Waldo Emerson,* edited by William H. Gilman et al., Cambridge, Mass.: The Belknap Press of Harvard University Press, Copyright © 1960, 1961, 1963, 1964, 1965, 1966, 1969, 1970, 1971, 1973, 1975, 1976, 1977, 1978, 1982 by the President and Fellows of Harvard College.

Reprinted by permission of the publishers from *The Letters of Ralph Waldo Emerson* (Vols. 1-6) edited by Ralph L. Rusk. Copyright © 1939 by Columbia University Press.

## Acknowledgments

I gratefully acknowledge the assistance of my editors, Bernard K. Duffy and Mildred Vasan, in the preparation of this book. I thank Sandra Stowe and Patsy Odam for typing portions of the manuscript. I thank Carolyn Simmons, Dean of the College of Arts and Sciences at UNC-Wilmington, for providing me with a summer grant that aided in the completion of the work.

I could not have finished this project without the aid of my wife, Diana, whose support and encouragement sustained me.

This book is dedicated to my wife, Diana.

# Contents

# Series Foreword

The idea for a series of books on great American orators grew out of the recognition that there is a paucity of book-length studies on individual orators and their speeches. Apart from a few notable exceptions, the study of American public address has been pursued in scores of articles published in professional journals. Yet, no matter how insightful their intellectual forebears, each generation of rhetorical critics must reexamine its universe of discourse, expand the compass of its researches, and redefine its purpose and methods. To avoid intellectual torpor, scholars and students cannot be content simply to see through the eyes of those who have gone before them. As helpful as article-length studies have been, none has or can provide a complete analysis of a speaker's rhetoric. Book-length studies, such as those in this series, will help fill the void that has existed in the study of American public address. In books, more than in articles, the critic can explicate a speaker's persuasive discourse that ranges over politics and history, theology and sociology, communication and law. The comprehensive research and sustained reflection that books require will undoubtedly yield telling examinations and enduring insights for the nation's most important voices.

This series chronicles the role of public discourse in the United States. American speakers shaped the destiny of the colonies, the young republic, and the mature nation. During each state of the intellectual, political, and religious development of the United States, great orators, standing at the rostrum, on the stump, and in the pulpit, persuaded their audiences with word and gesture. Usually striving for the noble, sometimes achieving the base, they urged their fellow citizens toward a more perfect Union.

Each book is organized to meet the needs of scholars and students who would evaluate the effects of American public address. Previously, if one desired to assess the impact of a speaker or a speech upon history, the path was, at best, not well marked and at worst, littered with obstacles. To be sure, one might turn to biographies to learn about an orator, but for the public address scholar these sources often prove unhelpful. Rhetorical topics, such as speech invention, disposition, style, delivery, and persuasive effect, are often treated in passing, if at all. Authoritative speech texts are often difficult to locate and the problem of textual accuracy is frequently encountered. This is especially true for early figures, or for those whose persuasive role, though significant, was secondary to other leading lights of the age.

Part I is a critical analysis of the orator and his or her speeches. Within the format of a case study, one may expect considerable latitude. For instance, in a given chapter an author might explicate a single speech or a group of related speeches, or examine orations that comprise a genre of rhetoric such as forensic speaking. but the critic's focus remains on the rhetorical considerations of speaker and speech, purpose and effect.

Part II contains the texts of the important addresses that are discussed in the critical analysis that precedes it. To the extent possible, each author has endeavored to collect definitive speech texts, which have often been found through original research in historical materials. In a few instances, because of the extreme length of a speech, texts have been edited, but the authors have carefully deleted material that is least important to the speech, and these deletions have been held to a minimum.

Each book contains a chronology of major speeches that serves several purposes. Pragmatically, it lists all of the orator's know addresses. Places and dates of the speeches are also given, although this information is sometimes difficult to determine precisely. But in a wider sense, the chronology attests to the scope of rhetoric in the United States. Certainly in quantity, if not always in quality, Americans are historically talkers and listeners.

Because of the disparate nature of the speakers examined in the series, there is some latitude in the nature of bibliographical materials that have been included in each book. But in every instance, authors have carefully described historical collections, and have gathered primary and secondary sources that bear on the speaker and the oratory. By combining in each book critical chapters with bibliographical materials and speech texts, this series notes that textual and research sources are interwoven in the act of rhetorical criticism.

May the books in this series serve as a fitting memorial to the nation's greatest orators as students and scholars study anew the history and criticism of American public address.

*Bernard K. Duffy*
*Halford R. Ryan*

# Foreword

Although one thinks of Emerson first for his acclaimed lectures delivered in later life, Professor Rohler demonstrates that to understand the rhetorical force of lectures such as "The American Scholar," one must first come to grips with Emerson's sermons, a part of his canon that has received far less attention. Emerson's ability to edify his audiences grew naturally from his ability to inspire his congregations. He did not change from preacher to lecturer by wraping himself in a cocoon and emerging in a wholly new form. His metamorphosis was not so complete as some scholars have claimed. Emerson the preacher, carefully schooled in homiletics, was always discernible in Emerson the lecturer.

Rohler also argues that Emerson has been unfairly criticized for lacking the polished and dramatic delivery of the greatesy orators of his day. He counters this claim with substantial historical evidence that Emerson was highly regarded for his ability as a speaker. Those who thought otherwise, including Midwestern newspaper editors, were often influenced by political considerations, such as Emerson's support for abolition. It would be tempting to say that Emerson was to Daniel Webster what Isocrates was to Demosthenes, more the philosopher and stylist than the spellbinder, but Emerson, unlike Isocrates, enjoyed and excelled at public performance. Finally, Rohler reminds us that it is not merely by Emerson's lectures that we should remember him but also by his extremely effective ceremonial oratory.

Despite the need to appreciate the full range of Emerson's prodigious rhetorical output it is undeniable that his lectures were most important, if only because of their enduring effects upon the culture. Emerson established the importance of the lecture as an instrument of popular education in America, no less than the medium of television has popularized such forms as the documentary or the interview. If one were to search television programming for parallels to Emerson's contributions through the medium of the platform lecture, one might think of the various series narrated by Jacob Bronowski,

Kenneth Clark or Bill Moyers. There were doubtless those in Emerson's day who complained that the lecture was an unnecessary intervention between the student and the text, as today educators complain that television spoon feeds a public still seeking a palatable education. Emerson was to accessible public education and "life-long learning" what someone like mythologist Joseph Campbell or historian Daniel J. Boorstin have been within the last decade.

When Rohler chose Albert Brisbane and American Fourierism as his dissertation topic in the American Studies program at Indiana University, he wrote a chapter on Brook Farm, a refuge for many of Emerson's friends. Like so many projects, the present book on Emerson, was begun almost by accident, and waited for many years before the threads of ideas presented as conference papers were carefully woven together into the theme of the present book. Currently the Editor of the *Journal of Communication and Religion*, Rohler's research focuses on how religious values inform and transform the larger culture. Emerson would certainly approve.

It is convenient to see Emerson as an icon and thereby to make him a somewhat bloodless character separated from a vibrant social context. Nietzsche has been described as standing at the precipice between traditional and modern culture. Much the same might be said of Emerson. Both responded intellectually and emotionally to the wrenching changes brought by science and technology in the last half of the nineteenth century. An explosion of scientific knowledge, including Darwinism; as well as rapid urbanization and industrialization and the steady weakening of traditional religion in daily life made this a socially and intellectually turbulent era. Nietzsche glibly asserted that God was dead and offered an existential philosophy to supplant religious belief, while Emerson offered the prescription of self culture and liberal loses of traditional Christian ethics. Both invited the individual to take responsibility for creating the ethical moorings and intellectual vitality needed in the new age.

Oratory of the kind Emerson was a master no longer captures the attention of the general public. Replacing it are technologies of communication that are in relative terms no more resplendent and much less sublime than was oratory in the last century. Professor Rohler contributes to our understanding of how the "winged words" of one of the nation's most influential orators shaped the American character. If Emerson has not received the attention he deserves from scholars of American public address, this book should correct that problem.

Truly great writers and speakers make rhetorical critics apprehensive about their own relationships with the literary muse. Professor Rohler speaks of the great light of nineteenth century American religious and ethical thought in a contemporary voice and a supple style well suited to his authoritative, yet sensitive, exposition. This book is a pleasure to read and, in addition to its substantive contribution, embodies the virtues of careful scholarship and lucid writing. Of this also, Emerson would heartily approve.

*Bernard K. Duffy*

# Preface

Although previous biographers and critics of Emerson have recognized the important role that preaching and lecturing played in his intellectual development, more attention has been paid to the activity of speaking and little to what he actually said. The editing and publication of his early lectures, his journals, and the publication of the complete sermon texts have provided scholars with the reliable texts that are so essential for any assessment of Emerson's achievement in this activity. The critical commonplace that the lectures served as a first draft for the *Essays* can now be seen as the hasty generalization that it is, and the sermons are finally receiving the attention that they deserve. This book is a contribution to the on going investigation of Emerson as a public speaker in pulpit and lecture platform. It will serve the needs of both scholars and students by providing bibliographic references, and criticism of important texts.

A study of Ralph Waldo Emerson certainly belongs in any series devoted to "Great American Orators" but the selection of speeches to reprint presents certain problems. The works of Emerson have not by any means been forgotten or allowed to go out of print. Indeed, a minor Emerson industry has published almost everything he ever wrote from his notebooks, to his sermons, lectures, and essays. Given such a richness of materials to choose from, I have had to make difficult choices in deciding what speeches to reprint in this book. I have reprinted three sermons even though a complete edition of the sermons was recently published on the grounds that this expensive scholarly edition may not be readily available in most undergraduate libraries. Two of his lectures are reprinted: "Manners" from his early lectures and "Eloquence" from a later series. Both are good examples of Emerson's achievement in the lecture format.

I have reprinted "The American Scholar Address," which is readily available in most collections of Emerson's writings, on the basis that it is, in Bliss Perry's words, "Emerson's most famous speech" and is central to any understanding of his thought and his impact on American culture. I have reprinted one other lecture, "The Young American" from this period because it is representative of Emerson's idealistic and optimistic attitude toward the pressing social and political problems of the day. I have also reprinted an example of his ceremonial speaking and a rare example of his political speaking. These speeches, representing the major genres, should provide a comprehensive view of Emerson's art as a public speaker.

My purpose in this study is to focus on Emerson as a speaker and for that reason I focus on the early Emerson as a minister and lecturer, rather than the later essayist. The voice and presence are gone and can never be recaptured. What remains are the texts and first hand observations and later recollections of Emerson preaching and lecturing. These materials have been used to provide context for his speeches, and to account for the powerful effect that Emerson had on his audiences. A full scale description of the audience and the occasion for each speech was not attempted. Given that most of the lectures were repeated many times to differing audiences, a generic description of the kinds of audiences that Emerson addressed seemed more useful. Also, some addresses such as "The American Scholar" have long since transcended the original purpose and audience for the speech and become defining texts absorbed into the canon of American thought. In analyzing Emerson's appeal, I have found it useful to return to the texts for a close analysis of his ideas and his techniques. The thesis of this study is that a continuity exists between Emerson's sermons and his lectures that can be found in his adaptation of sermonic form and homiletic techniques to the opportunities opened to him on the lecture platform. For this reason, I have identified the strategies in the written texts that contributed to their favorable reception by the audience.

Chapter One, "Self-Reliant Man," is a brief sketch of Emerson's life focusing on important events that influenced his development as a speaker. Chapter Two, "Preacher," examines Emerson's achievement in the pulpit by placing him in the tradition of New England Preaching. Particular attention is given in this chapter to the development of the sermon as an art form by Unitarian ministers and the adaptation of the traditional sermonic form to the needs of an inspirational address. Chapter Three, "The Rising Sun," examines Emerson achievement as a lecturer from a developmental perspective. The chapter stresses the continuity between Emerson's sermons and the early lectures and also demonstrates his growth as a lecturer and his development of a new form of lecture-essay. Chapter Four is a close reading of "The American Scholar Address" and "The Young American." Chapter Five examines Emerson's ceremonial and political speaking. The concluding chapter uses Emerson's ideas about eloquence as a means for evaluating his achievement as a preacher and lecturer. The last part of the book contains a selective bibliography of books and articles on Emerson's career as a public speaker. It is by no means definitive. The sheer quantity of materials published about

Emerson in the past few years mandate a selective approach. Included in this section is a selective chronology of Emerson's major speeches.

References to Emerson's own writings are cited within the main text. For example, a reference to EL, II, 100, would be *The Early Lectures*, vol. II, page 100. The following standard abbreviations are used:

CW *The Collected Works of Ralph Waldo Emerson*, Edited by Robert E. Spiller and Alfred R. Ferguson; vol. I: *Nature. Addresses. and Lectures.* Cambridge, Mass.: Harvard University Press, 1971.

Vol. 2. *Essays. First Series.* Edited by Joseph Slater, Cambridge, Mass.: Harvard University Press, 1979.

Vol. 3. *Essays. Second Series.* Edited by Joseph Slater, Cambridge, Mass.: Harvard University Press, 1983.

Vol. 4. *Representative Men.* Edited by Joseph Slater, and Wallace E. Williams, Cambridge, Mass.: Harvard University Press, 1987.

CS *The Complete Sermons of Ralph Waldo Emerson*, Edited by Albert J. von Frank, et. al. 4 vols., Columbia, Mo.: University of Missouri Press., 1989.

W *The Complete Works of Ralph Waldo Emerson.* With a Biographical Introduction and Notes, by Edward Waldo Emerson, Centenary Edition. Boston and New York: Houghton Mifflin Co., 1903-1904. 12 vols.

EL *The Early Lectures of Ralph Waldo Emerson*, Edited by Stephen E. Whicher, Robert E. Spiller, and Wallace E. Williams, 3 vols., Cambridge, Mass.: Harvard University Press, 1959, 1964, 1972.

JMN *The Journals and Miscellaneous Notebooks of Ralph Waldo Emerson.* Edited by William H. Gilman, et al. 16 vols., Cambridge, Mass.: Harvard University Press, 1960-1982.

L *The Letters of Ralph Waldo Emerson*, Edited by Ralph L. Rusk, 6 vols., New York: Columbia University Press, 1939.

YES *Young Emerson Speaks.* Edited by Arthur C. McGiffert, Jr. Boston: Houghton Mifflin Co., 1938.

# Part I

# CRITICAL ANALYSIS

# 1

# Self-Reliant Man

Emerson is a biographer's nightmare. His early life shows few signs of future greatness; in his maturity he blazes brightly for a few years, before gradually declining into senility. His life is outwardly uneventful, but his journal records an intense inner struggle that is difficult to dramatize. In Emerson we confront that peculiar combination of idealism and Yankee shrewdness that seems to run through the American character. The polarities of his mind constantly shift between experience and the ideal. Just when we think we have pinned him down, he slips away from us and shows us another way to see the world. His career as a lecturer is similarly filled with contradictions. A reserved, private individual, he seemed to thrive in contact with the frank, open manners of Midwestern farmers. An idealist, he found his greatest success among the hustling business class of booster cities on the make. A mediocre student, he gave the most famous literary oration in American history. Never a dynamic speaker, nor an entertainer, he enjoyed success on the lecture platform for over forty years. The formative influences of his career are in the family, the changing social conditions of Jacksonian America, and the impact of Romanticism on the Puritan-influenced culture of New England. [1]

Given that a family influences and molds the aspirations of a child, Emerson's family traditions pointed young Waldo toward a career as a minister. Born May 25, 1803, the son of the Reverend William Emerson and Ruth Haskins Emerson, Ralph Waldo Emerson's ancestors included eight ministers on both sides of the family since their arrival in the American colonies. The family was not wealthy, but respectable. Young Emerson went to the Boston Latin School and Harvard, where he was an undistinguished student unlike his older brothers whose academic records brought honor to the family. [2]

Following graduation, he taught school with his brother William for two years while contemplating a future vocation. His mediocre academic record promised little success as a university professor. Ministry and the law were the two professions traditionally open to men of Emerson's class who wanted to pursue a scholarly life outside the university. Emerson showed little aptitude for the legal intricacies of contracts and torts or courtroom confrontations. It seemed natural that a child whose whole life was shaped by the pastoral example of his father would eventually become a minister.

In February 1825 he formally enrolled in the Theological School at Harvard University. By October of the next year he presented his first sermon to the Middlesex Association and gained his license to preach.[3] Speaking in the pulpit presented no terrors to the young Emerson, for he had been training for this activity for most of his life. Emerson's training in public speaking reflected the classical precepts of observing good models, learning sound principles, and practicing regularly. He grew up in a society that valued good public speaking and he listened to his father and other ministers in the pulpit on a regular basis. At the Boston Latin School, he and the other pupils practiced public speaking every Saturday. At Harvard, he had weekly declamation exercises and participated in a club devoted to writing and speaking. He read Hugh Blair's *Rhetoric*, listened to the lectures of Edward T. Channing, the Boylston Professor of Rhetoric and Oratory, and memorized passages from Edward Everett's speeches.[4]

After studying theology at Harvard, Emerson was ordained and began his ministry at the historic Second Church in Boston where the Mathers had preached. He served the church for over three years and preached almost 200 sermons before resigning his ministry on October 28, 1832. During his years as pastor of the Second Church, he married Ellen Tucker, whose untimely death from tuberculosis greatly affected him. In poor health himself, and at loose ends following his resignation, Emerson used a small legacy from her estate to travel to Europe where he met Thomas Carlyle and other literary figures.[5]

The meeting with Thomas Carlyle on August 25, 1833, brought Emerson face to face with a sympathetic soul who had read widely in the German Idealism that was beginning to influence the younger generation in England and the United States. Although Emerson was familiar with the German philosophy through the intermediary sources of Wordsworth and Coleridge, his discussions with Carlyle brought him in direct contact with a major literary thinker who was conversant with the writings of Fichte, Schelling, and Hegel.[6]

Returning to the United States in October 1833, Emerson faced again the vexing problem of finding a vocation. His brother Charles suggested that Waldo be engaged for a series of lectures on natural history for the Boston Society for the Diffusion of Useful Knowledge. This organization and many more like it arose to meet the need for public education and were loosely organized into a lecture circuit. Emerson changed his pulpit for a lecture platform and created a new career for himself (L, 1, 397).

When Emerson began lecturing the lyceum movement was in its infancy. Its founder, Josiah Holbrook, saw the lyceum as a means to provide instruction and promote useful knowledge by drawing on the resources within the community. Individuals who had special expertise would be given an opportunity to share their knowledge with those who desired to learn. The lyceum reflected the democratic spirit of the Jacksonian era with its emphasis upon equal opportunity and its celebration of the ability of the common man. In an age when few attended let alone graduated from college, and the standards for practicing law and medicine were virtually undefined, the idea that individuals with special interests or talents could instruct others seemed reasonable. Unfortunately, in practice, the officers of the lyceum discovered the old truism that a prophet is without honor in his own country. Homegrown talent was too familiar to command the excitement and interest of the neighbors. Gradually, the focus of the lyceum changed from mutual education to providing a platform for visiting lecturers, many of whom provided more entertainment than instruction.[7]

When Emerson gave the first lectures on natural history he was a young apprentice following the example of other lecturers who popularized ideas for their audiences. Although an experienced speaker, he was new to the lyceum and lacked confidence in his ability to hold an audience with his own thoughts. These early lectures were all given under the sponsorship of organizations such as the Boston Mechanics Institution whose audiences expected a popular or at least interesting treatment of a vaguely educational subject. Although a relatively new phenomenon, the lyceum had already developed a formula for success. As a beginner without a reputation or a following, Emerson, at first, had to conform to the formula to succeed (EL, 1, xii- xxi).

While earning an income and a reputation lecturing around Boston in the next few years, Emerson read widely in philosophy, corresponded with Carlyle, and meditated on the relationship of man to the natural world. The result was the publication of his first book, *Nature*, in September 1836, which began an unusually productive period in his life. In the next few years he gave the major addresses, "American Scholar" in 1837 and the "Divinity School" in 1838, founded and edited *The Dial*, and published his first and second series of *Essays* and his first book of *Poems*.[8]

On October 5, 1847 Emerson left Boston on the *Washington Irving* and arrived in Liverpool on October 22, giving him a little over 10 days to rest before beginning a lecture tour of Great Britain at Manchester on November 2. This was Emerson's second visit to England but his first lecture tour. When he toured England in 1833, he met a several famous literary men including Wordsworth, Coleridge, and Carlyle. He also became an acquaintance of a young Scotsman, Alexander Ireland, who in later life became one of the leading spirits of adult education in Manchester and who in 1846 wrote to Emerson inviting him to return to England and give a series of public lectures.

Emerson was not unknown to the English public. His *Essays, First Series* and *Essays, Second Series* had both been published in England with introductions by Carlyle and widely reviewed in the press. The audience to whom Emerson spoke was familiar to him for the "Mechanics Institutions" that sponsored his lectures in England inspired the lyceum movement in the United States and followed a similar path of development.[9]

His English lecture tour confirmed Emerson's growing reputation as an intellectual, brought him into personal contact with some of the leading literary personalities in England, and rekindled his friendship with Carlyle. When he returned to the United States, he brought with him the mantle of English approval-a valuable commodity in a young nation that lacked an intellectual establishment that could give approbation to a young writer-lecturer.

Even when his lectures began to deal with his own ideas, Emerson spoke to audiences that knew something of him from his ministry or his occasional speeches. Until 1850 his lectures did not take him far from his home, but his growing reputation as an author and his acceptance by the English literati made him a "name" or public personality who began to receive invitations from lyceums far removed from his usual lecture circuit. His first major invitation came in the spring of 1850 from the members of the Literary Club of Cincinnati, who pledged money to support a course of lectures by Emerson in the city. Although traveling farther away from home would involve greater personal discomfort, the invitation to lecture in the Western states must have been a welcome assurance of continued popularity to Emerson, whose principal source of income until after the Civil War was his lecture fees. This invitation also provided the opportunity to recycle many old lectures previously given in New England and New York that would be fresh to these new audiences.[10]

The audiences were "new" not only in the sense that most had never seen or heard him before, but also in the sense that they heard Emerson's message in a different way. During this decade, Emerson took on the aura of a public figure who symbolized to the popular mind the prestige culture of New England as exemplified in the sobriquet, "The Yankee Sage." Mary K. Cayton studied this process in the city of Cincinnati and found that the new audience consisted of the rising young business class represented by such institutions as the YMCA which sponsored 'character-building' activities such as reading rooms, debating activities, and lectures as an alternative to taverns, gambling dens, and brothels. The young men who had migrated to the city in search of opportunities lived alone in rooming houses without the supervision or guidance of parents or familial friends. Institutions of self culture could provide these young men with the internal controls to confront the temptations of the big city. In a larger sense, the self culture movement represented the interests of the business class in disciplining the lower middle class work force of clerks and salesmen who carried on much of the business of the commercial organizations in the city.[11]

In the early lectures given from 1833 to 1842, Emerson used the lecture form as the primary vehicle to express his ideas. By the 1850s, the lecture had become secondary to the published essay and served primarily financial rather than artistic ends. Lectures were repeated more frequently as Emerson traveled farther afield in search of new audiences. Lectures in Boston and New York became social events, with the same people showing up year after year to see Waldo and be seen by others. Emerson became a public figure whose personality and presence on the platform were experienced by the cultivated classes much as going to a museum or an art exhibit might be. In this later stage of his life, Emerson became an icon of culture--the sage of Concord--and was used to promote the genteel culture of New England.[12]

The lectures "Power," "Wealth," and "Culture" given as part of the Conduct of Life series during the 1850s spoke directly to the concerns of the rising business class that formed his audience, and these lectures were especially popular in the West. Although the lectures are written to challenge his listeners' complacency, Emerson's indirect presentation of his ideas through metaphors and allusions allowed the audience to focus on his observations without comprehending the ideas they represented. Newspaper accounts reported the witty comments and brilliant aphorisms but not the framework of ideas that gave them coherence. As Emerson's reputation and popularity grew, he increasingly became identified as an optimistic seer who preached a progressive vision of self culture within a competitive commercial order.

This book focuses on the early lectures when Emerson was at the height of his powers. Following the Civil War, Emerson would continue to lecture, but both his physical strength and his mental abilities began to decline. For example, in 1867, Emerson gave 80 lectures and traveled to 14 states. By 1868 he reduced his schedule to a little over 30 lectures, and by 1869 his tours to the West were all but ended, as he stayed mainly within his old orbit of Massachusetts, New York, and Rhode Island. By 1872, his memory was so weak that he frequently read the same page of his lecture twice without realizing it. That year, following a series of six "conversations" given at Boston's Mechanics Hall during the afternoons and attracting primarily women who were old friends and admirers, Emerson limited himself to an occasional address usually before familiar audiences. His days as a traveling lecturer were over. His psychological balance was further disrupted when a fire swept through his house destroying the roof but thankfully not his papers or his books. His friends raised over $12,000 to restore the house and support him for the few remaining years of his life.[13]

Friends persuaded him to travel to Europe while the house was being restored. Although in declining health, he felt strong enough for one last trip to Europe, where he rekindled his friendship with Carlyle and met the leading literary figures of England and the Continent. When he returned to Concord, he was greeted by an overwhelming display of his neighbors' affection for him including a brass band and a floral arch leading to the newly restored house. In the remaining years he gave occasional speeches at literary meetings but declined most invitations. He gradually declined and on April 27, 1882, Ralph Waldo Emerson died after a brief struggle with pneumonia. He was buried in Sleepy Hollow Cemetery in a family plot not far from the graves of Hawthorne and Thoreau.[14]

## NOTES

1. The standard biography is Ralph Rusk, *The Life of Ralph Waldo Emerson* (New York: Charles Scribner's Sons, 1949). Several recent biographies are also excellent: John McAleer, *Ralph Waldo Emerson: Days of Encounter* (Boston: Little, Brown, 1984), and Gay Wilson Allen, *Waldo Emerson* (New York: Viking, 1981).

2. Rusk, *Life*, Chapters 1 and 7.

3. David M. Robinson, "The Sermons of Ralph Waldo Emerson: An Introductory Historical Essay," In *The Complete Sermons of Ralph Waldo Emerson,* ed. Albert J. von Frank, et al. 4 vols. (Columbia: University of Missouri Press, 1989) 1-32.

4. Herbert A. Wichelns, "Ralph Waldo Emerson," in *The History and Criticism of American Public Address,* ed. W. Norwood Brigance, 2 vols. (New York: McGraw Hill, 1943) 501-25.

5. Rusk, *Life*, Chapters 11 and 12.

6. Joseph Slater, ed. *The Correspondence of Emerson and Carlyle* (New York: Columbia University Press, 1964), 1-94.

7. Carl Bode, *The American Lyceum: Town Meeting of the Mind* (Carbondale: Southern Illinois University Press, 1968) 3-59.

8. McAleer, *Days of Encounter*, 228ff.

9. Townsend Scudder, "Emerson's British Lecture Tour, 1847-1848," *American Literature* 7 (1935): 35.

10. Mary K. Cayton, "The Making of an American Prophet: Emerson, His Audiences, and the Rise of the Culture Industry in Nineteenth Century America," *American Historical Review* 92 (1987): 597-620.

11. Cayton, "The Making," 605.

12. Rusk, *Life*, 388ff.

13. McAleer, *Days of Encounter*, 612ff.

14. McAleer, *Days of Encounter*, 661ff.

# 2

# Preacher

Living in a secular society at the end of the twentieth century, we may find it difficult to believe that at one time the sermon represented an art form that many educated Americans regarded as the best literature American culture produced. It was in this milieu that Emerson began his career as a preacher. Elizabeth Palmer Peabody, a close observer of Emerson, noted that he "was always pre-eminently the preacher to his own generation and future ones, but as much--if not more--out of the pulpit as in it." Although scholars have frequently quoted this remark, the suggestive implications of it have just as frequently been ignored. It seems that many critics view Emerson's career as a stark progression that required him to quit the ministry in order to achieve the great success as a lecturer and essayist that made him a leading figure in American letters. The logic behind this oversimplification of Emerson's career seems to be: Emerson quit the ministry; therefore, it must not have been very important to his career. Hence, the sermons need not be taken seriously.[1]

Thankfully, this long neglect of Emerson's sermons is finally coming to an end. The recent publication of the complete texts of the sermons edited by a team of scholars headed by Albert von Frank will provide a great stimulus to the important work that needs to be done.[2] Already chapters of books and articles discussing individual sermons and Emerson's preaching appear with increasing frequency. Scholars are recognizing that the ministry was the setting for Emerson's emergence as a thinker in his own right and his sermons are the record of a man struggling to free himself from the conventional pieties of society and to find his own voice. The sermons record his early efforts to find a form appropriate for his thought, and they demonstrate his growing confidence in his own inner vision as he goes his own way. Sherman Paul contends that the "sermons prepared his congregation for the precipitation of his character and he departed in peace."[3]

The journals of this period further document the struggle of a sensitive young man to overcome self doubt and to come to terms with his ambitions and the expectations of family and friends. They testify to his own intensely felt religious experience and to the gnawing fear that he would not be adequate to the task of communicating these deeply felt truths to others. His self analysis of his strengths and weaknesses as he contemplated entering the ministry is revealing. He confided to his journal that his "abilities are below my ambition" but he thought that since "the preaching most in vogue . . . depends chiefly on imagination for its success" that it was "within my grasp" (JMN, 1, 238). He noted the family influence recognizing that "I inherit from my sire . . . a passionate love for the strains of eloquence" (JMN, 1, 239).

When Emerson graduated from Harvard in 1821 with no immediate prospects, he began teaching school and three years would pass before he began to study theology informally with William Ellery Channing. He formally enrolled in Harvard Divinity School in 1825 but because of deteriorating health he did little work and left without graduating. He was licensed to preach on October 10, 1826, but shortly thereafter he went to the warmer climate of Charleston and St. Augustine for his health. Upon his return to Cambridge in 1827, he began a regular practice of supply preaching, which gave him steady employment almost every Sunday for the next year. During this time, he built his stock of sermons and carefully considered where he might find a permanent parish. His engagement to Ellen Tucker in December 1828 gave him good reason to seek a secure tenure. When Henry Ware, Jr., the minister at Boston's Second Church collapsed while returning from a speaking engagement, Emerson was hired to supply the pulpit on a regular basis. When Ware realized that he could not resume his duties full time, the church offered Emerson a position as his assistant and on March 11, 1829, he was finally ordained a Christian Minister.[4]

The Unitarian culture of New England and particularly Boston and Harvard College that Emerson absorbed as the child of a father who occupied a distinguished pulpit and took an active part in the intellectual life of the community molded Emerson and influenced his decision to become a minister. Emerson's subsequent career as a serious philosophical thinker is in many ways a continuation and development of ideas that grew out of the controversies surrounding the emergence of Unitarianism as a major intellectual force in New England. Emerson's leading ideas of the relationship of man to nature and the importance of self culture did not magically appear from his readings or meditations. As David Robinson writes, Emerson "was molded by the religious culture of New England Unitarianism and . . . he was given much of his intellectual impetus by that . . . culture, especially by the doctrine of self-culture."[5]

Growing up in a deeply religious family, Emerson at an early age developed an appreciation for preaching. The first letters he wrote when he had just turned thirteen record hearing sermons by Horace Holley and Nathaniel Frothingham at First Church in Boston, and in the same year he mentions a new collection of sermons by John Jebb and says, "I like them very much indeed" (L, I, 26). In his first year at Harvard, he so delighted in hearing a sermon preached by Edward Everett that he wrote a two-page letter recounting the experience to his brother, William, and boasted that he could "say half the sermon the night after it" (L, II, 90).

By the time Emerson entered the ministry in the 1830s, the forceful Puritan preaching style that shaped the New England consciousness had waned. The Puritan sermon in its full glory was an intellectual exercise in which the minster read a Biblical text, interpreted its meaning to the congregation, derived a doctrine from it, and showed its uses or applications to their lives. Derived from *The Arte of Prophesying*, the canonical homiletic text by William Perkins, this structure, although ideally suited to a dogmatic religion, had to be modified to meet the flexibility needed by the liberal ministers of the Congregational churches who would become known as Unitarians. The Perkins model involves a progressive movement from the text to the applications of the text in the lives of the congregation. When liberal ministers moved away from instruction in theology with a stress on doctrine, they modified the model to focus more on the applications of the text to the lives of the congregation. Thus the sermon became an exhortation to do good and to lead moral lives. [6]

Moreover, Channing and his associates, by defining Christianity in ethical terms rather than as a body of Biblical-based doctrine freed the ministers to employ secular as well as sacred texts in their sermons. Gradually, the text lost its sacred power to instruct and came to be judged on its usefulness in inculcating moral principles that could be applied in everyday life. While outwardly retaining the Perkins structure, the preaching in Unitarian churches shifted the emphasis from instruction to persuasion. The ministers' task on Sunday was to present the ethical implications of ideas derived from reason, nature and human experience for the moral improvement of the congregation. The validation of his efforts came to depend on audience response. Channing recognized this and challenged his fellow Unitarians to "substitute interesting views for those they would remove" by exhibiting "Christianity in all its sublime encouragements, its solemn warnings, its glorious assurances."[7] As Lawrence Buell notes "Unitarian preachers were the first of any American sect to move in significant numbers in the direction of the literary sermon." [8] Both social and theological conditions unique to the Unitarian congregations favored this development. Composed of individuals who possessed a literary refinement and served by a ministry that was highly educated, they used an order of worship flexible enough to allow innovation. These ministers usually received training in rhetoric and came from a homiletic tradition that encouraged appeals to the intellect made through written texts.[9]

Emerson's preparation for the pulpit pointed in precisely this direction. When Emerson began his studies in the Divinity School in 1825, Professor Henry Ware, Sr., conducted weekly exercises in preaching for all students during the fall semester. During the spring semester, Ware led a discussion of preaching on Wednesday evenings and conducted exercises on Saturdays. From a reading of his journals, we can surmise that Emerson attended these exercises and heard various practice sermons. We do know that Emerson was a member of the Society for Extemporaneous Speaking founded in 1825 and that he proposed one of the questions to be discussed.[10]

The reading list in homiletics for the divinity students in 1825 included the works of Jeremy Taylor, Campbell's *Lectures on Pulpit Oratory*, and Robinson's "Note on the Composition of Sermons." William Ellery Channing, who compiled the list, also emphasized the works of Blair. Emerson's journals for the period include references to Blair, Taylor, Channing, and Joseph Stevens Buchminster, a noted preacher. Kenneth Cameron has documented that Emerson withdrew from the Harvard Library all of South's sermons, and those of Tillotson and Butler.[11] These readings in homiletics and the model sermons emphasize the literary quality of pulpit oratory. For example, Tillotson drew upon French models for his sermons; Jeremy Taylor was famous for the "metaphysical" style of his sermons; and Robinson's essay was a translation and precis of the leading French homiletic text. Hugh Blair, the Scottish rhetorician whose ideas were expounded at Harvard by Edward T. Channing, shifted the emphasis of the sermon from instruction by the minister to persuasion: "The end of all preaching is, to persuade men to become good. Every sermon therefore should be a persuasive oration."[12]

Blair urged the minister to adapt his discourse to the needs of the audience by "plac[ing] himself in the situation of a serious hearer." He advised the minister to "study above all things to render your instructions interesting to the hearers . . . . The great secret lies in bringing home all that is spoken to the hearts of the hearers, so as to make every man think that the preacher is addressing him in particular. As much as possible the discourse ought to be carried on in the stream of direct address to the audience . . . and mix[ing] what is called application or what has an immediate reference to practice with the doctrinal and didactic parts of the sermon. Select the most useful, the most striking and persuasive topics which the text suggests and rest the discourse upon these."[13]

Blair's advice was useful to Unitarian ministers whose sermons became inspirational orations designed to promote self-improvement or self culture. The liberal Unitarians of Emerson's generation viewed mankind's life on earth as a probationary period during which the character of the individual developed. As Henry Ware, Jr., Emerson's predecessor at the Second Church in Boston expressed it, a human being is a "free moral agent capable of choosing between right and wrong and is accountable for his choice." In the world, he "is placed in a state of trial and probation for the purpose of forming and bringing out his character in preparation for a final allotment of condition in conformity with his character."[14] Unitarian ministers found their calling in the promotion of self culture as a means of elevating the soul toward an ideal of moral perfection.

Emerson drew upon his homiletic training at Harvard and his observation of many different ministers to develop his own preaching style. He recognized that it differed from what his congregation at Boston's Second Church was accustomed to and in one of his early sermons he gave a forthright exposition of his ideas about preaching: "I shall labour . . . as far as my poor abilities will reach to use a freedom in my preaching befitting the greatness of the Gospel and its universal application to all human concerns. I shall not be so much afraid of innovation as to scruple about introducing new forms of address, new modes of illustration, and varied allusions into the pulpit when I believe they can be introduced with advantage. I shall not certainly reject them simply because they are new." Emerson knew how easy it was for the minister to repeat the time worn formulas of the past instead of meeting the demands of "the times before us." He criticized conventional preaching as too "narrow" because it does not "apply itself to all the good and evil that is in the human body." He complained that "men imagine that the end and use of preaching is to expound a text and to unfold the divisions and subdivisions of meaning . . . and forget that Christianity is an infinite and universal law which touches all action, all passion, all natural being" (CS, I, 235).

Emerson's journals record his difficulty in writing sermons. One frequent complaint common to all professional speakers is the necessity of having something to say that is appropriate to the occasion. He expresses his frustration that "When the sermon is done he is aware that . . . a good deal of it . . . is unworthy . . . . But tomorrow is Sunday. He must take this or write worse or have nothing" (JMN, III, 182). In a letter describing his new pastoral duties he admits, "I fear nothing now except the preparation of sermons. The prospect of one each week, for an indefinite time to come is almost terrifick" (L, I, 182).

On another occasion he wrote to his brother, "Prithee, dear William send me some topics for sermons . . . . For much of my time is lost in choosing a subject & much more in wishing to write" (L, I, 211). He was also "discouraged by learning the motives that brought his great congregation to church. Scarcely ten came to hear his sermon" (JMN, V, 37). We hear him protesting against the irrelevance of much of the preaching he hears "the minister in these days, how little he says!" (JMN, V, 37). All this meditation gave him an ideal to aim for: "A preacher should be a live coal to kindle all the church" (JMN, V, 197).

Emerson wrote his sermons and lectures in long-hand several days prior to delivering them. He established a routine of writing the weekly sermon on the Friday before the service. This practice worked for him not because he was gifted with unusual inspiration, but because he had for years collected ideas and supporting material in his journals and regularly reviewed and cross-indexed them to make them useful in the composition process. Reading the journals, one finds quotations from his current reading, maxims, observations about his friends, chance remarks overheard in public, facts culled from newspapers or magazines, dreams, lines of poetry--indeed, it seems that everything he read or heard or saw became grist for his mill.

To a great extent, this process of composition admirably suited Emerson's means of expressing his ideas to others. His temperament did not incline him to the legal model of sustained argument. He preferred to present several different perspectives of the issue under discussion, moving not in a straight line from one point to another, but circling it and seeing how one view may be changed by another. His mind worked by analogy, by comparison and contrast. The materials in his journals served the same function as the bits of glass in a mosaic. Emerson arranged them into a pattern that revealed the overall design underlying the diversity of his materials.

Evidently Emerson's theorizing about the art of preaching had practical effect. Frederick Henry Hedge recalled that "Emerson's early sermons were characterized by great simplicity and an unconventional, untheological style, which brought him into closer rapport with his hearers than was commonly achieved by the pulpit in those days."[15] Another observer wrote to Ezra Stiles Gannett, secretary of the American Unitarian Association: "We want a man of force & popular address . . . such a man was Mr Emerson, the society was constantly increasing while he was here, & our meeting fully attended" (L, I, 222, n. 135).

The three sermons reproduced in this text represent different stages in Emerson's development as a preacher and show the growth of his thinking during this period. The first sermon, "Pray Without Ceasing," was originally preached before the Middlesex Association of Ministers on October 10, 1826, as Emerson's trial sermon. Emerson reports that the inspiration for the sermon came from a farmer and the sermon itself is a religious gloss on the old observation, "Be careful what you wish for; you might get it" (JMN, II, 98n). It achieved its purpose, as Emerson was granted a license to preach. Given the circumstances, Emerson wrote a fairly conventional sermon that proved to be one of his most popular, being repeated fourteen times.

Images of seeing predominate in this sermon, which contrasts the seen and the unseen; the visible and the invisible. The opening sentence establishes the opposition: "we judge men by their action," which can be seen by our faculty of sight because we cannot "see the soul," which is the source of their inner thoughts. Emerson explains that human beings straddle two worlds, the world of matter and the world of spirit, one seen, the other unseen: "our bodies belong to one; our thoughts to another." Recognition of this leads some men to the false conclusion that they can "retreat from the public eye and hide themselves to conceal in solitude guilty recollections or guilty wishes," but in fact the "great congregation of moral natures . . . angels and archangels, the Son of God, and the Father everlasting, open their eyes upon them and speculate on these clandestine meditations" (the choice of words is exact as the verb comes from the Latin meaning to view or to see and reinforces the central idea). The knowledge of God which illuminates the "arts of hypocrisy . . . and artifice" and reveals all as "naked" is contrasted with images of the unseen "grave," the "deep," and "gulfs of chaos." He returns to this unseen world of death and the grave toward the end of the sermon, describing it as "though shadows, clouds and darkness rest upon it." This time the unseen is not the mind of the sinner, but the spiritual world that we should be preparing for, consisting of "this mysterious eternity about to open upon us."

The images of the seen and unseen, the visible and the invisible, unify the topics of the sermon: the two worlds of the spirit and matter, and the two phases of man's existence as an embodied soul in this world and as a disembodied soul in the next. In this first sermon, we hear Emerson announcing the earliest formulation of the idea that would be central to his mature thought: the unity of the material and the spiritual world. Although Emerson had studied the Scottish common-sense philosophers Steward and Reid at Harvard--indeed much of his education had been based on them--during his ministry he read widely in the Cambridge Neo-Platonists and discovered Samuel Taylor Coleridge. The Scots accepted the Lockean model of the mind dependent on the senses to provide external sensations that through association produced ideas, but they also posited a "sixth sense"--the common sense--that would function in the same way as the others to recognize right and wrong. They believed that through moral instruction it could be trained to be even more effective. To the Romantics and the Neo-Platonists this reduced the moral sentiment to a mere reflex action and bound the individual to the traditional moral codes and laws of whatever society he lived in. Believing that the human mind could play a more active part in discovering the universal moral laws that governed the universe, they asserted a unity between mind and matter, between the physical universe and the spiritual, between the mind of God and the mind of man. Coleridge in the *Aids to Reflection* located the source of this unity in Reason, which was distinct from human understanding. The understanding as a faculty of the mind dependent on sensation apprehended the particular and the material. In contrast, Reason, a spiritual faculty, focused on the unity of phenomena and looked behind and beyond the particular to the universal. Emerson, at this stage in his life deeply immersed in the thinking of the neo-Platonists, does not elaborate upon these ideas in his first sermon, but they are the philosophical basis for it.

After the introduction, Emerson announces his doctrine: "We pray without ceasing. Every secret wish is a prayer. Every house is a church, the corner of every street is a closet of devotion." He immediately reassures his audience: "There is no rhetoric, let none deceive himself; there is no rhetoric in this." Perhaps he was concerned that the congregation would be startled by such a bold statement. He clarifies his meaning by reminding his audience that God's knowledge is "perfect and immense" and the minds of men are surely open to him. This leads him to restate the doctrine as "every desire of the human mind, is a prayer uttered to God and registered in heaven."

He finds in the application of the doctrine the idea that "our prayers are granted." He hastens to add that he does not mean in the vulgar sense that every passing wish when prefaced by ceremonial words will be granted. No. He means that true prayers bear testimony to the character of the soul and that we become the kind of person we intend to be. He illustrates this idea by three parallel examples of answered prayers: those of the rich man, the sensualist, and the good man. He does not really develop arguments or proof for his propositions. Rather, he uses images and rhetorical questions to evoke feelings in the audience and thus move them emotionally to accept the truth of his doctrine. Emerson concludes by showing how each member of the congregation can use the doctrine to "cleanse his thoughts" for, as he reminds them, from out of the heart "pure or impure" arise "the issues of life and DEATH."

This sermon has interest not only in documenting Emerson's growth as a preacher and revealing the early undeveloped state of some of his ideas, but in demonstrating the source of his ethical appeal: his intense piety. There is an uncritically examined generalization that the Unitarians were coldly rational in their religious beliefs. This sermon reveals another side to the Unitarian temper: an intensely felt need to experience the fervor of the religious life, which Daniel Howe described as "a very special type of emotional sensitivity, a combination of religious affection and moral taste."[16]

Sermon XXXIX, "Summer" is a good example of Emerson's developing ideas about man and nature and of his willingness to "introduc[e] new forms of address, new modes of illustration, and varied allusions into the pulpit when I believe they can be introduced with advantage." It is also tempting to read in this sermon the genesis of some of his mature works. For example, scholars have noted that the opening lines of "Summer" prefigure the opening of the "Divinity School Address" and the sermon contains the ideas of *Nature* in embryo. Not only does this sermon have importance for any study of the development of Emerson's thought, it is an important artistic production in its own right, demonstrating Emerson's achievement in composition and his increasing willingness to abandon traditional forms and find his own.[17]

The subject of the sermon is the immanence of God in nature. The form of the sermon suggests this by exploring a series of natural images that reveal the power of the Creator. Emerson's introduction does not really announce a topic; it invites the audience to meditate on the idylls of nature with the preacher: "the most careless eye is caught by the beauty of the external world. The green tree with its redundant foliage and its fragrant blossoms shows fairer than it did a few weeks since when its arms were naked and its trunk was sapless." The next few lines contrast the full glory of nature on view in the country side to the narrow one available to those in the city "imprisoned in streets of brick and stone, in tainted air and hot and dusty corners, [with] only glimpses of the glorious sun . . . and of [the] matchless beauty [of] one wide garden." But Emerson is not preaching a sermon on the stock topic of the city versus the country. He reminds his listeners that even in the cramped and crowded city, "something of the mighty process of vegetation forces itself on every human eye." This process and its evidence of "Divine power and goodness" will be the central theme of the sermon. Some people know that this "organized creation of every new year indicates the presence of God" but others "fail to derive from the changes of nature that lesson which to a pious, to a Christian mind they ought to."

Emerson announces the doctrine that "all nature is a book on which one lesson is written." That lesson is "the omnipresence of God." What is distinctive about the sermon is that the congregation is not presented with a structured argument to "prove" the doctrine but with a meditation that invites them to see again scenes that they have experienced many times and recognize God's presence in the natural world. This sermon may reflect Emerson's evolving belief that the speaker and the audience must cooperate in the development of the meaning in the discourse. Indeed, Toulouse believes that "Summer" shows the influence of Emerson's reading in Coleridge, particularly of the idea of suggestive form as a means for involving the audience in the process of discovering the "truth" of a sermon through the experience of hearing it spoken.

Thinking that the rules of composition and formal argument were of secondary value in opening the human mind to spiritual truth, Coleridge claimed, "it is an immutable truth that what comes from the heart, that alone goes to the heart."[18] Neither external forms nor the method of rhetorical devices will suffice if the speaker and the audience are not open to the movement of the Holy Spirit. Having experienced the Divine presence by listening to its voice within, the minister when he addresses the congregation is a medium by which the Divine voice speaking through him animates the heart of each member of the congregation. This Romantic view of preaching, with its emphasis on the sincerity of the minister and the participation of the audience, heightens the expectations and places a greater burden on both in the creation of a genuine religious experience.

It is true that Emerson frequently meditated on the role of the inner voice or the Holy Spirit in preaching. He wrote in his journal,"It is God within you that responds to God without or affirms his own words trembling on the lips of another" (JMN III, 302). Another journal entry noted that "the best part of any discourse is that which is unspoken" (JMN IV, 278). Thus a suggestive form or one that invited the audience to participate in the unfolding of its meaning both heard and unheard could invoke the presence of the Holy Spirit. This reasoning justified Emerson's experiments with forms that are more intuitive than logical and his willingness to abandon logical demonstration and exposition in favor of metaphor and suggestive imagery.

Whatever the reason for it, "Summer" is a good example of his continuing experiments with metaphor, image, and sound as a substitute for externally imposed form. The introduction gains power from Emerson's use of consonance in repeating the similar sound of "glory" and "glimpses of the glorious" and "green," "great," and "garden." The word "glory" or "glorious" is repeated three times in three lines in relation to the earth, sun, and clouds, and the linking of "green," "garden," and "grass" in the same paragraph conveys the power of seasonal change and vegetative power. Emerson also uses rhythm effectively by writing clauses containing one-syllable words, "with which rain and sun shall act on the seed," and triplets, "to the rain and the sun and the soil." He accumulates example upon example in a vast catalogue of nature: "On the glorious sky it is writ in characters of fire; on earth it is writ in the majesty of the green ocean; it is writ on the volcanoes of the south, and the icebergs of the polar sea; on the storm, in winter; in summer on every trembling leaf; on man in the motion of the limbs, and the changing expression of the face, in all his dealings, in all his language it is seen and may be read and pondered and practiced in all."

Visual images predominate of seeing, looking, and examining from the opening line that "the most careless eye is caught by the beauty of the external world" to the announcement that "all nature is a book in which one lesson is written and blessed are the eyes that can read it." He uses visual verbs that connote and denote visual activity in looking, recognizing, exploring, opening, hunting, detecting, and examining. He even calls science "eagle-eyed" as it "explores" by opening "its microscopes."

A second group of images clusters around the words "seed," "kernal" and "grain." These are images of growth and vegetative life, of transformation, of becoming, of process, which suggest the presence of God in creation. Emerson calls the process of growth a "perpetual miracle more unaccountable" than any "tale of metamorphosis in poetry" or "fabulous transformation . . . in the Arabian Tales." These images convey the idea of nature as commodity, as the seeds develop and produce more products that are useful to mankind. Emerson uses familiar images of the beauty of nature and the seasonal process of change not to construct an argument but to invite the audience to participate with him in a meditation on its meaning. The congregation recognizes and understands these ideas. There are no unfamiliar situations or customs that need to be explained; no historical context is necessary; no abstract doctrine need be explicated. Emerson's description of nature as beauty, commodity, and a source of images to discuss the Divine presence drew upon ideas common to all. By inviting the congregation to meditate upon these with him, Emerson is trying to speak an "immutable truth" that they can sense in their own hearts and affirm from their own experience: All nature testifies to the immanence of God. This idea is not developed logically, nor supported by exegesis of

Biblical texts or learned commentaries. It is an actual experience of the Divine presence engendered by the Holy Spirit manifesting itself in the shared experience of preacher and congregation.

By the time he preached "Genuine Man" just before resigning his pastorate, Emerson was more confident in his abilities to work within the outward sermonic form while radically transforming it. The sermon foreshadows the organizational techniques that Emerson will later bring to fruition in his lectures: the abandonment of argumentative or logical patterns in favor of association or juxtaposition of divergent views organized around a central image or controlling metaphor. Although the sermon retains the outwardly familiar form of text, doctrine, uses, and applications, Emerson makes no effort to develop the sermon by advancing a proposition and developing it logically with rigorous argument.

Instead, as Toulouse has noted, Emerson "makes a proposition, follows with an image which expands or clarifies it, then repeats the proposition only to have it serve as the introduction to a new repetition of the pattern."[19] Thus "the audience hears repeated patterns that are juxtaposed, not analyzed." The sermon moves through three levels of increasingly higher spirituality as Emerson first describes the individual man, then the true self, and lastly the genuine man who speaks with the voice of God. The first two of these sections are introduced by a rhetorical question: "A finished man--who has seen?" and "Is it not true to your experience brethern that this the man is the least part of himself?" Each of these sections follows the pattern identified by Toulouse, although Emerson, not trusting the audience to follow his pattern, intrudes with a very obvious summary that slows down the movement of the sermon. He then picks up where he left off, even using the familiar masculine pronoun as he uses a series of statements to "counterbalance" the outward circumstances of a man's life with the true object of life which is to form the real self-the genuine man.

Emerson next moves to the third and highest level of spirituality by linking the soul to God. He refers to the inward voice as the "voice of God" which speaks to all men. Again Emerson interrupts the movement of the sermon with an exhortation to the congregation not to be "dazzled by circumstances" but to recognize that what society views as adverse occurrences such as failure in business or death of a close relative or friend may provide opportunities for inward spiritual growth. Emerson now returns to the theme of the sermon by enumerating the "conspicuous marks of the genuine man." Images of seeing dominate the first part of the sermon; images of hearing control this section. The genuine man does not use speech to dissemble or conceal. In a passage that foreshadows the famous transparent eyeball image in *Nature*, Emerson describes the genuine man as "transparent. His intention shines through all his words and deeds." When he speaks, "reason" speaks through him. The genuine man hears God's voice--the inner voice in his soul--and gives it utterance. He "speaks in the spirit of truth." Everything he says, he says with "all his heart and soul."

The genuine man is "distinguished by the heartiness of his actions." The genuine man, by listening to this inward voice, has the power to "make God responsible for him." In doing so, he is "following God's finger" and "God will take care of the issues." Emerson tells the congregation that "this truth of character is identical with a religious life, that they are one and the same thing; that this voice of your own mind is the voice of God." He concludes by propounding the uses of the sermon to the congregation: "What is the practical end of the views we have taken? This, and this only,-Be Genuine. Be girt with truth."

"The Genuine Man" shows how far Emerson had moved beyond the traditional format of a Perkins sermon with its need for enumeration and summaries in his search for a form that would through indirection and suggestion invite audience participation in developing the meaning of his discourse. The sermon develops the relationship between outward circumstances and inward spiritual states through juxtaposing descriptions of fleeting and transient externals to the immortal universals of inward truth found in the soul.

Emerson quit his pastorate over doubts as to his ability to administer the communion rites in good conscience. His readings had convinced him that Christ did not mean to institutionalize a ritual celebration for all Christians throughout the succeeding centuries. Although a committee of parishioners attempted to compromise with their minister's desire not to administer the sacrament regularly, he was firm in his objections and in the end, on October 28, 1832, the congregation by a vote of 34 to 25 reluctantly accepted his resignation. Without doubting Emerson's sincerity, it is possible to see this incident as providing a sufficient justification for leaving his parish. Emerson left the pastorate of the Second Church; he did not resign from the ministry itself. He continued to preach to supplement his income and to repay obligations to other ministers. He preached his last sermon January 20, 1839, at Concord almost ten years after his ordination.[20]

Emerson wrote 171 sermons and preached 885 times. Several of the sermons were preached 15 or 16 times and one, "On Showing Piety at Home," was preached 27 times. The record is a clear indication that Emerson was an effective preacher and in demand in the pulpit.[21] Yet only one sermon was published during his lifetime and Emerson, himself, seemed to hold the sermons in low regard. He once mentioned burning them to his daughter, provoking John Cabot, his literary executor, to exclaim that he was "no judge whatever of their value."[22] What is their value today? Wesley Mott provided the best answer to this question: "Claims for the significance and inherent quality of the sermons must . . . be tempered. Some are limp exercises reflecting the constraints of writing-to-order on a regular basis; some are one time occasional pieces, curiosities, some are interesting chiefly for historical reasons . . . . Others are stirring, even impassioned oratory." [23]

This is a just estimate of the literary quality of the sermons. Although they may never take the place of the great essays or lectures, they are more than the seedbed of Emerson's inspiration. If they are not the full flower of his sunny days, they are at least the root and stalk of his ideas. They are the catalyst for Emerson's developing ideas about language and form, the first statements of his central ideas about nature and the self, and the expression of his view of the relationship between doctrine, faith, works, and tradition to the Christian life. Moreover, the demanding task of preparing 171 sermons for weekly delivery inspired the habits of reading, reflecting, and writing that served Emerson throughout his speaking and writing career.

After accepting his resignation, the congregation voted to pay Emerson through the end of 1832. In poor health, and without a regular position, Emerson decided to use the money and some savings, and travel to Europe in hopes that a sea voyage would aid his recuperation. Upon his return, he would face anew the vexing question of a vocation. His decision to trade his pulpit for a lectern would test the new possibilities for the intellectual in Jacksonian America and explore the potential for developing a democratic culture in the newly formed institution of the lyceum. The next chapter will explore the continuity between Emerson as Preacher and Emerson as Lecturer.

## NOTES

1. Elizabeth Palmer Peabody, "Emerson as Preacher" in *The Genius and Character of Emerson*, ed. Frank B. Sanborn (Boston: Houghton Mifflin, 1898), 146.

2. *The Complete Sermons of Ralph Waldo Emerson*, Albert J. von Frank, et al., eds., 4 vols. (Columbia: University of Missouri Press, 1989).

3. Sherman Paul, *Emerson's Angle of Vision: Man and Nature in American Experience* (Cambridge, Mass.: Harvard University Press, 1952), 7.

4. John McAleer, *Ralph Waldo Emerson: Days of Encounter* (Boston: Little, Brown, 1984)

5. David Robinson, "The Sermons of Ralph Waldo Emerson: An Introductory Historical Essay," in *The Complete Sermons*, 31.

6. W. Fraser Mitchell, *English Pulpit Oratory from Andrews to Tillotson* (New York: Russell & Russell, 1962), 99-100.

7. Teresa Toulouse, *The Art of Prophesying. New England Sermons and the Shaping of Belief* (Athens: University of Georgia Press, 1987), 92.

8. Lawrence Buell, "The Unitarian Movement and the Art of Preaching in 19th Century America," *American Quarterly* 24 (1972): 167-190.

9. Buell, "The Unitarian Movement," 168.

10. George H. Williams, *The Harvard Divinity School* (Boston, 1954) 63.

11. A. M. Baumgartner, "'The Lyceum is My Pulpit': Homiletics in Emerson's Early Lectures," *American Literature* 34 (1963): 477-78.

12. Hugh Blair, *Lectures on Rhetoric and Belles Lettres*, ed. Harold F. Harding, 2 vols. (Carbondale: Southern Illinois University Press, 1965) 2: 105.

13. Blair, *Lectures*, 111.

14. Cited in Robinson, "Sermons," 5.

15. Quoted in James Eliot Cabot, *A Memoir of Ralph Waldo Emerson* vol. 1 (New York: AMS reprint, 1965), 150.

16. Daniel Walker Howe, *The Unitarian Conscience: Harvard Moral Philosophy, 1805-1861* (Cambridge, Mass.: Harvard University Press, 1970), 153.

17. Teresa Toulouse, *The Art of Prophesying,* 155ff.

18. Cited in Toulouse, *The Art of Prophesying*, 137.

19. Toulouse, *The Art of Prophesying*. 165ff.

20. John McAleer, *Ralph Waldo Emerson: Days of Encounter* (Boston: Little, Brown, 1984), 117ff.

21. Arthur McGiffert, ed., *Young Emerson Speaks* (Boston: Houghton Mifflin, 1938), 261.

22. Nancy Craig Simmons, "Arranging the Sibylline Leaves: James Elliot Cabot's Work as Emerson's Literary Executor," *Studies in the American Renaissance* 1983: 361.

23. Wesley T. Mott, *"The Strains of Eloquence": Emerson and His Sermons* (University Park: Pennsylvania State University Press, 1989), 3.

# 3

# "The Rising Sun"

When Emerson returned to the United States on October 9, 1833, after seven months traveling in Europe, he faced the vexing question of what to do with his life. For the next few weeks, he earned some income by preaching on a temporary basis and contemplated the possibilities of becoming a lecturer. Moving to the lecture platform offered him both the freedom to succeed in a new venue and the prospect of failure. The relationship between a minister and his congregation was bound by settled expectations on both sides. The newly developing relationship between the lecturer and the audience was still being defined. His brother Charles and his cousin George, taking advantage of their personal contacts in Boston, forced the issue by making arrangements for Waldo to lecture before the Natural History Society on November 5, 1833, on "The Uses of Natural History."[1] His brother Charles, who was in the audience, wrote that "young and old opened their eyes and ears--I was glad to have some of the stump lecturers see what was what and bow to the rising sun" (L, I, 397). The success of this first effort brought invitations to lecture from such diverse groups as the American Institute of Instruction, the Franklin Lectures, and again the Natural History Society. These early lectures on natural history gained Emerson both needed money and a growing reputation, but he rapidly outgrew the confines of the lyceum system with its emphasis on a formulaic mixture of seriousness, entertainment, and practicality.

Perhaps the best way to understand Emerson's achievement in the lectures is to examine them from a developmental perspective. When Emerson gave his first lectures he was a young apprentice who popularized the thoughts of others. These first lectures included colorful descriptions of the zoos he visited in Europe with their unusual and often rare specimens, presented within a framework of general ideas drawn from Emerson's reading in natural history. In his first lecture he described the "Garden of Plants in Paris," listing "all stripes of tygers, hyenas, leopards, and jackals; a herd of monkeys; not to mention the great numbers of sheep, goats, llamas, and zebras" (EL, I, 7-9).

Although the lectures on natural history achieved their purpose of supplementing his income and gaining him personal recognition, he was dissatisfied with the amount of work required to write lectures to meet the demands of his sponsors. He wrote in his journal: "I will say at public lectures and the like those things which I have meditated for their own sake, and not for the first time with a view to that occasion" (JMN, III, 361). His success in these early lectures also gave him the confidence to attempt a more ambitious course of lectures focusing on a common theme. By providing sufficient time to discuss a subject in greater depth, this format allowed Emerson to establish a framework of ideas in an introductory lecture that could be elaborated in subsequent ones. Because tickets were sold on a series basis, he could presume that as the course developed, most of the audience retained some knowledge of previous lectures. Thus he avoided the necessity of repeating his ideas, and he had a greater opportunity to discuss similarities and differences among the various divisions of his overall theme.

Emerson first utilized this format in a course of public lectures on the subject of biography beginning on January 29, 1835, with a different lecture read each Thursday night before the Society for the Diffusion of Useful Knowledge at the Masonic Temple. The course opened with an "Introductory" lecture whose text is lost to us, and considered "Michel Angelo Buonaroti," "Martin Luther," "John Milton," "George Fox," and "Edmund Burke" in turn. Emerson examined the lives of "Great Men" not primarily to inform or amuse the audience but to make a moral point. In the introduction to his lecture on Michelangelo, Emerson stated his thesis that "this truth, that perfect beauty and perfect goodness are One, was made known to Michael Angelo, and I shall endeavor by sketches from his life to show the direction and limitations of his search after this element" (EL, I, 100). To make certain that members of his audience understood the implications of this idea to their own lives, Emerson pointedly said, "let not the laborer, the accountant, the manufacturer, the mechanic, the farmer turn away with ill-will or indifference as if this might be a very pretty subject for an idle hour but promised nothing of interest to them. It does concern them if they take an interest in . . . useful, noble, religious men" (EL, I, 100). In the conclusion, he reiterated that Michelangelo "was a brother and friend to all who acknowledge the beauty that beams in universal nature and who seek by labor and denial to approach its source in Perfect Goodness" (EL, I, 117).

The success of this series confirmed Emerson's judgment that an audience would willingly pay to hear a sustained discussion of a subject. In June, he wrote to Frederick Henry Hedge that he was planning another series of lectures on English literature, and his journal contains alternative outlines for the course. His preparation for this series had to be worked into a busy schedule that included buying a house in Concord, marrying Lidian, and giving a long historical address commemorating the founding of Concord. On November 3 the Boston *Daily Advertiser* carried an announcement of the course of lectures, and two days later Emerson read the introductory lecture before the Society for the Diffusion of Useful Knowledge. The other lectures in the series include: "Permanent Traits of the English National Genius"; "The Age of Fable"; "Chaucer"; "Shakspear" (two lectures); "Lord Bacon"; "Jonson, Herrick, Herbert, and Wotton"; "Ethical Writers"; and "Modern Aspects of Letters." This series represents a further stage in the development of Emerson as a lecturer. In giving these lectures, Emerson moved beyond his sources and with a greater confidence in his own ideas gave rein to his own speculations. This growing confidence in his own abilities extended also to the business of lecturing. This series on English Literature would be the last that he would give under the sponsorship of others.[2] Thereafter, he would be his own manager. When the next series of lectures was announced, it was under Emerson's own name and not that of a sponsoring organization. He hired the hall, advertised, and sold tickets to the series himself. To increase the return, he repeated the series in nearby communities.[3]

In the years 1836-1838, Emerson gave two courses of lectures: The Philosophy of History, and Human Culture. Coming between the publication of *Nature* in 1836 and the publication of the *Essays* in 1841, these lectures trace the development of Emerson's thought during this important period of his life, which included such other significant speeches as "The American Scholar" and "The Divinity School Address." The journal entries for the period record his struggle to find a theme and a title for the series of lectures. He asked himself, "shall I call my subject the Philosophy of modern History, and consider the action of the same general causes upon Religion, Art, Science, Literature?" (JMN, V, 218). Several days later after a walk around Walden Pond, he had decided "what principles I might lay down as the foundations of this course of lectures I shall read to my fellow citizens" (JMN, V, 221). These constitute the foundation of his thinking: "There is one mind common to all individual men. . . . Underneath all appearances and causing all appearances are certain eternal laws which we call the Nature of Things" (JMN, V, 221-222).

Although the two series share a common origin in *Nature*, it is a mistake to see them as merely a popular statement of his developing "first philosophy." As Robinson has convincingly argued, the Philosophy of History series is in its own right a significant working out of the progressive expression of Spirit in human affairs.[4] The twelve lectures turn on two axes--the individual and society--with the first six lectures exploring how the individual expresses spirit in such forms as science, art, literature, politics, and religion and the last six exploring the social dimensions in manners, trades and the professions, society, and ethics. Both of these courses deserve to be read as a whole; individual lectures resonate with meaning as they participate in the development of the central theme. This is especially true of the Human Culture series, which possesses a dialectical unity of paired lectures expressing the dual perspectives of the individual and society. Although individual lectures still radiate with the intensity of Emerson's inspiration, the series as a whole represents a systematic exposition of his thought that approaches the best of his later work.

In these principles and in the lectures that followed, Emerson is still working out the implications of the ideas of *Nature* for a general theory of human culture. Not surprisingly, the central theme of the series on history is the discovery of the eternal laws of "the Nature of Things." The twelve lectures in the Philosophy of History series began with an introductory lecture read December 8, 1836 at the Masonic Temple in Boston and concluded with the lecture, "The Individual" on March 2, 1837. In the introductory lecture, Emerson raised the question "What is history?" and described it as the "vague account . . . . the wearisome chronicle . . . . [and] the superficial enumeration of Olypiads, of troops, of towns, of taxes." He emphatically denied this commonplace answer: "This is not History . . . it's the shell from which the kernel is fallen. History is the portraiture in act of man, the most graceful, the most varied, the most fertile of actors. The true History will be commensurate . . . . It will traverse the whole scale of the Human faculties" (EL, II, 8-9). Emerson proclaimed his intention to show the "defects of actual History . . . by comparing it with its ideal. That is, of course, with the Nature of Man. We are compelled in the first essays of thought to separate the idea of Man from any particular men. We early arrive at the great discovery that there is one Mind common to all individual men . . . . Of this mind who can enumerate the elements? Religion is its self respect; science its insight of matter; poetry its language; music its voice; philosophy the announcement of its laws" (EL, II, 11-12). He drew the conclusion that "of this one Mind, History is the record" (EL, II, 13). In these lines he not only introduced his method but foreshadowed the five lectures that would constitute the first part of the course. Next, he turned to the other axis, man in nature as a social being. "Another fact of no less importance is the position of man in nature. Nothing but God is selfdependent. Every being in nature has its existence . . . connected with other beings . . . Man is powerful only by the multitude of his affinities, or because his life is intertwined with the whole chain of organic and inorganic being" (EL, II, 17). Having divided his subject into two parts, he confidently announced that "under the light of these two facts, that the mind is one and that nature is its correlative, history is to be read and written" (EL, II, 19).

Although the series was a financial success, some members of the audience voiced what would become a common criticism of Emerson's limitations as a lecturer. The Unitarian clergyman Convers Francis heard Emerson's lecture on "Ethics" on February 16, 1837 and complained to his journal, "His style is too fragmentary and sententious. It wants the requisite words or phrases of connection and transition from one thought to another. This defect and his habit of expressing a common truth in some uncommon . . . way of his own, are the reasons perhaps that it is so difficult to retain and carry away what he says. I find that his beautiful things are slippery and will not stay in the mind."[5]

This difficulty in following Emerson's thought is the result of his experimentation with the form of the lecture, which is not designed for the logical exposition of an idea nor for the sustained development of an argument. Based on the traditional sermonic form of text, doctrine, exposition, and uses, it permits the audience to participate with Emerson in examining from several perspectives the multiple meanings involved in the central idea. Much as a minister might take a simple text and, through opening up its multiple meanings, help the congregation to understand it, so Emerson invites his audience to participate in the process of thinking through the complex meanings and teachings that History has for us in its multiple forms. This indirect method that characterizes Emerson's lectures allows the audience to participate in the process through which the "meaning" of the lecture is created. As Emerson examines first one aspect and then another of the question, the audience is drawn into the dialectical process that leads to the discovery of a "truth" or "meaning" for them.

In doing so, Emerson perfected an inspirational oration exploring the possibilities of self culture that urged his listeners to realize their better selves. We can trace the origination of this in some of the sermons preached to his congregation based on such unconventional themes as "Summer," "Trifles," "Conversation," "Hymn Books," "Astronomy," and "Self Culture."[6] Thus, when Emerson embarked on his lecturing career he had already experimented with the possibilities of using a sacred format, the sermon, to preach cultural values to an increasingly secular age. Shorn of its dogmatism, the format was flexible enough to encompass the themes of self culture and the spiritual nature of the universe that formed the core of Emerson's thought.

The lecture "Manners," which was part of the course, illustrates this pattern. His text was the unifying idea of the philosophy of history rightly construed, and Emerson began the lecture with a short preface placing the individual lecture within the context of the overall theme. Emerson introduced the doctrine by reminding the audience that in writing the history of the nature of mankind, manners are an important element but so subtle and evanescent as to elude analysis. The "silent and mediate expression of character," they are affected by "climate, religion, occupation, commerce, age" and represent a compound product of circumstances and character. This is the doctrine he will explore by examining manners in different historical ages: Greece and Rome, France and England during the eighteenth and nineteenth centuries, and the United States at the present. He developed the exposition of the doctrine by a series of contrasts between the manners of the ancients and the moderns, the cannibals and the Christians, the "Hindoo" and Chinese, Parisians and

Londoners, Native Americans and European settlers. In developing these topics, Emerson did not logically examine how the climate, religion, occupation, and commerce affected each pair, but used them to suggest the differences he had in mind.

This led him to the idea that the value of manners to the historian is that they are the unconscious account that the individual gives of himself and are very useful in understanding his character. He developed this with various examples drawn from the behavior of the Saxons, Spartans, Athenians, Romans, and King Alfred. These led him to the next topic, that manners impress us in proportion to the dignity of spirit that they betray--a topic that is further developed with examples from Greece and Rome.

Having identified Greek manners with the simplicity of the noble savage who shows reverence for such personal qualities as strength, beauty, self, command, swiftness, and fierceness, Emerson contrasted these with the manners of the Christian era, which tended toward the subjugation of the body. Next he suggested that manners are determined by "body, habits of life and the genius of the individual." This topic was developed with examples of the manners of countrymen--whose rustic charm rests on the simplicity of their manners; the nobility--whose marked and impressive manners strike the attention and obtain obedience; and the Court of Fashion--whose manners rest upon claims of power, wealth, and elegance. Having examined different aspects of this doctrine, he next showed his audience how they could benefit from it.

Emerson concluded the lecture and his survey of manners with the idea that the manners of individuals are only approximations of the "Idea of the hero, in modern times, the gentleman or Man of Honor." This is the topic toward which the lecture builds: the idea of men as "self sustained persons . . . . governed by reason and not by the senses or the understanding." This is the "Genuine Man" he preached about and this is the self-reliant man he would write about in his great essay. Emerson ends with a description of this ideal: "the man of reason is he who walks by the light of his own mind and so becomes a mountain of honor round which other stars revolve . . . . The gentleman sees . . . that glory is a light which shines from us on to others not from others on us." He concluded with an inspirational line assuring his audience that these "ways of glory seem to me to be opened to every man and these gates never shut from everlasting to everlasting."

Why did Emerson find this format so useful? The most obvious answer is that he was trained as a minister and it was natural to him. Obviously, he did not confuse preaching in the pulpit with lecturing in the lyceum, but he did see similarities in the relationship that he hoped to establish with the audience. His journals are filled with references to his occasional addresses and lectures as "sermons." Although this might reflect the habitual designation of a minister for his discourse, in a man as conscious of language as Emerson it represents his awareness that he was delivering a secular sermon to his audience. For example, he wrote to his mother, "I have relinquished my ecclesiastical charge at E Lexington & shall not preach more except from the Lyceum" (L, II, 120). And in a journal note of ideas for the American Scholar Address, he refers to "that Sermon to Literary Men which I propose to make" (JMN, V, 164). In another passage he writes of "another fact to be remembered in the scholar's sermon" (JMN, V, 167). On still another occasion, he called the lecture room, "the true church of today & the home of . . . eloquence" (JMN, VII, 277-278). The format provided him with the flexibility to combine exposition with inspiration to become the "poet-priest", the secular preacher he aspired to be. In contrast to many lyceum lecturers who spoke primarily on informative topics and imparted incidental information to the audience sometimes with a practical bent, Emerson's early lectures aimed at a high moral purpose. Another practical reason for using this format was that his audiences found it familiar. In a church-going age, when most of his listeners were familiar with homiletic techniques, Emerson's use of the sermonic form would have been recognizable and even comforting.

Although Emerson drew upon the familiar sermonic structure in organizing his lectures, he recognized the new freedom available to him in the lyceum. "Here is a convertible audience & here are no stiff conventions that prescribe a method, a style. . . . Here everything is admissible. . . . Here is a pulpit that makes other pulpits tame & ineffectual. . . . Here he may lay himself out utterly, large, enormous, prodigal, on the subject of the hour. Here he may dare to hope for ecstasy & eloquence" (JMN, VII, 265).

The success of this first sustained lecture course under his own management encouraged Emerson to try his had again the following winter with a series of lectures entitled Human Culture that continued where the last left off with an examination of the development of the individual. In ten lectures read between December 6, 1837 and February 7, 1838, Emerson outlined his concept of self culture. The lectures in this series possess a dialectical unity, with paired lectures examining opposite sides of the same phenomenon as is evident from his working outline in EL, II, 208:

I. Culture
II. Culture from the Convenient & Common;
III. " " Vocation, or The Hands
IV. " of the Intellect; or The Head
V. " of Art; or The Eye
VI. " of Society; or The Heart
VII. " from the Laws of Life
VIII. " from the Individual or The Name
IX. " of the Heroic
X. " of the Holy

Although Emerson modified the sequence of lectures before giving them, he maintained the dual perspective of the individual and society. The course represents a systematic exposition of Emerson's thought that approaches the best of his later work. The introductory lecture proclaimed Emerson's vision of culture: "His own Culture, the unfolding of his nature, is the chief end of man. A divine impulse at the core of his being, impels him to do this" (EL, II, 215). He identified "the basis of Culture" as "that part of human nature which in philosophy is called the Ideal" (EL, II, 217), and proclaimed, "the universal presence of this vision of the Better in all parts of life is the characteristic of human nature" (EL, II, 217). While admitting the "utter incompetency of a single mind to draw the chart of human nature," he proclaimed "that confidence may be inspired in the powers of the Will and in the aspirations of the Better by the voice and the faith of a believing man." He concluded, "I wish to inspire hope and shall esteem it the highest success if any ingenuous mind shall own that his scope has been extended; his conscience fortified and that more has been suggested than said" (EL, II, 229).

As the editors of the lectures remark, "Culture in this high sense had little precise definition but was one of the magic words, like Reason, Freedom, Virtue, etc., by which he hoped to issue the call of worth and conjure man's slumbering higher nature to rush full grown into day" (EL, II, 210). Emerson himself joked that "the notes I collect in the course of a year are so miscellaneous that when our people grow rabid for lectures . . . I huddle all my old almanaks together & look in the encyclopaedia for the amplest cloak of a name whose folds will reach unto & cover extreme & fantastic things. . . . The name [of Culture] is sky high & cannot easily be clutched & monopolized" (L, II, 121). The audience responded to the call and even Emerson admitted to himself in his journal that the audience showed "a gratifying interest" in "the views" expressed. He further noted that "the ten lectures were read on ten pleasant winter evenings on consecutive Wednesdays" (EL, II, 211). The success of this series confirmed Emerson's commitment to lecturing. He wrote to his brother William that "henceforth perhaps I shall live by lecturing which promises to be good bread. I have relinquished my ecclesiastical charge at E. Lexington & shall not preach more except from the Lyceum" (L, II, 120).

Convers Francis, who had heard the previous series, noted the same problems in the introductory lecture, December 6, 1837: "The fault is that of too quick and easy generalization--the natural fault of a mind that dwells habitually on ideas and principles. But every sentence in it was a gem of thought. His description of the ideal, the universal aspiration toward the better, was admirable, and what some of his statements are not, it was clear." After hearing Emerson's lecture on "The Head" he wrote, "The lecture, on the whole, I think superior to any I have heard from Mr. E., more methodical, and coherent."[7]

With the lecture series, The Present Age, given from December 1839 to

February 1840 in Boston, Emerson's role as the inspired teacher or seer who announced his own vision to the audience changed to that of an objective observer who reported what he saw of the world to the audience. In searching for a subject for his course of lectures, Emerson mused in his journal, "Shall I not explore for the subject of my new lectures the character, resources & tendencies of the Present Age" (JMN, VII, 283). Later after deciding on a subject, he reflected on the method he would use: "I cast myself upon the Age & will not resist it. Passive I will think what it thinketh & say what it saith. All my hope of insight & of successful reporting lies in my consciousness of fidelity & the abdication of all will in the matter" (JMN, VII, 283). The introductory lecture announced the problem of the age as Emerson saw it: "The whole hope and vigor of the period centres in the new importance of the individual man" (EL, III, 199). He explored this theme in ten lectures given from December 4, 1839 to February 12, 1840 at the Masonic Temple in Boston.

Emerson forthrightly confided to his journal his aim as a secular preacher on the eve of the commencement of a new course of lectures. He wrote: "I am to indicate constantly, though all unworthy, the Ideal and Holy Life, the life within life . . . . I am to celebrate the spiritual powers in their infinite contrast to the mechanical powers & the mechanical philosophy of this time. I am to console the brave sufferers under evils whose end they cannot see by appeals to the great optimism self-affirmed in all bosoms" (JMN, VII, 271).

This series was written and delivered while Emerson worked on the manuscript for the *Essays* and several of the lectures were used extensively in that volume. Although he preferred to work on his manuscript, financial necessity compelled him to turn to the lecture room for money. He wrote to his brother William, "I see plainly I shall have no choice about lecturing again next winter; I must do it" (L, II, 218). The demands on his time made it difficult for Emerson to devote as much time to the preparation of the lectures as he felt necessary. He complained that "I have not done what I hoped when I said, I will try it once more. . . . And why? . . . I can only expend say, twenty one hours on each lecture. . . . Could I spend sixty hours on each . . . I should hate myself less" (JMN, VII, 338-339). He calculated that the "average attendance at a lecture consisted of about 400 persons" but that included the 120 free passes that he gave to his friends (JMN, VII, 338). Emerson found personal if not financial satisfaction in the series, noting that "the young people are so attentive & out of the hall ask me so many questions, that I assume all the air of Age & sapience" (CEC, 261). Still pressed for funds, Emerson used his brother William's contacts to schedule three lectures in New York City, using an old lecture "The Philosophy of History" and two lectures from the newly delivered "Present Age" course on three nights starting March 10 and concluding March 17. Emerson's first appearance in New York City did not attract much attention from the press, but the lectures were so well attended that the president of the lyceum reported that "more single tickets were sold to your lectures than to all the rest" (L, II, 272, ft. note 112).

## THE BUSINESS OF LECTURING

The publication of *Essays* in March of 1841 did not bring enough money to meet the increasing financial responsibilities of his growing household. By the end of the year Emerson supported himself, his wife, three children, his mother, and Henry David Thoreau; partially supported a retarded brother Bulkeley; employed a boy, a cook, and a maid; and paid for the education of Hillman Sampson, a family friend. He also entertained extensively his Concord neighbors such as the Bronson Alcotts and friends such as Margaret Fuller, Caroline Sturgis, and Sam Ward. He acted as the literary agent in the United States for Thomas Carlyle, advancing his American publishers money to cover printing costs. The publication of *Essays* also marked a decided change in Emerson's method of composition as he developed his own genre of the lecture-essay. No longer would he write solely for oral presentation. His compositions would be written so that with minimal change they could be printed. His writing style became more concentrated as the connective passages were dropped. Single sentences condensed so much meaning that the effect of hearing them was analogous to hearing "the explosion of a cannon."[8] These lectures on The Times represent Emerson's achievement in the lecture-essay, a form that retained the discursive nature of the lecture with its informal and even colloquial tone but held it under the tighter control of organic form.

As his style matured, he moved further away from the overt sermonic structure toward what Richard Adams has called the organic method of development based upon a central or unifying metaphor.[9] Emerson expressed this idea as "a process in the mind very analogous to crystallization in the mineral kingdom. I think of a particular fact of singular beauty & interest. In thinking of it I am led to many more thoughts which show themselves first partially and afterwards more fully. But in the multitude of them I see no order" (JMN, III, 316). It was this refusal to be bound by the conventions of composition that led many of his auditors to complain that his lectures were unorganized and difficult to follow.

The New York *Evening Post* on February 28, 1842 advertised Emerson's course of six lectures on "The Times" to be given at the Society Library from March 3 to March 14. Emerson opened with an introductory lecture and considered in order: "The Poet," "The Conservative," "The Transcendentalist," "Manners," and future "Prospects." His brother William, always an admirer, wrote to Mary Moody Emerson that the course "produced a marked sensation in the best part of our community & has created for him many lovers & admirers here" (L, III, 21 note 73). William Cullen Bryant, editor of the New York *Post*, used his column to welcome Emerson to the city and noted that he "is one of the most interesting public speakers whom we . . . have heard. He possesses great powers of language . . . and a very impressive delivery."[10] Emerson wrote to his wife that "we had a pretty good company in the lecture room, although the hall is small & I see not how it will hold people enough to answer any of my profane & worldly purposes which you & I at this moment have so much at heart" (L, III, 21). Although the lectures did not earn enough money to pay his increasing debts, they did attract "some interesting persons" including "Henry James [Sr.] who paid me a long visit after my first lecture" and whom Emerson found to be "a very manlike thorough seeing person" (L, III, 23). Not all his encounters in New York City were so congenial. Emerson found himself pursued by Horace Greeley, the reform-minded editor of the New York *Tribune*, and Albert Brisbane, the ardent social reformer who popularized Fourierite socialist communities in the United States. At a meeting at their Grahamite boarding house, Brisbane invited Emerson "with all my party to come in directly & join him." A bemused Emerson realized, "They are bent on popular action: I am in all my theory, ethics & politics a poet and of no more use in their New York than a rainbow or a firefly" (L, III, 15-23).

For the first time in his career, Emerson encountered full press coverage of his lectures. The *Tribune* sent stenographically trained reporters to take notes on them and published fairly complete summaries in the weekly *Tribune*, which had a vast circulation not only in the immediate vicinity but also in western New York and Ohio. These reports helped to make Emerson's reputation in those areas before he actually lectured there, but they also affected his ability to continue to repeat the lectures in other towns and earn additional return on his intellectual capital. He reported to his friend Carlyle, "the penny papers *reported* my lectures, somewhat to my chagrin when I tried to read them; many persons came & talked with me, and I felt when I came away that New York is open to me hence-forward whenever my Boston parish is not large enough" (CEC, 321). Unfortunately, his finances continued to worsen. A month later wrote to his brother William, "I learn today that the City Bank again declares *No dividend*, which makes me a loss of $900.00 in 18 months" (L, III, 40). He would have no other choice but to continue to lecture.

As he prepared a lecture series for the following year, he wrote Margaret Fuller, "I have in my portfolio the value of three pretty good lectures on New England which may become five before they get spoken" (L, III, 107-108). He opened the series at Philadelphia on January 23, 1843 with the first lecture on "New England" which did not seem to make a great impression on the lecture going public. He complained to his wife that in "the monstrous city of Phila. our hammer makes but a small dent therein. The first evening I thought the audience very small, perhaps 200. . . . I am not in the way of paying my debts pecuniary, which I dimly call to mind was one of my wife's reasons for sending me forth into this remote field" (L, III, 133). His lectures in Philadelphia would prove memorable, as he reported to Margaret Fuller, "at the end of my last lecture, one of the ladies rose as the audience were dispersing & gave us a good Quaker sermon" (L, III, 137-38).

He was already making plans to lecture in New York City and wrote to his brother William asking his help in arranging them. Even with his brother's aid, Emerson found that the Berean Society, the lyceum that engaged him, lacked competent management. The *Tribune* in its review of the lecture noted that "the audience [was] thinner than it would have been in a more accessible place, and on a less inclement evening"[11] After two more disappointing lectures, Emerson began the series anew at the Society Library on February 11, and concluded it on February 22, 1843. Even with the new location and the added publicity, the results were disappointing. He reported that "as far as money results go, my lecturing in N. Y. has had no success. The price of tickets is one half the price of last year & the expenses of the hall &c are the same as last year. . . . So that my payment for my work is as I counted something less than $9.00 per lecture the modestest compensation I ever received except once," (L, III, 150). As a consequence he advised Lidian "you must hold off all claimants for a little time & I will either earn some more pence, or, if not, borrow some for the present distress." A postscript to the letter adds, that "William has money to lend me, so I enclose a cheque for $25.00" (L, III, 142).

Emerson was also angry with the newspapers, claiming their "report is so ruinous to what truth & proportion is in my stories, that I cannot read them. Odious, Odious. It is just as if I had read a poem and the N. Y. Herald should then say, Mr. E. said thus & so, from stupidity to stupidity, & from fatuity to fatuity. I have sometimes heard that some of my auditors like the reports better than the speech" (L, III, 149).

Although the lectures on The Times given in New York City did not meet Emerson's financial needs, they did mark another important transition in his career. By taking his lectures to New York City and Philadelphia, Emerson moved out of the familiar circuit of New England to seek a wider audience. These first steps foreshadowed the direction of his career: a tour of England, and further travel in America including the western states of Ohio, Indiana, Illinois, Iowa, and Wisconsin.

## EMERSON ON "ELOQUENCE"

The lecture "Eloquence," reprinted in this book, is an example of Emerson's new format for the lecture-essay that proved popular as a single performance on the lecture circuit in the Midwestern states. On December 29, 1846, Emerson wrote to his brother William, "I have just now been writing a new paper on 'Eloquence' which interests me & which I am shortly to read as a lecture to the Mercantile Library in Boston" (L, III, 366). Although this was to be his first formal lecture on eloquence, it was not the first time he had spoken on the topic in conjunction with another subject in his lectures. His early biographical lecture on Edmund Burke contained several passages defining "the idea of eloquence" (EL, I, 198ff). The lecture on "Art" in the Philosophy of History series considered eloquence as one of the fine arts and noted that "architecture and eloquence are mixed arts, whose end is sometimes beauty and sometimes use" (EL, II, 45). And in the lecture on "Society" in the same series, Emerson pronounced eloquence "an example of a perfect society" in its effects on mankind. It is surprising that, given his long interest in the subject and his many reflections on it in his letters and journals, Emerson did not lecture on eloquence until after more than a decade as a public lecturer. The lecture on Eloquence became one of his most popular especially on the lyceum circuit in the Midwest.

## SOURCES FOR THE LECTURE

Emerson received a classical education at Harvard, where he read the Greek and Latin classics including Plato. His Bowdoin Prize essay written in 1820 was a study of "The Character of Socrates." In 1842, the Concord Lyceum gave him the thirteen-volume set of Victor Cousin's translation of Plato as a means of thanking him for lecturing before them without fees. Before that, his library contained several volumes of Plato, and he frequently copied passages from Plato into his journal. Not surprisingly, Plato is quoted twice by name in the lecture. Shortly before he began the composition of this lecture, Emerson wrote a lecture on Plato for the Representative Men series. Perhaps the experience of reading and reflecting on Plato's life and work was the immediate inspiration for the lecture on eloquence.

Certainly Hugh Blair, whose *Lectures* Emerson read during his second year at Harvard, provided the majority of the topics for the lecture. Although Emerson in his mature years developed his own ideas about rhetoric, Blair's influence is still evident in the many parallels between Blair's lecture, "Means of Improving in Eloquence," and Emerson's. For example, Blair lists the requirements of the eloquent speaker as:

1. A strong lively imagination
2. Quick sensibility of the heart
3. Solid judgment, and good sense, presence of mind
4. Personal character and disposition
5. Fund of knowledge
6. Habit of industry and application

Emerson discusses the following topics as characteristic of the eloquent speaker:

1. Imagery
2. Substantial personality
3. Sane man able to communicate his sanity
4. Strength of character
5. Have command of the facts
6. Method

The overlap between the two lists is obvious, and not only suggests Blair's influence but Emerson's familiarity with classical rhetoric as systematized by Cicero and Quintilian. Most of the topics on the lists can be subsumed under the familiar Aristotelian classification of the three forms of proof into *ethos* or character, *logos* or rational appeals, and *pathos* or psychological appeals.

Edward T. Channing, who became Boylston Professor of Rhetoric and Oratory at Harvard in 1819, further stimulated Emerson's thinking about the changing nature of eloquence. In his inaugural lecture, which Emerson heard, Channing distinguished between the eloquence of the ancients and the moderns by insisting that the development of educational institutions that have dispersed knowledge widely among the population has been responsible for the decline of the orator's power to sway an audience. His characterization of the modern audience closely matches Emerson's: "They are not assembled to be the subjects upon which he (the orator) may try the power of his eloquence, but to see what eloquence can do for the question. The subject is more thought of than the orator and what he says must come from the subject rather than his art."[12] Channing also insisted upon the moral dimension of eloquence: "I would mention the importance of character to all successful eloquence."[13]

Obviously, not all of Emerson's ideas about eloquence came second-hand from books. The son of a minister, Emerson grew up in a household that valued public speaking and in a time when the spoken word had great cultural authority. He lived during the Golden Age of American oratory, when Webster, Calhoun, and Clay held sway in Congress, when Edward Everett graced many public platforms, and when Wendell Phillips could be heard speaking against slavery throughout New England. As a minister and lecturer, he had first hand experience with many different audiences. His own observations went into the composition of this lecture, as is evident from the personal references in it to listening to ministers and attending trials.

## THE COMPOSITION OF THE LECTURE

Emerson collected ideas, observations, sentences, proverbs, and lines of poetry from his vast reading and recorded them in his journal along with chance observations, random thoughts, and casual comments made by his many visitors and Concord neighbors. The journal entries were cross-referenced and indexed to facilitate retrieval of the material. When Emerson needed to prepare a new lecture to meet a deadline, the journals show an increase in the number of entries dealing with the proposed subject. The entries may range from a single sentence to a long paragraph; in the composition of the lecture, the journal entry may be expanded or reduced to a single word. The finished manuscript resembled a mosaic of brilliant sentences--some original and some quoted--set off against a background of ideas whose connection to each other and to the individual sentences is not always readily apparent.

Emerson made a preliminary outline for the lecture in Journal O, which is contained in JMN, IX, 384. Under the heading "Eloquence" he lists the following topics:

Intellect 1. Method
2. Imagination
power of symbols
"rugged & awful crisis"

Irish Eloquence of common people
examples of the animal heat division
There must be spirit too

The composition of this lecture follows the pattern outlined above. Since Emerson had been writing a lecture on Plato for the Representative Men series just before beginning on the lecture on "Eloquence," several quotations from Plato copied from the journal are used in the lecture but transformed to meet fit the topical requirements. For example, the quotation from the *Republic*, "Plato. The fine laid on the just if they refuse to govern is the punishment of being governed by a base person" (JMN, IX, 184), becomes in the lecture an analogous warning to the eloquent person, "Plato says, that the punishment which the wise suffer, who refuse to take part in the government, is, to live under the government of worse men; and the like regret is suggested to all the auditors, as the penalty of abstaining to speak, that they shall hear worse orators than themselves."

After reflecting on the experience of hearing Father Taylor, the famous Methodist evangelist, Emerson wrote: "One orator makes many. How many orators sit mute there below. They come to get justice done to that ear & intuition which no Chatham & no Demosthenes has begun to satisfy" (JMN, X, 402). He combines that sentence with another entry from his journal to complete the thought: "No one can survey the face of an excited assembly, without being apprised of new opportunity for painting in fire human thought, and being agitated to agitate. How many orators sit mute there below! They come to get justice done to that ear and intuition which no Chatham and no Demosthenes has begun to satisfy" (JMN, IX, 70).

Emerson changes the wording of quotations to suit his own sense of style, in some cases substituting Latinate words for the simpler words in his journal. He recorded Isocrates' definition of eloquence from an English translation of Plutarch as, "To make the great little, & the little great," Isocrates said "was the orator's part" (JMN, IX, 231). When he used this in the lecture, it became, "Isocrates described his art, as "the power of magnifying what was small and diminishing what was great."

Sometimes a list of words or names in the journal serves as a reminder to Emerson of paragraphs he intends to write. Thus, the words, "Eloquence, True Thomas, Pied Piper, Le Menetrier de Meudon" become in turn a paragraph comparing the power of eloquence to "that despotism which poets have celebrated" in the stories of the Pied Piper, and in the story by Meudon of the minstrel who made the pall-bearers dance around the bier (JMN, X, 77).

An entry in the journal that uses the personal pronoun becomes transformed for the lecture into the more impersonal and formal third person: "I well remember my stay at the Hotel Giaccheri, in Palermo, where I listened with pleasure to the novelty of the melodramatic conversation of a dozen citizens of the world" (JMN, IX, 18), becomes "The traveller in Sicily needs no gayer melodramatic exhibition than the *table d'hote* of his inn will afford him." He delighted in aphoristic sentences and frequently copied them into his journal. One that he used exactly as copied is, "Every bullet will hit the mark, which is first dipped in the marksman's blood." This sentence was recopied into Journal W, which served as the working journal for the "Eloquence" lecture from an earlier journal (JMN, X, 202).

In composing this lecture, Emerson borrowed freely from earlier lectures, lifting whole passages and examples from them. For example, the passage containing the testimony to the great eloquence of Demosthenes and Warren Hastings is taken directly from the lecture on "Edmund Burke," as is the line that Demosthenes wrote on his own shield as a motto, "Good Fortune" (EL, I, 199).

## EMERSONIAN ELOQUENCE

Virtually the entire lecture, including the introduction, can be found in some form in passages Emerson copied into his journal or working notes that he recorded there. Given this compositional process in which sentences or even whole paragraphs are rearranged to make a lecture, it is easy to see why the lecture does not follow a linear pattern or systematically consider the idea of eloquence. As with most of Emerson's lectures, this one circles around the idea of eloquence--focusing now on one aspect, now on another. When Emerson introduces various definitions of eloquence, he never seriously investigates them or even attempts to compare them. There is no argument with any of them--although they are a very heterogeneous lot--and there is only one passing comment that gives any indication of what Emerson thinks about them. The quotation from the Koran that seems to deny the possibility of eloquence is thrown in with the rest of the quotations with no explanation. This habit of juxtaposing odd quotations from unfamiliar sources is a feature of Emerson's style that was frequently noted and parodied. At the end of this series he simply asserts, using a rhetorical question, that "the end of eloquence is--is it not?--to alter in a pair of hours, perhaps in a half-hour's discourse, the convictions and habits of years." This is asserted as though the question were settled, but if the idea is so obvious, what was the purpose of introducing the quotation from the Koran? Was it to show a diversity of opinion on the topic? Or to show that different cultures view the idea differently? We have no idea, because Emerson doesn't really use the quotation to develop an argument or even an observation.

Emerson's view of eloquence closely follows his classical sources, particularly Plato's *Phaedrus*. He insists that the speaker must be in command of the facts and have knowledge that provides a context for them. The eloquent speaker teaches the audience to see the world through his eyes, which to Emerson means to see the truth that underlies the phenomenal experience of everyday life. The speaker may need to resort to symbols to express this truth by putting "the argument into a concrete shape, into an image." A crisis in public affairs precipitates a rhetorical situation that demands an eloquent speech for its resolution. This will be the "best speech of the best soul," based on the moral sentiment as the orator sees through all masks to the eternal truth and communicates this truth to the audience. In describing the eloquent speaker, Emerson could not help but describe himself.

## EMERSON SPEAKING

This study focuses on the early lectures for which reliable texts can be established. In the early lectures given from 1833 to 1842, Emerson used the lecture form as the primary vehicle to express his ideas. By the 1850s the lecture had become secondary to the published essay and served primarily financial rather than artistic ends. Lectures were repeated more frequently as Emerson traveled farther afield in search of new audiences. When Emerson began his extensive lecture trips to the Midwest, he began to patch together "new" lectures from older ones, transposing whole paragraphs or even pages from previous lectures to produce a composite. Published as essays in the later collections such as *The Conduct of Life*, and *Letters and Social Aims*, these composite productions were much worked-over versions of what he had actually spoken several years before in some small town in Ohio or Indiana. Nancy Simmons, whose investigation of the editorial work that produced these works is definitive, reports that "the state of the surviving manuscripts . . . for the later lectures" [consists of] "bundles of loose leaves. . . . Often introductions and conclusions were lacking or one bundle might contain two or more introductions used at different times." For example, "Social Aims" had "undoubtedly undergone much change . . . in more than seventy readings from Boston to Milwaukee." As printed "the first third of the printed essay closely follows the outlines provided by an 1864 account in the Boston *Commonwealth*," while "the remainder incorporates material on conversation largely from "Table Talk."[14] Under the circumstances, the editors of the critical edition of Emerson's works at Harvard University Press have decided not to publish any lectures beyond the ones already released.

Lectures in Boston and New York became social events, with the same people showing up year after year to see Waldo and to be seen by others. Emerson became a public figure whose personality and presence on the platform were experienced by the cultivated classes much as going to a museum or an art exhibit might be. In this later stage of his life, Emerson became an Icon of culture--the sage of Concord--and was used to promote the genteel culture of New England.[15] It is during this period that Emerson adopted the highly successful persona of "Mr. Emerson, lecturer." Although Emerson had many motives for becoming a lecturer, at bottom he needed a vocation that would pay enough money to support his household. He was shrewd enough to realize that his idealist message would not be credible if his listeners thought he was only lecturing for money. Thus he always conveyed an aura of earnestness--of moral elevation--that was reinforced by his traditional ministerial garb of black suit, black tie, and white shirt, and his formal demeanor. He was always, "Mr. Emerson," not "Waldo," to the lecture committees or the many people he encountered on his travels. His reserved manner protected his privacy and projected an image of a lofty thinker more comfortable with big ideas than the minutia of small talk. He was not an entertainer like Barnum, nor a sophisticated world traveled like Bayard Taylor, nor even a handsome, publicity-seeking popular preacher like Beecher. He was Mr. Emerson, of Concord, reputed a transcendentalist thinker and (later in his career) a Yankee Sage.

Judged by almost any criteria, Emerson was a successful lecturer. He supported himself by lecturing; he was constantly in demand; he was invited back again and again by the same lecture committees; he was acclaimed for his lectures. And yet when many of today's critics examine reports of Emerson's lectures written by competent observers, they find it hard to believe that a lecturer so artless in his presentational skills could have held audiences in thrall. One of his English admirers, George Gilfillan, who arranged for the highly successful English tour said of him: "He reads his lectures without excitement, without energy, scarcely even with emphasis. . . . There is no betrayal of emotion except now and then when a slight tremble in his voice proclaims that he has arrived at some spot of thought to him peculiarly sacred or dear."[16]

Perhaps the most complete portrait of Emerson lecturing is the following:

> Precisely at four o'clock the lecturer glided in, and suddenly appeared at the reading-desk. Tall, thin, his features aquiline, his eye piercing and fixed; the effect as he stood quietly before his audience, was at first somewhat startling, and then nobly impressive. Having placed his manuscript on the desk with nervous rapidity, and paused, the lecturer then quickly, and, as it were, with a flash of action turned over the first leaf, whispering at the same time, "Gentlemen and ladies." The initial sentences were next pronounced in a low tone, a few words at a time, hesitatingly, as if then extemporaneously meditated, and not, as they really were, premeditated and forewritten. There was, however, nothing like acquired elocution, no regular intonation, in fact none of the usual oratorical artifices, but for the most part a shapeless delivery (only varied by certain nervous twitches, and angular movements of the hand and arms, curious to see and even smile at), and calling for such cooperation on the part of the auditor to help out its shortcomings. Along with all this, there was an eminent bonhomie, earnestness, and sincerity, which bespoke sympathy and respect,-nay, more, secured veneration.[17]

All observers agreed that Emerson had few gestures, A reporter who heard him lecture in Cincinnati described him as standing "at an acute angle toward his audience" and using no gestures "beyond the motion of the left hand at his side, as if the intensity of his thought were escaping, like the electricity of a battery at that point"[18] Most commented on the characteristics of Emerson's voice. The literary critic Edwin Whipple recalled that "There was nothing sensual, nothing even sensuous, nothing weakly melodious, in his utterance; but his voice had the stern keen, penetrating sweetness which made it a fit organ for his self-centered, commanding mind."[19] Other listeners agreed that "His voice is full, strong, and rich, but he speaks with a sort of hesitation, not unpleasant but the contrary, as if he were struggling with thought too great for immediate utterance."[20]

This hesitation in his delivery was noted by many observers. Bronson Alcott suggested that Emerson had consciously adopted this manner of reading to suggest a sense of spontaneity to his delivery: "In speaking he pleases, practicing a sort of hesitancy between the readings of his paragraphs, as of the springs of locks or choice of keys at the showing of cabinet specimens."[21] John Jay Chapman observed that "On the platform his manner of speech was a living part of his words. The pauses and hesitation, the abstraction, the searching, the balancing, the turning forward and back of the leaves of his lecture, and then the discovery, the illumination, the gleam of lightning which you saw before your eyes descend into a man of genius--all this was Emerson.

He invented this style of speaking."[22] Some were put off by his peculiar "style of oratory . . . full of quaint jerks and turns of thought and quaint halts and modulations of speech, . . . devoid of the slightest suggestion of a desire to let either help the other by any grace of ornament or oratory."[23]

And yet listening to Emerson could be an intensely emotional experience, as Samuel Bowles testified in a letter to Austin Dickinson, brother to Emily: "It is pictures, landscapes, poetry, music, babies, and beautiful women rolled up in an hour of talk. It takes the place of making love in our young days."[24] Henry Wadsworth Longfellow wrote to a friend, "Don't fail to hear Emerson's lectures. The difference between him and most other lecturers is this. From Emerson you go away and remember nothing save that you have been much delighted, you have had a pleasant dream in which angelic voices spoke. From most other lecturers you go away and remember nothing save that you have been lamentably bored."[25]

Emerson's effectiveness as a lecturer derived in large part from the ethical appeal of his persona--a persona that he developed in his apprenticeship on the lecture platform. In part, this persona derived from and was reinforced by his conscious use of sermonic structures, which gave an ethical cast to his secular speeches. In time, the sermonic structures receded further and further in the background as Emerson developed other forms more suited to his needs. But the persona remained and was strengthened through countless performances. This is not to suggest that there was any lack of sincerity on Emerson's part in the public portrayal of his personality. Rather, this complex man chose to present to the public one side of his sensibility as a means to reinforce the appeal of his message. Certainly a man who could write the following about his aims for a new course of lectures had a vision and a purpose that rings true: "But truly I would not be frivolous or conventional in this attempt however slight at expounding the spirit & tendency of my day. Let us in the one golden hour allowed us be great & true, be shined upon by the sun & moon, & feel in our pulse circulations from the heart of nature" (L, II, 246).

## NOTES

1. The introductions and notes to each volume of *The Early Lectures of Ralph Waldo Emerson*, 3 vols., ed. Stephen E. Whicher, Robert E. Spiller, and Wallace Williams (Cambridge, Mass.: Harvard University Press, 1959-1972), 1: xxi.

2. Ralph Rusk, *The Life of Ralph Waldo Emerson* (New York: Charles Scribner's Sons, 1949), 238-39.

3. Rusk, *Life*, 247-8.

4. David M. Robinson, *Apostle of Culture: Emerson as Preacher and Lecturer* (Philadelphia: University of Pennsylvania Press, 1988), 103-111.

5. Quoted in John McAleer, *Ralph Waldo Emerson: Days of Encounter* (Boston: Little, Brown, 1984) 271.

6. Arthur Cushman McGiffert, Jr., *Young Emerson Speaks. Unpublished Discourses on Many Subjects by Ralph Waldo Emerson* (Port Washington, N.Y.: Kennicat Press, 1968), xxi-xxii.

7. McAleer, *Days of Encounter*, 277.

8. New York *Tribune*, February 25, 1843, p. 2.

9. Richard Adams, "Emerson and the Organic Metaphor," *PMLA* 69 (1954): 117-30.

10. New York *Post*, February 28, 1842.

11. New York *Tribune*, February 11, 1843, p. 1.

12. Edward T. Channing, *Lectures Read to Seniors in Harvard College*, ed. Dorothy I. Anderson and Waldo W. Braden (Carbondale: Southern Illinois University Press, 1968), 17.

13. Channing, *Lectures,* 23.

14. Nancy Craig Simmons, "Arranging the Sibylline Leaves: James Elliot Cabot's Work as Emerson's Literary Executor," *Studies in the American Renaissance* 1983: 347.

15. Rusk, *Life*, 388ff.

16. McAleer, *Days of Encounter,* 489.

17. Quoted from *Jerrold's Newspaper* in George Willis Cooke, *Ralph Waldo Emerson: His Life, Writings, and Philosophy* (Boston: James R. Osgood, 1882), 115-16.

18. Cincinnati *Times*, January 28, 1857.

19. Edwin Percy Whipple, *Recollections of Emminent Men* (Boston, 1887) 131-32.

20. Cincinnati *Times*, January 28, 1857.

21. Bronson Alcott, *The Journals of Bronson Alcott*, 2 vols. ed. Odell Shepard (Port Washington, N.Y.: Kennikat Press, 1966), 2: 338.

22. John Jay Chapman, *Emerson and other Essays* (New York: 1904), 33.

23. Indianapolis *Journal*, January 28, 1863.

24. McAleer, *Days of Encounter*, 491.

25. Henry Wadsworth Longfellow, *The Letters of Henry Wadsworth Longfellow*, 6 vols., ed. Andrew Hilen (Cambridge, Mass.: Harvard University Press, 1966-1982), 2: 215.

# 4

# From "The American Scholar" to "The Young American"

During the period from the "The American Scholar" address in 1837 to the "The Young American" lecture in 1844, Emerson's thought underwent a significant shift from a position of critical idealism to a resigned acceptance of life. Stephen Whicher identified a crisis in Emerson's life occurring about 1840 as Emerson became aware "that the pattern of his convictions is undergoing an unforeseen modification" from "a subjective toward an objective idealism" that conceives of nature in the general idea of evolution.[1] This tendency is first notable in the lecture series The Present Age given in the winter of 1839-1840 in Boston. The editors of the lectures note Emerson's new role as "observer" or "reporter" and suggest that in editing his lecture manuscripts for publication in the *Essays*, Emerson recognized the two voices or personas of the teacher or reporter in them (EL, III, xv). Increasingly it was the voice of the reporter that he used in his lyceum lectures in the West and it is this voice, with its serene optimism, that has become part of the common culture with half-remembered aphorisms such as "Hitch your wagon to a Star." The two texts included in this section can be read as Emerson teaching Americans the importance of a critical intelligence and Emerson reporting to Americans the social and economic constraints upon it.

The circumstances of Emerson's "most famous speech" did not begin auspiciously. On June 22, 1837, Professor Felton issued a written invitation to Emerson to give the address for the August 31, meeting explaining that the Reverend Jonathan Wainright had declined. Although the lateness of the invitation did not give the speaker much time to prepare the address, it was all that was necessary to call forth from Emerson his celebrated address on the American Scholar. Emerson's preparation for this occasion had a long foreground in his early manhood. Coming of age during a period of great economic expansion and change in the character of American society, Emerson witnessed the changing status of the minister-scholar as the values of business and trade came to dominate the times. His early journals are filled with his meditations on the problematic role of the scholar in a bustling entrepreneurial age. The speech could as easily be addressed to Emerson, himself, as to anyone else in his immediate or extended audience.[2]

The speech was accompanied by all the pomp and ceremony of an academic occasion, including a gowned procession from University Hall to the First Church where the over 200 graduating Seniors joined by faculty and alumni filled the small church to capacity. Graduating Seniors including Richard Henry Dana, James Russell Lowell, and Henry Thoreau were joined by the President of Harvard, Josiah Quincy, and prominent alumni, some of whom served on the Board of Overseers. What might this distinguished company have been thinking of their featured speaker as they awaited his introduction? They would be aware that he came from an old family and that both his brothers had distinguished themselves as scholars. But Waldo himself might have seemed an unusual choice to them as the featured speaker of the day. He was a mediocre student at best. It was true that he had occupied a prominent pulpit for three years, and had published a slim volume of philosophical thought, but for the past few years he had no regular position save that of an occasional lecturer and may have seemed to these accomplished men to be drifting. He had a slight reputation for being controversial.[3]

Following a prayer by Reverend Rogers of Boston, the speaker was introduced. The audience saw a tall, young man of thirty-four with thinning brown hair and blue eyes ascend the pulpit and arrange his manuscript in front of him. His theme, "The American Scholar," was not original, having served countless speakers before him as a source of inspiration. Few, perhaps, expected to hear anything original that day. Others may have suspected that this unconventional young minister would not be content with the usual cliches and platitudes that had been the staple fare of past occasions. Whatever their expectations or doubts, the audience listened respectfully as Emerson began his formal salutation.

It is a critical commonplace to discuss the address as the cultural equivalent of the political Declaration of Independence. It is more than that. The occasion called for a ceremonial address, but Emerson used the opportunity to issue a manifesto not so much of American literary independence but of intellectual independence from the dead weight of tradition and the hostility of the commercial society. In his journal Emerson stated the purpose of his address: "The hope to arouse young men at Cambridge to a worthier view of their literary duties prompts me to offer the theory of the Scholar's function. He has an office to perform in society. What is it? To arouse the intellect; to keep it erect & sound; to keep admiration in the hearts of the people; to keep the eye open upon its spiritual aims" (JMN, V, 364-365).

Indeed, Emerson spent little time acknowledging the ceremonial aspects of the occasion but quickly revealed his intention to challenge the complacence of the audience, "Our anniversary is one of hope, and perhaps, not enough of labor." The following sentences contrast this meeting unfavorably with past gatherings of scholars in Ancient Greece, Medieval France, and contemporary meetings of learned societies in Britain and Europe. The rest of the introduction foreshadows the central ideas of the speech that in America the scholar is indolent, marginal, and remote from the essential activity of society. Even his proclamation of hope in "the precious sign of an indestructible instinct," for the love of letters is immediately qualified by the recognition that "the sluggard intellect of our continent" has not yet fulfilled the world's expectations. His optimism is expressed not in a declarative sentence but ambiguously in a rhetorical question, "Who can doubt that Poetry will revive and lead in a new age," which implies that poetry is now as moribund as the other arts in America. After hearing these words, the audience must have sensed that they were not about to hear a conventional ceremonial address filled with platitudes praising the American scholar.

This speech mocks the critical commonplaces that Emerson writes in sentences and is incapable of sustained argument. The speech is well organized and develops large units of thought in a systematic manner. The organizing principle of the speech is based on the metaphor of the whole man contrasted with the partial man produced by the specialization of the commercial and industrial age: "The state of society is one in which the members have suffered amputation from the trunk, and strut about so many walking monsters,-a good finger, a neck, a stomach, an elbow, but never a man. . . . In this distribution of functions, the scholar is the delegated intellect. In the right state, he is Man Thinking. In the degenerate state, when the victim of society, he tends to become a mere thinker, or, still worse, the parrot of other men's thinking."

Having introduced the ideal of the scholar as Man Thinking, Emerson divides the speech into two parts: what influences create the scholar and what are the duties of the scholar? The first section is clearly introduced by a topical sentence: "Let us see him [the scholar] in his school and consider him in reference to the main influences he receives." The three influences are nature, books, and action. Emerson clearly numbers these, uses transitions between sections, and at the end of this part of the exposition, summarizes: "I have now spoken of the education of the scholar by nature, by books, and by action. It remains to say somewhat of his duties."

Beneath this conventional pattern can be detected the outline of the sermonic form that Emerson adapted to his inspirational lectures. The text is the fable of the whole man divided into separate men who perform different functions. The doctrine of "Man Thinking" is derived from the fable and contains "the whole theory of his office." Emerson invites us to "see him in his school, and consider him in reference to the main influences he receives." This is the explication of the doctrine in which Emerson identifies nature, books, and action as the influences and constraints operating on Man Thinking. Lastly, Emerson shows the audience the "uses" to which the doctrine may be put as he describes the "duties" of the scholar: "The office of the scholar is to cheer, to raise, and to guide men by showing them facts amidst appearances." He will conclude with an inspirational vision of the future.

The speech is not only united by the progression of ideas but by the choice of images. Within each section of the speech, Emerson selects images appropriate to the influences on the scholar. In the first section on nature the images are of force, movement, growth, and change: "Ever the winds blow; ever the grass grows. Every day, men and women, conversing, beholding and beholden. . . . There is never an end to the inexplicable continuity of this web of God, but always circular power returning into itself." The scholar in studying nature is dealing with elemental forces "whose beginning, whose ending he never can find," that nonetheless follow a law that is also a law of the human mind. Both man and nature "proceed from one root: one is leaf and one is flower." Nature's "beauty is the beauty of his own mind. Its laws are the laws of his own mind. . . . The ancient precept, 'Know thyself' and the modern precept, 'Study nature' become at last one maxim." The images reinforce one of his central ideas that there is a correspondence between the natural universe and the human mind.

He next considers the influence of the past as represented by books. This is perhaps the most disjointed section of the speech as Emerson both affirms the importance of past knowledge learned through books and warns against a complacent acceptance of received dogma. He is particularly eager to distinguish the creative scholar from the stereotype of the bookworm-that "booklearned class, who value books, as such . . . the emendators, the bibliomaniacs of all degrees." This section is dominated by images of diet, food, and health which Emerson foreshadowed in his introduction, "millions that around us are rushing into life, cannot always be fed on the sere remains of foreign harvests." Emerson sees the scholar as "transmuting life into truth" in the process of writing a book. He compares it to the process of distilling pure and imperishable truth from the raw materials of experience. But nothing comes from nothing. To be creative, the scholar must test the learning of books against his own experience: "When the mind is braced by labor and invention, the page of whatever book we read becomes luminous with manifold allusion." He warns against a thin diet of books only: "We all know that as the human body can be nourished on any food, though it were boiled grass and the broth of shoes, so the human mind can be fed by any knowledge. And great and heroic men have existed who had almost no other information than by the printed page. I only would say that it needs a strong head to bear that diet." Again, he warns that "man thinking must not be subdued by his instruments." When the scholar can "read God directly, the hour is too precious to be wasted in other men's transcripts of their readings." He calls for "creative reading" of "only the authentic utterance of the oracle." In deference to the audience he is addressing, he concedes that "there is a portion of reading quite indispensable to a wise man. History and exact science he must learn by laborious reading. Colleges, in like manner, have their indispensable office,-to teach elements."

Action, the third influence on the scholar, is subordinate but "essential." Without it, "he is not yet man. Without it, thought can never ripen into truth." Emerson is eager to correct the "notion that the scholar should be a recluse . . . unfit for any handiwork or public labor." He sees action as the natural corrective for the scholar's tendency to depend on the thin abstractions of books and the love of system building. This section of the speech is dominated by images of growth and change. He compares action to "the raw material out of which the intellect moulds her splendid products. A strange process too, this, by which experience is converted into thought, as a mulberry leaf is converted into satin."

Having diagnosed the condition of the intellectual in a materialistic society, Emerson prescribes "his duties. They are such as become man thinking." In the last part of the address, Emerson challenges the educated class "to guide men by showing them facts amidst appearances. He calls for a "free and brave" intellect that can serve as the critical intelligence for the age that shall "wake [men] and they shall quit the false good and leap to the true."

He concludes by identifying "some of the auspicious signs of the coming days." One of these is the democratic spirit that is invigorating the cultural life. This idea inspires Emerson: "I ask not for the great, the remote, the romantic; what is doing in Italy or Arabia; what is Greek art, or Provencal Minstrelsy; I embrace the common, I explore and sit at the feet of the familiar, the low. Give me insight into today, and you may have the antique and future worlds. What would we really know the meaning of? The meal in the firkin; the milk in the pan; the ballad in the street; the news of the boat; the glance of the eye; the form and the gait of the body;-show me the ultimate reason of these matters"

A second auspicious sign is the "new importance given to the single person." A growing recognition of individual moral responsibility is necessary in Emerson's mind for "true union as well as greatness."

Having identified causes for optimism that the mission of the scholar is vital to the health of the society and that it is gradually having a salutary effect, Emerson returns to his theme of literary nationalism: "This confidence in the unsearched might of man, belongs by all motives, by all prophecy, by all preparation, the American Scholar. We have listened too long to the courtly muses of Europe. . . . What is the remedy? . . . . If the single man plants himself indomitable on his instincts, and there abide, the huge world will come round to him." His conclusion unites the theme of literary nationalism with his optimism in the democratic spirit of the times and his confidence in the salutary power of the intellectual class. In a series of declaratory sentences he affirms: "We will walk on our own feet; we will work with our own hands; we will speak our own minds. The study of letters shall be no longer a name for pity, for doubt, and for sensual indulgence. The dread of man and the love of man shall be a wall of defense and a wreath of joy around all. A nation of men will for the first time exist, because each believes himself inspired by the Divine Soul which also inspires all men."

What did the audience make of the speech? At a dinner following the speech, Edward Everett, one of Emerson's youthful heroes, and at the time the Governor of Massachusetts, complimented him on the speech, and Charles Warren proposed a witty toast, "The spirit of Concord. It makes us all of one mind," punning on Emerson's newly adopted town. Emerson was so pleased that he recorded it in his journal (JMN, V, 376). Oliver Wendell Holmes who was present wrote many years later that to the "young men" it was "as if a prophet had been proclaiming to them." The only immediately recorded observation by anyone in the audience is a note by John Pierce, an old alumnus who never missed such occasions. He wrote: "Rev. Ralph Waldo Emerson gave an oration, of 1 1/4 hour, on The American Scholar. It was to me in the misty, dreamy, unintelligible style of Swedenborg, Coleridge, and Carlyle. He professed to have method; but I could not trace it except in his own annunciation. It was well spoken, and all seemed to attend but how many were in my own predicament of making little of it I have no means of ascertaining." Perhaps he spoke for many who heard Emerson that day. We do know that there was sufficient interest in the speech that an edition of 500 copies printed on September 23, 1837 sold out within a month and a second edition was printed.

When he read a copy of the speech, Thomas Carlyle wrote strong words of encouragement to Emerson: "lo, out of the West, comes a clear utterance, clearly recognizable as a mans voice and I have a kinsman and brother: God be thanked for it. I could have wept to read that speech; the clear high melody of it went tingling thro' my hear" (CEC, 173). He prayed, "may God grant you strength, for you have a fearful work to do!" (CEC, 174).

The speech still challenges the American intellectual today. Although the material conditions of the intellectual class have changed since Emerson's day-the expansion of higher education has provided more opportunities for employment-the psychological sense of alienation from the real business of the society still exists. Many intellectuals find that the opportunities to participate in government decision making compromise their independent judgment, as the memoirs of those who served in the Kennedy and Johnson administrations during the escalation of the Vietnam war testify. Although literary nationalism is a minor theme in the address, Emerson's few words on that subject remind us that recent social and literary criticism in the United States is still enthralled with French and Continental models. Because its theme of self-trust resonates so strongly with the individualistic values of Americans, it is now universally recognized as one of the essential statements about the cultural life of Americans.[4]

**THE YOUNG AMERICAN**

"The Young American," read before the Mercantile Library Association in Boston on the 7th of February, 1844, is a good example of Emerson's inspirational style. The very title, "The Young American," alludes to the "Young American" movement in literature centered around the *Democratic Review*, which called for a distinctly American literature. In the 1840s a generational sense of "newness" developed in some circles, which was a mixture of optimism, romanticism, and nationalism. Although not directly addressing the literary or esthetic issues posed by this group, Emerson does express the optimism of "manifest destiny" that motivated many of the young leaders of the movement. [5]

Emerson's language in the lecture is discursive, as befits an oral presentation. The introduction is long and filled with vivid images to convey the movement of his thought. He begins with the observation that much of American culture is derived from aristocratic European cultures: "We are sent to a feudal school to learn democracy." Introducing the theme of nationalism, he suggests that this cultural lag is being corrected as "America is beginning to assert itself to the senses and to the imagination of her children." He then considers the role that the railroad has in nationalizing the culture and reflects upon the importance of immigrant workers in building it. This leads to a consideration of their unjust treatment and to a reflection that in the future their lives will improve. Abruptly, he remembers that "I have abstained too long from speaking of that which led me to this topic--its importance in creating an American sentiment." And now he clearly identifies the railroad as the instrument for realizing America's destiny--it is "a magician's rod, in its power to evoke the sleeping energies of land and water." It is thus within the power of Americans to embrace the broad region of the continent and "appreciate the advantages opened to the human race in this country." Emerson celebrates "the land" as "the appointed remedy for whatever is false and fantastic in our culture. The great continent we inhabit is to be physic and food for our mind, as well as our body. The land, with its tranquillizing, sanative influences, is to repair the errors of a scholastic and traditional education, and bring us into just relations with men and things."

He next considers "the uprise and culmination of the new and anti-feudal power of Commerce, [as] . . . the political fact of most significance to the American at this hour." He celebrates America as "the country of the Future. . . . It is a country of beginnings, of projects, of vast designs and expectations. It has no past: all has an onward and prospective look." He ascribes this fertile activity to "Trade," and argues that "Trade was the principle of Liberty; that Trade planted America and destroyed Feudalism; that it makes peace and keeps peace and it will abolish slavery." Having been an effective instrument of change (like the railroad?), Trade must give way to something "broader and better whose signs are already dawning in the sky."

In his last topic, he cites the communal movements of the 1840s as signs that cooperative endeavors for the common good may be replacing the cutthroat competition inspired by Trade. He sees this as inspired by a moral sentiment embraced by eminent citizens who are "willing to stand for the interests of general justice and humanity." This is the challenge to the Young American: "obey your heart and be the nobility of this land." He summarizes his argument: "The development of our internal resources, the extension to the utmost of the commercial system, and the appearance of new moral causes which are to modify the state, are giving an aspect of greatness to the future. . . . One thing is plain for all men of common sense and common conscience, that here, here in America is the home of man." He then moves to an inspirational conclusion filled with images of the freedom and promise of America: "Let us live in America, too thankful for our want of feudal institutions. Our houses and towns are like mosses and lichens, so slight and new; but youth is a fault of which we shall daily mend. And really at last all lands are alike. Ours, too, is as old as the Flood, and wants no ornament or privilege which nature could bestow. Here stars, here woods, here hills, here animals, here men abound and the vast tendencies concur of a new order. If only the men are well employed in conspiring with the designs of the Spirit who led us hither, and is leading us still, we shall quickly enough advance out of all hearing of other's censures, out of all regrets of our own, into a new and more excellent social state than history has recorded."

One can be charitable and say that Emerson takes a long view and that the immediate problems caused by industrialization and immigrant labor have receded into the dim memory of past time. When the speech was given, the terri-torial expansion of the United States had already caused war with Mexico, and the displacement and annihilation of numerous Native Americans tribes, and disputes over organizing the newly acquired territories fueled the sectional conflict over slavery and would lead to the outbreak of the Civil War. The power of Trade might not have seemed so benign to the families whose fathers worked twelve-hour days, six days a week, and who often saw their young children work alongside them in mills and mines. Nor did it seem benign to Emerson himself, who once mused in his journal: "A question which well deserves examination now is the Dangers of Commerce. This invasion of Nature by Trade with its Money, its Credit, its Steam, its Railroad, threatens to upset the balance of man, and establish a new, universal Monarchy more tyrannical than Babylon or Rome" (JMN, VII, 268).

We may assume that few if any Irish laborers heard Emerson commend their "grim day's work of fifteen or sixteen hours . . . [as] a better police than the sheriff and his deputies." Probably not a few members of his audience profited from the stock of the Boston & Fitchburg Railroad Company and they could be expected to see great benefits from this "rage for road building" that was mapping the land in a "network of iron." Drawn from the educated class of the city and including members of the rising middle class and business community, Emerson's audience might well be inspired by visions of expansive progress and calls to assume their rightful role as leaders of the community.

Few members of the audience could doubt to what class of men the inspirational challenge at the end of the speech was directed: "In every age of the world, there has been a leading nation, one of a more generous sentiment, whose eminent citizens were willing to stand for the interests of general justice and humanity. . . . Which should be that nation but these States? Which should lead that movement, if not New England? Who should lead the leaders, but the Young American?"

In the structure of the lecture, we can discern the basic sermonic form of text, doctrine, exposition of doctrine and uses. The long introduction serves as the text by giving vivid illustrations of the changes in society and culture occurring during the 1840's. Emerson announces the doctrine that these changes are creating "an American sentiment" and explores the consequences of this change as it affects commerce and changing concepts of social relations. The conclusion of the lecture shows the "uses" that the audience of "Young America" can derive from these changes and directly challenges them to assume the leadership in making the United States "into a new and more excellent social state than history has recorded."

By 1844, Emerson had found the formula that would make him one of the most popular lecturers of the time. By adapting the sermonic format to lectures that embraced social and cultural ideals, using homiletic techniques carefully polished in the pulpit, emphasizing his ethical appeal, and artfully using appeals to audience self-interest clothed in moral pieties, his lectures became inspirational orations that gave his audiences a vision of their better selves. Emerson reflected on the occasion in his journal and recorded satisfaction with his own performance: "When I address a large assembly, as last Wednesday, I am always apprised what an opportunity is there: not for reading to them as I do, lively miscellanies, but for painting in fire my thought, & being agitated to agitate. One must dedicate himself to it and think with his audience in his mind, so as to keep the perspective & symmetry of the oration and enter into all the easily forgotten secrets of a great nocturnal assembly & their relation to the speaker" (JMN, IX, 70).

## NOTES

1. Quoted in Milton R. Konvitz, ed., *The Recognition of Ralph Waldo Emerson* (Ann Arbor: University of Michigan Press, 1972), xii-xiii.

2. Bliss Perry, "Emerson's Most Famous Speech," in *The Praise of Folly and Other Papers* (Boston: Houghton Mifflin, 1923), 81-113 contains a complete but rather

romantic description of the occasion. I have relied on this account for details.

3. Perry, "Emerson's Most Famous Speech," 81-85.

4. Perry, "Emerson's Most Famous Speech," 110-113.

5. Robert Riegel, *Young America, 1830-40* (Norman: University of Oklahoma Press, 1949).

# 5

# Occasional Addresses: Ceremonial and Political Speaking

The bulk of Emerson's public speeches took the form of sermons or lectures, but Emerson was also an accomplished ceremonial speaker. He was frequently asked to give eulogies of friends and commemorative speeches marking anniversaries of important historical occasions, and he was even invited to dedicate both a church and a school. The two great addresses, "The American Scholar" and "The Divinity School Address," were both delivered on ceremonial occasions. As he grew older and his powers diminished, he limited himself to this form of public address. The ceremonial speech is a genre particularly suited to Emerson's talents. The speaker praises an individual or celebrates an action or event that has significance to the community. In doing so, the speaker identifies common values represented by the individual or the action. Frequently these will be the virtues celebrated by both classical and Christian tradition. Emerson's background as a minister enhanced his ethical appeal on such occasions, as did his well-known reputation for moral earnestness. His sincerity in praising the moral character of his friend Thoreau or commemorating the Harvard men who died in the Civil War was unquestioned. Since ceremonial speeches also lend themselves to highly stylized writing and to emotional appeals, Emerson's experience in the pulpit gave him effective training in the use of metaphors and other figures of speech to rouse the emotions of his audience.

Shortly after he began his lecture career Emerson moved to Concord, Massachusetts, where he found a congenial community that would sustain him for the rest of his life. His reputation as a speaker preceded him, and he was asked to prepare "A Historical Discourse" to be delivered at the Second Centennial Anniversary of the founding of Concord on September 12, 1835. Emerson took his assignment seriously. His research involved not only a review of the town records, but interviews with survivors of the famous Revolutionary battle. The resulting oration which combined a thorough exposition of the historical record with lively personal interest stories took an hour and forty-five minutes to deliver, and earned Emerson much praise. Phillip Hone, the wealthy New York merchant who as guest of the governor of Massachusetts heard the oration, wrote in his diary, "an excellent oration spoken by Rev Ralph Waldo Emerson, a young clergyman of distinguished talents and eloquence. It was full of interesting details . . . . [which] gave a vivid interest to the oration."[1] Although the address is too long to reprint in this book, it is still readable and proves that Emerson could write well-organized expository prose when he wanted to.

Emerson's talent for compressing his thoughts into aphoristic phrases and the graceful oratorical cadences of his speech made him a welcome after-dinner speaker. He graced many a table to pay tribute to famous visitors such as Louis Kossuth or various New England friends. Perhaps the speech that had the greatest impact on an audience was his tribute to Robert Burns, delivered before the Boston Burns Club on January 25, 1859. The speech itself is generous in its praise of Burns and carefully crafted to avoid any slight to the sensitivities of the Scottish people. While Emerson recognizes that Burns is the favorite son of Scotland, he claims that his poetry has become the common property of all mankind. In this short tribute he magnifies his subject by associating him with the democratic revolution represented by "The Confession of Augsburg, the Declaration of Independence, the French Rights of Man, and the Marseillaise." This is high praise indeed, but the audience felt that his tribute was just. James Russell Lowell, who was present, described its reception in extravagant terms: "Every sentence brought down the house, as I never saw one brought down before."[2] Aside from his use of shared values, Emerson achieves part of his effect through his use of balanced phrases whose rhythm conveys a sense of forward movement. Many of his sentences echo the language of Burns and are themselves musical if not poetic. The long sentence beginning "He has given voice to all the experiences of common life" is completed by a series of balanced phrases that could be arranged in verse form:

farm house and cottage
patches and poverty
beans and barley
ale, the poor man's wine
hardship, the fear of debt
the dear society of weans and wife
of brothers and sisters
proud of each other, knowing so few
and
finding amends for want and obscurity
in books and thought.

The sentence immediately following repeats the same syntactical patterns and achieves the same oratorical cadence. The speech ends in a torrent of words whose musicality evokes the music of Burns's verse. Throughout the speech, Emerson demonstrates his sensitive understanding of the rhythm of English prose and the effective use of alliteration and assonance. Oliver Wendell Holmes, who was present, recalled that "His words had a passion in them not usual in the calm pure flow most natural to his uttered thoughts."[3] By concealing his manuscript among the serving dishes on the table, Emerson intimated that the speech was extemporaneous or even impromptu. He used several rhetorical techniques to enhance the effect, most notably that hoary old device of pleading incapacity to do justice to the subject through his lack of Scottish ancestry: "the worse Scotsman of all." Yet, his identification with the subject and with the audience is so complete by the end of the speech that the final lines that proclaim Burns' universal appeal seem apt.

On his second English lecture tour, Emerson was asked to speak at a dinner given by the Manchester Atheneum, the literary society that sponsored his lectures. It was a glittering occasion graced by the presence of two of the foremost reformers of the day, John Bright and Richard Cobden. In this situation, Emerson briefly addressed the assembly as both a visitor and an outsider, making a speech of tribute to his hosts. He graciously allowed that he knew the political reformers in the hall by their reputation long before he met them: "When I was at home they were as near to me as they are to you." The rest of the speech is similarly adroit at being gracious without being too effusive, and achieves its purpose by praising those enduring values that have given England both its moral and political influence: "its commanding sense of right and wrong." Emerson did not indulge himself or his audience in any fantasies that England was a "lotus-garden, [or] paradise of serene sky and roses and music and merriment." He recognized it as a "cold foggy mournful country where nothing grew well in the open air, but robust men and virtuous women . . . of a wonderful fibre and endurance." This surprising turn of phrase, which is characteristic of Emerson, praises his hosts for succeeding in spite of difficulties posed by an inhospitable climate through the moral resources of themselves. This is high praise, indeed, and would be most gratifying to his audience. He ends with a stirring vision of England not in decline but "young and still daring to believe in her power of endurance and expansion. Seeing this, I say, All hail! mother of nations, mother of heroes with strength still equal to the time; still wise to entertain and swift to execute the policy which the mind and heart of mankind requires in the present hour, and thus only hospitable to the foreigner, and truly a home to the thoughtful and generous who are born in the soil." This generous speech and its subsequent notice in the press contributed to Emerson's growing reputation and his warm reception throughout his English tour.

Emerson read political speeches, listened to politicians speak, and even once campaigned for a congressional candidate, but he was always uncomfortable making a political speech. Believing as he did in the necessity of affirming an individual moral vision, Emerson regarded concerted political action as tending to compromise moral integrity. Politics, by substituting collective action for individual responsibility, allows the individual to avoid the dictates of his own conscience by participating in largely symbolic activities. Although Emerson professed a devotion to democracy as an ideal, both by temperament and by inclination, he was more an observer than a participant in political activities. His natural reserve and his scholarly life led him to view the spectacle of political campaigning and its backslapping camaraderie with distaste. His belief in the sanctity of the individual conscience and the importance of the self led him to view organized effort by the mass of men as futile and self defeating. He often found the machinery of a democratic state and the men who ran it distasteful. One theme runs through his commentaries on the reformers and politicians he encountered: both lack a comprehensive view of the public good and both tend to underestimate the importance of inculcating an individual moral vision in the common man. When some citizens of Concord prevailed upon him to write a letter to President Van Buren to protest the removal of the Cherokee Indians, he brooded over the action for weeks, proclaiming to a friend that: "I hate myself when I go out of my sphere." [4]

But situated in the environs of Boston, he could not ignore the growing antislavery protest nor the coming political storm that would soon wreak the Whig Party and diminish the reputation of one of his boyhood heroes, Daniel Webster. The passage of the Fugitive Slave Law of 1851 as part of the great compromise supported by Webster and Clay aroused his ire as nothing had before, for now a political question involved his own individual sovereignty. The law required that the citizens of Massachusetts, through their magistrates, give aid and comfort to slavecatchers from the South to transport back into slavery individuals who had escaped from the grips of the slaveholders.

John Palfrey, a former Divinity Professor at Harvard, ran as the Free Soil candidate for Congress from Emerson's district and Emerson supported him by speaking several times in Middlesex County, starting in his own town of Concord and then at Lexington, Cambridge, and Fitchburg. At Cambridge, Emerson faced heckling by some twenty or so Harvard students. James Thayer, a member of the audience, recalled, "the hisses, shouts, and cat-calls made it impossible for Mr. Emerson to go on. . . . He stood with perfect quietness until the hubbub was over, and then went on with the next word. It was as if nothing had happened: there was no repetition, no allusion to what had been going on, no sign that he was moved, and I cannot describe with what added weight the next words fell." [5] Palfrey, in spite of Emerson's efforts, lost to the Whig candidate.

Emerson confided to his journal his unease and his frank recognition of the contradictory impulses that moved him: "I waked at night, & bemoaned myself, because I had not thrown myself into this deplorable question of Slavery, which seems to want nothing so much as a few assured voices. . . . [However,] in hours of sanity, I recover myself. . . . I have quite other slaves to free than those negroes, to wit, imprisoned spirits, imprisoned thoughts . . . which important to the republic of Man, have no watchman, or lover, or defender, but I" (JMN, III, 80). He managed to suppress these doubts on several other occasions, most notably before a meeting of the Anti-Slavery Society in New York City marking the fourth anniversary of the passage of the Fugitive Slave Law. Although his speech is ostensibly a political address, Emerson does not follow the classical model for a deliberative speech by giving reasons to support a policy and answering the objections that might be made against it. Instead, he utters a political jeremiad that adapts the sermonic form to a political occasion. What is particularly striking about the speech is his personal attack on the character of Daniel Webster that reveals much about Emerson's own disillusionment with his former hero. Even a superficial reading of the early journals will reveal a multitude of favorable comments about Webster and his eloquence. Since Emerson in his early years took Webster as something of a role model, it is interesting to compare quotations from the early journals with this speech to see how greatly Emerson changed his opinions. Compare this entry from his journal for March 3, 1830 with his denunciation of Webster in the speech: "Read with admiration & delight Mr Webster's noble speech in answer to Hayne [delivered January 26, 1830]. What consciousness of political rectitude & what confidence in his intellectual treasures must he have to enable him to take this master's tone! . . . . The beauty & dignity of the spectacle he exhibits should teach men the beauty & dignity of Principles. This is one that is not blown about by every wind of opinion, but has mind great enough to see the majesty of moral nature & to apply himself in all his length & breadth to it & magnanimously trust thereto" (JMN, III, 184).

Emerson in this speech is also extending his critique of what was regarded by the general public as the democratic eloquence of the time. Although Webster has all the attributes of a great speaker such as voice, accent, intonation, attitude, manner, and propriety, his lack of concern for what is morally right produces a counterfeit eloquence that misleads. He accuses Webster of misusing his considerable talents: "The history of this country has given a disastrous importance to the defects of this great man's mind. . . . It was the misfortune of his country that with this large understanding he had not what is better than intellect. . . . If his moral sensibility had been proportioned to the force of his understanding, what limits could have been set to his genius and beneficent power? . . . . In the final hour, when he was forced by the peremptory necessity of the closing armies to take a side, did he take the part of great principles, the side of humanity and justice, or the side of abuse and oppression and chaos? "

The speech gains considerable power from Emerson's use of antithesis to contrast the moral position of the slaveholders and the abolitionists: "For one would have said that a Christian would not keep slaves; but the Christians keep slaves. Of course they will not dare to read the Bible? Won't they? They quote the Bible, quote Paul, quote Christ, to justify slavery. If slavery is good, then is lying, theft, arson, homicide, each and all good, and to be maintained by Union societies."

Ultimately the speech is more than a personal attack directed against Webster. Emerson forces the audience to consider their own (and his) responsibility for the outrageous action. In a striking series of parallel sentences he reminds his audience that their reliance on men and forms to prevent evil failed: "You relied on the constitution . . . . on the Supreme Court . . . . on the Missouri Compromise . . . . on State sovereignty . . . . and these dismal guarantees infamously made in 1850." What has been the result? "These things show that no forms, neither constitutions, nor laws, nor covenants, nor churches, nor Bibles, are of any use in themselves. The Devil nestles comfortably into them all." What is the only answer? It is the self reliance of honest men. "To make good the cause of Freedom, you must draw off from all foolish trust in others. . . . He only who is able to stand alone is qualified for society." His political speech turns out to be an Emersonian sermon on a familiar topic: the consciousness of individual moral responsi- bility and the need to rely on the inviolate self.

The speaker's demeanor considerably heightened the effect of the speech. A reporter who was present described the scene: "When Ralph Waldo Emerson stood up in the Tabernacle last night, one could have heard a pin drop." Although Emerson "had entered the hall with that shy, shrinking manner" that made him resemble a "frightened country clergyman in a great city church," when Emerson's voice "broke the silence with those well-compacted sentences" the vast audience "was hushed into a close attention." The reporter noted little applause, but claimed that "every eye was on the speaker, and no word fell upon inattentive ears." In concluding his review, the anonymous reporter praised Emerson: "those who had entered the hall, thinking that the speaker could find no new form in which to exhibit his hackneyed subject, no felicity of illustration that had not been pressed into service, found that, in the hands of the master, the old theme wears a new beauty when clothed with the graces of his thought." [6]

The occasional addresses, the ceremonial speeches, and the political speeches demonstrate that Emerson had command of the major genres of public speaking. The long occasional addresses, in particular the address celebrating the second centennial of Concord, show that Emerson could write well organized expository prose in contrast to the less clearly organized lectures. The ceremonial speeches, particularly the tributes, show Emerson's ability to write rhythmical lines using inspiring images that move his audiences. He is less successful in the few political speeches that we have because they require sustained argument rather than assertion of the truth.

## NOTES

1. *Diary of Philip Hone 1828-1851,* ed. Allan Nevins 2 vols. (1927; New York: Kraus Reprint Co., 1969), 1: 176.

2. James Russell Lowell, *My Study Windows* (Boston: 1871), 359.

3. Olvier W. Holmes, *Ralph Waldo Emerson* (Boston: Houghton, Mifflin and Company, 1895), 224.

4. Ralph Rusk, *The Life of Ralph Waldo Emerson* (New York: Charles Scribner's Sons, 1949), 237.

5. James Eliot Cabot, *A Memoir of Ralph Waldo Emerson*, 2 vols. (New York: AMS Press reprint, 1965), 2: 586.

6. Article in Boston *Transcript* reprinted in the *Liberator*, March 17, 1854.

# 6

# Conclusion: Emerson's Achievement

Although Alcott's claim that "Emerson made the lecture" is an exaggeration of historical fact, it does express an important perception of Emerson's accomplishment at the lectern.[1] It would be more accurate to say that the lecture made Emerson and Emerson's lectures sustained the educational aims of the lyceum founders. Lecturing provided Emerson with a vocation at a critical juncture in his life and a forum to test and refine his ideas. In turn Emerson and other educated men of his class drawn primarily from the ministry and law provided the initial impetus for the lyceum movement. Having primarily a local reputation, they filled the lecture rooms provided by the lyceum in its early stage. When the local committees began to look to outsiders with more of a reputation to provide more variety and the attraction of novelty, Emerson again led the way traveling to New York City, western New York, Philadelphia and Rhode Island to lecture. Soon he was among the first of the New England writers to venture to Ohio, Indiana, Illinois and Iowa to answer the call for distinguished lecturers. After the Civil War, when the lyceum turned more commercial, and entertainment rather than education came predominate, Emerson became a representative figure of New England Culture whose lectures became an opportunity for the audience to experience the aura of the Yankee Sage and to participate in a cultural event. As the lyceum changed, Emerson changed and so did his lectures. In the early lectures, Emerson is a teacher working out in public the implications of his ideas. In the second stage, in his lectures given in the 1840's and 1850's, Emerson is the observer--reporting and assessing the civilization he sees developing. In the last stage of his career, after the Civil War, he is a cultural icon whose powers of observation and analysis have diminished, but who speaks with the voice of authority from bits and pieces of old lectures patched together to give the semblance of newness.

What was it like to listen to Emerson lecture? The answer to this question depends on what stage in his career you heard him. As Emerson aged, his mental and physical powers declined. His lungs which had never been strong did not support a forceful voice. Over the years his ability to project his voice declined so severely that in his later years many people complained that he spoke so softly as to be barely audible. However, in his prime Emerson was recognized by many as an effective speaker. Unfortunately this fact has been obscured by those writers who selectively quote from his worst reviews without providing a context for evaluating them.

Emerson's delivery of his lectures was artless by nineteenth century standards. In an age dominated by elocutionists, Emerson eschewed flamboyant or extravagant gestures, preferring to use his voice and countenance to convey his emotional involvement with his ideas. He always spoke from a manuscript. He did not use props as did the lecturers on scientific subjects nor did he dress in costume like the travel lecturers. He was not as extraordinarily handsome as Henry Ward Beecher, nor did he entertain the audience with comic characters as did Artemus Ward. Always appearing in the severe and formal ministerial black suit, he was "Mr. Emerson" to the lecture committees. Yet in reading his lectures, Emerson practiced an art of his own. Through long training in the ministry and extensive practice on the lecture circuit, he learned how to read a manuscript so that it sounded more extemporaneous than recited. He had a trick of pausing at the end of his sentences as if searching for the right word and when he found it exactly as he had written it, his faced beamed as he spoke it to the audience. The effective uses of pauses for emphasis and hesitations as if considering a newly found word or phrase conveyed a sense of spontaneity to his performance. He was especially effective in using his voice to convey enthusiasm and excitement for his ideas. A rich baritone, his vocal modulations and inflections charmed his audience. His voice, never strong, lost the power to fill a hall in the later years, but when he had command of it, he was the possessor of an instrument attuned to his needs.

Emerson's first lecture audiences in the Boston area were not much different in kind from his congregation and probably the two overlapped to a considerable extent. These audience were accustomed to hearing sermons read and many had heard Emerson preach. The audiences were representative of a certain type of New Englander: serious, informed, pious, and public spirited. No newspaper review of Emerson's lectures are available for this period because he actively discouraged them to protect his ability to repeat the lectures and editors during this phase of the lyceum abided by this request. We do have passing comments on the lectures written in letters that speak highly of them.

Even when Emerson ventured further away from his home to New York City, he still lectured before essentially the same audiences. Several studies of Lyceum audiences exist and they agree that the typical audience was "made up of both men and women, ranging in age from the mid-teens through the late fifties or early sixties, and drawn from an occupational spectrum that included artisans, mechanics, farmers, lawyers, teachers, professors, doctors, clergymen, shopkeepers, and merchants, as well as people in a wide range of commercial and service trades."[2] Oliver Wendell Holmes, who lectured in many of the same towns as Emerson, left this description of a typical audience: "Front seats: a few old folks--shiny-headed--slant up best ear towards the speaker--drop off asleep after a while .... Bright women's faces, young and middle-aged, a little behind these, but toward the front ... Here and there a countenance, sharp and scholarlike, and a dozen pretty female ones sprinkled about. An indefinite number of pairs of young people--happy, but not always very attentive."[3] Holmes recognized that the motives for attending a lecture were not always to hear the lecturer. In many small communities the lyceum provided a convenient and respectable reason for young men an women to spend an evening together. Scott also notes that although the lyceum aimed at self improvement, "very few if any factory operatives participated in the institution while almost all the young professionals in a town would be members of the sponsoring societies."[4]

Given the educational purpose of the early lyceum, the audience expected to benefit from the lecture by gaining knowledge that could help them advance in their careers. This did not necessarily mean a narrow focus on facts or technical information, but knowledge that could contribute to the development of a comprehensive view of life--that could develop a deeper understanding of the times. Later, in its second phase, the public lecture was also expected to be a lively performance that delighted the audience while instructing them.

When Emerson accepted an invitation to lecture in Cincinnati in 1850, he began a new career in the middle west and faced new audiences. It is from this stage in his career that the unflattering reviews collected in various articles or books helped to create the myth that Emerson was a poor speaker whose halting delivery audiences endured for the sake of his "pearls of wisdom." These western audience were different from those in Boston and New York City primarily because the cities and towns lacked the cultural institutions and the traditions that sustained a sophisticated and knowledgeable audience. Some of the larger towns in the west such as Cincinnati had the trappings of culture and a rising middle class to support it--Emerson's lecture tour coincided with a concert tour by Ole Bull, the great violinist--but when he ventured further west to Indiana and Illinois, the cultural level declined to a very low level. Without accepting all the stereotypical contrasts between Easterners and Westerners, we can none the less recognize some differences in the orientations of the audiences. These audiences were less educated than the early ones and perhaps contained a greater number of the merely curious who came to see what all the fuss over this man Emerson was about. The western audiences were cruder, more heterogeneous, and more accustomed to an emotional preaching done extemporaneously, which was not conducive to the intellectual sermon so familiar to New England audiences. Charles G. Finney whose revivals set the tone for the region in one of his pamphlets on preaching, claimed that one sure way to preach so as to convert nobody was to write your sermons with a high degree of literary polish.[5] Emerson, with his written text filled with literary and philosophical references, was clearly outside the usual experience of many of his auditors. Dressed in his ministerial black suit, with his formal manners, and Yankee twang, Emerson might have bemused some of his listeners at times. Secondly, the expectations of the audience may have worked against Emerson who was frequently invited to lecture by the local literary society with extravagant publicity extolling his reputation as a thinker, philosopher, poet, writer and lecturer all rolled into one--the Sage of Concord. Although Emerson certainly looked the part, and with his Yankee accent sounded the part, even he could not satisfy such exalted notices.

To be fair to the audiences, we should consider their needs as well. Life on the western prairies was not easy. Many of the farmers who came to hear Emerson lecture at the end of the day had already been up since early in the morning and had done a full day of physically tiring labor. These were not highly educated men and women; for most of them the family library consisted of the Bible. When they went to a lecture they may have expected some relief from their rather monotonous existence. Artemus Ward could make them laugh; Bayard Taylor could entertain them with descriptions of faraway lands, but Emerson came to challenge them to think.

Too much as been made of a few critical notices in the press from this period without considering the context of those reviews. We must recognize that the editors who wrote the reviews were not the professional reviewers we are accustomed to today. Few had college degrees; most were self-made, entrepreneurs who were trying to succeed financially in the growing economy of the middle west. Some of them may have succumbed to the temptation to put the celebrated "Yankee Sage" in his place. Given the rough and tumble ethos of the journalism of the day, the temptation to expose Emerson's transcendental nonsense as humbug and to poke fun at his genteel ways might have been too much to resist. The lack of professionalism raises another point. In some cases, editors attacked Emerson for his political views and not for what he said in his lecture. Louise Hastings in her close examination of the reporting of his lectures in Cincinnati noted that before his appearance in 1860, Emerson was greeted with a furious denunciation in the Democratic paper the *Enquirer* as a speaker of "blasphemous and traiterous [*sic*] sentiment" for his outspoken support of John Brown and she concluded from a comparison of the reviews of the *Enquirer* with rival papers that "much of the opprobrium was carried over into the *Enquirer*'s report of Emerson's lecture.[6]

Obviously, Emerson was not animated on the platform, and his humor tended more toward word play than the tall tales or exaggerated effects of the comic lecturers. Clearly some members of the audience were disappointed in him. On occasion some walked out. However, during the 1850's, Emerson spoke to large and generally appreciative audiences. He was invited back to the major towns in the middle west to lecture again and again. It is during the next stage of his career, after the Civil War, when his physical and mental abilities decline that more and more auditors begin to complain that his voice is so soft as to be inaudible and that his presentation is so disorganized that it is difficult to follow him. As Emerson's mental ability declined, he stopped writing new lectures and began to recycle old ones, frequently transferring entire pages from one lecture to another. Given that many of the lectures discussed the same themes, he could easily combine an early lecture on "Poetry" with a later lecture on "Eloquence" and produce a "new" lecture that could be used in a town where he had lectured previously without repeating word for word a lecture his audience had heard before. In doing this, Emerson took advantage of the way he wrote his lectures by folding a large folio sheet in half and then folding it again. This produced the effect of a note card with four sides to write on. When Emerson wanted to add material to the lecture, he could tuck the new sheet into the pocket formed by the folds in the old one. Thus, on the platform he sometimes paused, to reach inside one sheet to retrieve a different example or an additional paragraph to supplement his original lecture. This is the origin of the familiar complaint that Emerson shuffled his papers and presented his paragraphs in random order. In fact, he knew precisely what he was looking for because he had "filed" it there previously.

## DARE TO HOPE FOR ECSTASY AND ELOQUENCE

In 1824 shortly before he began Divinity School, young Ralph Waldo Emerson took stock of his abilities and his ambitions and confessed to his journal: "I derive from [my father] or his patriot parent a passionate love for the strains of eloquence .... I have hoped to put on eloquence as a robe and by goodness and zeal and the awfulness of virtue to press & prevail over the false judgments, the rebel passions & corrupt habits of men" (JMN, II, 239). Emerson meditated about the nature of eloquence over the better part of his adult life. His early journals are filled with quotations defining eloquence taken from classical authors or with observations about speakers he had heard. In his young manhood, he idealized Daniel Webster and made frequent references in his journals to the role that an eloquent leader could play in a democratic society. In the early journals, one can trace Emerson's own aspirations to be an eloquent speaker. Such aspirations would not be unwarranted in a youth with Emerson's background. But all the declamation exercises at Boston Latin and Harvard could not change the stubborn fact that Emerson lacked the temperament and skills to be a political leader. In his own eyes, his arena of eloquence would be confined to the pulpit. At first he saw the possibilities of pulpit eloquence and exhorted himself to avoid the common mistakes he observed in others. In time, he discovered that the pulpit was too constricting a theatre for his talents. His move to the lecture room opened up new possibilities for him and he celebrated its freedom: "Here are no stiff conventions that prescribe a method [or] a style [or] an exact respect to certain books person or opinions. No, here everything is admissible .... Here is a pulpit that makes other pulpits tame & ineffectual.... Here [the speaker] may dare to hope for ecstasy & eloquence" (JMN, VII, 265).

In his new role as lecturer, Emerson thought anew about the meaning of eloquence and the role that it could play in the developing democratic society. Emerson witnessed at first hand the political revolution ushered in by the election of Jackson in 1828. Unhappy with the substitution of political spectacle and party slogans for reasoned political discussion, he became disenchanted with politics, even discovering that his old heroes Webster and Everett were not the giants he first thought them to be. Not only had they become bores speaking in "stereotyped phrase & scarcely originat[ing] one expression to a speech" (JMN, V, 92), but in their failure to confront the moral issues posed by slavery, "they have dishonored themselves" (JMN, IX, 17). Nor was he impressed by the various reform gatherings that he attended. He saw them as mainly substituting emotional excitement for "depth of interest." He observed that: "the words flow, & the superlatives thicken, & the lips quiver, & the eyes moisten, & an observer new to such scenes would say, here was true fire; the assembly were all ready to be martyred, & the effect of such a spirit on the community would be irresistible. But they separate & go to the shop, to a dance, to bed, & an hour afterwards they care so little for the matter that on slightest temptation each one would disclaim the meeting" (JMN, V, 479).

In his early writings, Emerson showed a conventional understanding of eloquence as an art, classifying it as a fine art "modified by the material organization of the orator, the tone of voice, the physical strength, the play of the eye and countenance" (EL, II, 41). Later, he realized that if eloquence were to have a permanent effect and not just a momentary emotional one, it must aim at more than virtuoso display of technique by the speaker. In his lecture, "Eloquence," he affirmed: "the highest platform of eloquence is the moral sentiment. It is what is called affirmative truth, and has the property of invigorating the hearer." Achieving this involves the speaker and his hearers in a process that enables the individual members of the audience to participate in the common mind which is able to understand the universal truth or moral basis of the universe. Emerson saw this as analogous to the process by which "the generic soul overcome with sleep .... hearing some deeper voice, ... lifts his iron lids, & his eyes straight pierce through all appearances" (JMN, V, 161-62). Thus, "in perfect eloquence, the hearer would lose the sense of dualism, of hearing from another; would cease to distinguish between the orator and himself; would have the sense only of high activity and progress"

(JMN, VII, 52).

How to accomplish this was a question that Emerson pondered. He had witnessed first hand the debasement of rational discourse in the Jacksonian electoral campaigns and the substitution of symbolic gestures for depth of commitment in the reform activities of the day. Perhaps one way to restore the effectiveness of eloquence was to make effective audiences. When both audience and speaker become Man Thinking they are able to achieve a unity of purpose and understanding that makes democratic government possible. In today's jargon, the audience must be empowered through access to information and encouraged to develop its critical thinking abilities. In Emerson's terms, it must be inspired to become "self reliant men." Emerson had no formal program to accomplish this task. Given his antipathy to collective action, he favored individual action to bring people to self awareness of the latent powers they possessed.

The lyceum was one instrument available to him. As a "self supporting, locally controlled, voluntary association," it was the "most effective means of popular education during the nineteenth century" and "played a vital role in the development of American Culture." [7] For almost forty years, Emerson devoted himself to the task of educating the American public on the platform and through his writings. This embodiment of New England culture, this reserved Yankee, forced himself to travel over uncomfortable roads, stay in seedy hotels, and endure the awkward courtesy of innumerable lecture committees to bring his message to the people. He may not have had the easy manner of Lincoln, but his dedication to his mission was equal. Lincoln wanted to save the Union; Emerson wanted to save its soul.

Arriving at a just estimate of Emerson's achievement in the pulpit and on the lecture platform presents obvious difficulties. Both the sermons and the lectures were originally written for public performance. Like all public performances, they consume themselves in their enactment living on in memory but never entirely resurrected from the cold corpse of the text. We have no way of assessing his effect on the many people who came to listen to him out of curiosity or as a break from their daily routine. We cannot know precisely how many individuals heard him preach or lecture. What evidence we do have of his impact is partial and suspect. His friends almost universally testify to the positive impact that his character and thought had on the audience; his detractors (and they are many) complain of the lack of systematic development of his ideas and his weak delivery.

Even with this conflicting evidence, many scholars have tried to place Emerson's work in the context of major changes in the relationship of the individual to an increasingly complex and highly organized society. For example, Frederick J. Antczak in his study of the development of the lecture system in sustaining the values conducive to a democratic society suggests that Emerson along with Twain and James tried to improve the "thought and character" of the democratic audience. In Emerson's case, Antczak identifies Emerson's ethical appeal as his major rhetorical strategy. Emerson was able to embrace the paradox of being both "like and unlike his audience. Like enough in character to tap the resources of common ethical authority, yet still sufficiently unlike in order not to compromise his thought." In Emerson's own words, "he speaks that which they recognize as part of them but which they were not yet ready to say" (EL, II, 57). In short, Emerson "represented" the audience--showed them in his own person what they themselves could become. This is best illustrated by the following perhaps apocryphal story:

"'Do you understand Mr. Emerson?' a washerwoman was asked as she was eagerly making ready to attend his lecture. 'Not a word, but I like to go and see him stand up there and look as though he thought everyone was as good as he was.'"[8]

When Alex de Toqueville visited the United States in 1831, the Lyceum was in its infancy but he saw more clearly than many native commentators the promise and the difficulty posed by the democratic audience. His description of the democratic taste in literature sounds presciently like the lecture system as it developed: "Style will be frequently fantastic, incorrect, overburdened, and loose--almost always vehement and bold .... Small productions [lectures?] will be more common than bulky books: there will be more wit than erudition, more imagination than profundity; and literary performances will bear marks of an untutored and rude vigor of thought--frequently of a great variety and singular fecundity. The object of authors will be to astonish rather than to please, and to stir the passions more than to charm the taste."[9] Emerson's experience on the platform confirmed Toqueville's prediction: he had to compete for an audience with spiritualists, phrenologists, humorists, dramatic readers, bell ringers, singers, temperance lecturers, abolitionists, explorers, and other fantastic types. Toqueville was very prescient in seeing the effect that the audience would have on this institution and the literary men who flocked to it. Even in Emerson's case this may explain why one of our major thinkers produced mainly lectures that were later collected into books and why his style took the often fantastic direction it did.

But still Emerson persisted and year after year he was invited back to address the same audiences. In one period of three years from 1852 to 1855, he delivered one hundred and ninety lectures traveling as far west as Milwaukee. Perhaps Josiah G. Holland had Emerson in mind when surveying the lyceum system some thirty years after its promising beginning, he admitted that it had its share of "buffoons and triflers" but claimed that their careers were always "short." He argued that "only he who feels that he has something to do in making the world wiser and better, and who in a bold and manly way, tries persistently to do it is always welcome."[10] In answer to the question, "what good has the popular lecture accomplished," Holland claimed that it had increased toleration for unorthodox opinions by being "the common ground for the representations of all our social, political and religious organizations.[11] Thomas Wentworth Higginson also saw the lecture as creating a public when he described the lecturer as "moving to and fro, a living shuttle, to weave together this new web of national civilization."[12]

Donald M. Scott argues that this was the great achievement of the public lecture system that it "created and embodied a American public."[13] Echoing Holland's comment quoted above, he sees the public lecture as "transcending the divisions that fragmented society" by providing a neutral ground on which all members of the community could meet. With its regular meetings, its rules, and its corp of lecturers traveling around the country, it created a public opinion. In a sense, it became a ritualized means for enacting the creation of a public--a public that was thought to embrace more than local opinion. As one of its most faithful lecturers traveling thousands of miles and giving more lectures than most others, Emerson clearly deserves some credit for forming and sustaining this public. As Carl Bode emphasizes, "Emerson is perhaps the only lecturer in the movement who could unhesitating be called great. The amazing thing is that he was also enormously popular."[14]

We may never be able to separate out from the larger social forces such as the growth of the transportation system that brought a national distribution network for books and periodicals or the rapid growth of the school system or even the development of popular newspapers the impact on the public mind of a single institution such as the lyceum or of a single individual such as Ralph Waldo Emerson. But when all the commentary is read and the conflicting opinions sifted, there remains a solid body of work that reveals a critical intelligence grappling with important religious and philosophical questions and providing original answers. In the sermons, the early lectures, and the addresses, Emerson is ultimately the "American Scholar"--the critical intelligence that our busy materialistic civilization desperately needs. He still calls us to accept responsibility for our own actions and to establish high standards of achievement for ourselves. That is achievement enough.

## NOTES

1. Bronson Alcott, *The Journals of Bronson Alcott*, ed. Odell Shepard (Boston, 1938).

2. Donald M. Scott, "The Popular Lecture and the Creation of a Public in Mid-Nineteenth Century America," *Journal of American History* 66 (1980): 800.

3. Oliver Wendell Holmes, *The Autocrat of the Breakfast Table* (New York: E.P. Dutton, 1906), 193.

4. Scott, "The Popular Lecture," 801.

5. Charles G. Finney, *How to Preach so as to Convert Nobody* (Boston: Willard Tract Repository, n.d.) 4.

6. Louise Hastings, "Emerson in Cincinnati," *New England Quarterly* 11 (1938):

465.

7. Russell B. Nye, *Society and Culture in America 1830-1860* (New York: Harper & Row, 1974), 360.

8. Quoted in Frederick J. Antczak, *Thought and Character: The Rhetoric of Democratic Education* (Ames: Iowa State University Press, 1985), 98-107.

9. Alexis de Tocqueville, *Democracy in America*, ed. Andrew Hacker (New York: Washington Square Press, 1964), 162.

10. Josiah G. Holland, "The Popular Lecture," *Atlantic Monthly* 15 (1865): 366.

11. Holland, "The Popular Lecture," 368.

12. Thomas Wentworth Higginson, "The American Lecture System," *MacMillan's Magazine* 18 (1968): 49.

13. Scott, "The Popular Lecture," 808.

14. Carl Bode, *The American Lyceum: Town Meeting of the Mind* (Carbondale: Southern Illinois University Press, 1968), 221.

# Part II

# COLLECTED SPEECHES

# Pray Without Ceasing

Pray without ceasing. First Thessalonians V, 17.

It is the duty of men to judge men only by their actions. Our faculties furnish us with no means of arriving at the motive, the character, the secret self. We call the tree good from its fruits, and the man, from his works. Since we have no power, we have no right, to assign for the actions of our neighbor any other motives than those which ought in similar circumstances to guide our own. But because we are not able to discern the processes of thought, to see the soul --it were very ridiculous to doubt or deny that any beings can. It is not incredible that the thoughts of the mind are the subjects of perception to some beings, as properly as the sounds of the voice, or the motion of the hand are to us. Indeed, every man's feeling may be appealed to on this question, whether the idea, that other beings can read his thoughts, has not appeared so natural and probable, that he has checked sometimes a train of thoughts that seemed too daring or indecent, for any unknown beholders to be trusted with.

It ought to be distinctly felt by us that we stand in the midst of two worlds, the world of matter and the world of spirit. Our bodies belong to one; our thoughts to the other. It has been one of the best uses of the Christian religion to teach, that the world of spirits is more certain and stable than the material universe. Every thoughtful man has felt that there was a more awful reality to thought and feeling, than to the infinite panorama of nature around him. The world he has found indeed consistent and uniform enough throughout the mixed sensations of thirty or forty years, but it seems to him at times, when the intellect is invigorated, to ebb from him, like a sea, and to leave nothing permanent but thought. Nevertheless it is a truth not easily nor early acquired, and the prejudice that assigns greater fixture and certainty to the material world is a source of great practical error. I need hardly remind you of the great points of this error. I need not ask you if the objects that every day are the cause of the greatest number of steps taken, of the greatest industry of the hands and the feet, the heart and the head, are the perishable things of sense, or the imperishable things of the soul; whether all this stir from day to day, from hour to hour of all this mighty multitude, is to ascertain some question dear to the understanding concerning the nature of God, the true constitution and destination of the human soul, the proper balance of the faculties and the proper office of each; or (what of immortal thought comes nearer to practical value) whether all men are eagerly intent to study the best systems of education for themselves and their children? Is it not rather the great wonder of all who think enough to wonder that almost all that sits near the heart, all that colours the countenance, and engrosses conversation at the family board are these humble things of mortal date, and in the history of the universe absolutely insignificant? Is it not outside shews, the pleasures of appetite, or at best of pride; is it not bread and wine and dress and our houses and our furniture, that give the law to the great mass of actions and words? This is the great error which the strong feeling of the reality of things unseen must correct. It is time greater force should be given to the statement of this doctrine; it is time men should be instructed that their inward is more valuable than their outward estate; that thoughts and passions, even those to which no language is ever given, are not fugitive undefined shadows, born in a moment, and in a moment blotted from the soul, but are so many integral parts of the imperishable universe of morals; they should be taught that they do not think alone; that when they retreat from the public eye and hide themselves to conceal in solitude guilty recollections or guilty wishes, the great congregation of moral natures, the spirits of just men made perfect; angels and archangels; the Son of God, and the Father everlasting, open their eyes upon them and speculate on these clandestine meditations.

I. The necessary inference from these reflections, is the fact which gives them all their importance, and is the doctrine I am chiefly anxious to inculcate. It is not only when we audibly and in form address our petitions to the Deity, that we pray. We pray without ceasing. Every secret wish is a prayer. Every house is a church, the corner of every street is a closet of devotion. There is no rhetoric, let none deceive himself; there is no rhetoric in this. There is delusion of the most miserable kind, in that fiction on which the understanding pleads to itself its own excuse, when it knows not God and is thoughtless of him. I mean that outward respect, that is paid to the name and worship of God, whilst the thoughts and the actions are enlisted in the service of sin. "I will not swear by God's name" says the wary delinquent; "I will not ask him to lend his aid to my fraud, to my lewdness, to my revenge; nor will I even give discountenance to the laws I do not myself observe. I will not unmask my villainy to the world, that I should stand in the way of others, more scrupulous, nay, better than I."

And is it by this paltry counterfeit of ignorance that you would disguise from yourselves the truth? And will you really endeavour to persuade yourself, that God is such an one as you yourself, and will be amused by professions, and may, by fraudulent language, be kept out of the truth? Is it possible, that men of discretion in common affairs, can think so grossly? Do you not know that the knowledge of God is perfect and immense; that it breaks down the fences of presumption, and the arts of hypocrisy; that right, and artifice, and time, and the grave, are naked before it; that the deep gives up its dead, that the gulfs of chaos are disembowelled before him; that the minds of men are not so much independent existences, as they are ideas present to the mind of God; that he is not so much the observer of your actions, as he is the potent principle by which they are bound together; not so much the reader of your thoughts, as the active Creator by whom they are aided into being; and, casting away the deceptive subterfuges of language, and speaking with strict philosophical truth, that every faculty is but a mode of his action; that your reason is God, your virtue is God, and nothing but your liberty, can you call securely and absolutely your own?

Sincc, thcn, we are thus, by the inevitable law of our being, surrendered unreservedly to the unsleeping observation of the Divinity, we cannot shut our eyes to the conclusion, that *every desire of the human mind is a prayer uttered to God and registered in heaven.*

II. The next fact of sovereign importance in this connection is, that our prayers are granted. Upon the account I have given of prayer, this ulterior fact is a faithful consequence. What then! if I pray that fire shall fall from heaven to consume mine enemies, will the lightning come down? If I pray that the wealth of India may be piled in my coffers, shall I straightway become rich? If I covet my neighbor's beauty, or wit, or honourable celebrity,--will these desirable advantages be at once transferred from being the sources of his happiness, to become the sources of mine? It is plain there is a sense in which this is not true. But it is equally undeniable that in the sense in which I have explained the nature of prayer, and which seems the only proper sense, the position is universally true. For those are not prayers, which begin with the ordinary appellatives of the Deity and end with his Son's name and a ceremonial word--those are not prayers, if they utter no one wish of our hearts, no one real and earnest affection, but are formal repetitions of sentiments taken at second hand, in words the supple memory has learned of fashion. O my friends, these are not prayers, but mockeries of prayers. But the true prayers are the daily, hourly, momentary desires, that come without impediment, without fear, into the soul, and bear testimony at each instant to its shifting character. And these prayers are granted.

For is it not clear that what we strongly and earnestly desire we shall make every effort to obtain; and has not God so furnished us with powers of body and of mind that we can acquire whatsoever we seriously and unceasingly strive after?

For it is the very root and rudiment of the relation of man to this world, that we are in a condition of wants which have their appropriate gratifications within our reach; and that we have faculties which can bring us to our ends;

that we are full of capacities that are near neighbors to their objects; and our free agency consists in this, that we are able to reach those sources of gratification, on which our election falls. And if this be so, will not he who thinks lightly of all other things in comparison with riches; who thinks little of the poor man's virtue, or the slave's misery as they cross his path in life, because his observant eye is fixed on the rich man's manners and is searching in the lines of his countenance, with a sort of covetousness, the tokens of a pleased contemplation of the goods he has in store, and the consideration that, on this account, is conceded to him in society; will not such an one, if his thoughts daily point towards this single hope, if no exertion is grateful to him which has not this for its aim; if the bread is bitter to him that removes his riches one day farther from his hand, and the friends barren of comfort to him that are not aiding to this dishonourable ambition;--will not such an one arrive at the goal such as it is, of his expectation and find, sooner or later, a way to the heaven where he has garnered up his heart? Assuredly he will.

And will not the votary of other lusts, the lover of animal delight, who is profuse of the joys of sense, who loveth meats and drinks, soft raiment and the wine when it moveth itself aright and giveth its colour in the cup; or the more offensive libertine who has no relish left for any sweet in moral life, but only waits opportunity to surrender himself over to the last damning debauchery; will not these petitioners who have knocked so loudly at heaven's door, receive what they have so importunately desired? Assuredly they will. There is a commission to nature, there is a charge to the elements made out in the name of the Author of events, whereby they shall help the purposes of man, a preexistent harmony between thoughts and things whereby prayers shall become effects, and these warm imaginations settle down into events.

And if there be, in this scene of things, any spirit of a different complexion, who has felt, in the recesses of his soul, "how awful goodness is, and virtue in her own shape how lovely," who has admired the excellence of others, and set himself by precepts of the wise, and by imitation, which, a wise man said, is "a globe of precepts," to assimilate himself to the model, or to surpass the uncertain limit of human virtue, and found no model in the universe, beneath God, level with his venerated idea of virtue; who looks with scorn at the cheap admiration of crowds, and loves the applause of good men, but values more his own; and has so far outstripped humanity, that he can appreciate the love of the Supreme; if he aspire to do signal service to mankind, by the rich gift of a good example, and by unceasing and sober efforts to instruct and benefit man; will this man wholly fail, and waste his requests on the wind? Assuredly he will not. His prayers, in a certain sense, are like the will of the Supreme Being:

> "His word leaps forth to its effect at once,
> He calls for things that are not, and they come."

His prayers are granted; all prayers are granted. Unceasing endeavours always attend true prayers, and, by the law of the universe, unceasing endeavours do not fail of their end.

Let me not be misunderstood as thinking lightly of the positive duty of stated seasons of prayer. That solemn service of man to his maker is a duty of too high authority and too manifest importance to excuse any indifference to its claims. It is because that privilege is abused, because men in making prayers forget the purpose of prayer, forget that praying is to make them leave off sinning, that I urge it in its larger extent where it enters into daily life.

I have attempted to establish two simple positions, that, we are always praying, and that it is the order of Providence in the world, that our prayers should be granted. If exceptions can be quoted to me out of the book of common life, to the universality of either of these doctrines, I shall admit them in their full force, nor shall I now detain you by any inquiry into the abstract metaphysical nature of that happiness human beings are permitted to derive from what are called possessions, and how far it belongs to the imagination. I shall content myself, at present, with having stated the general doctrine and with adverting to its value as a practical principle.

And certainly, my friends, it is not a small thing that we have learned. If we have distinctly apprehended the fact which I have attempted to set in its true light, it cannot fail to elevate very much our conception of our relations and our duties. Weep no more for human frailty, weep no more for what there may be of sorrow in the past or of despondency in the present hour. Spend no more unavailing regrets for the goods of which God in his Providence has deprived you. Cast away this sickly despair that eats into the soul debarred from high events and noble gratification. Beware of easy assent to false opinion, to low employment, to small vices, out of a reptile reverence to men of consideration in society. Beware, (if it teach nothing else, let it teach this) beware of indolence, the suicide of the soul, that lets the immortal faculties, each in their orbit of light, wax dim and feeble, and star by star expire.--These considerations let our doctrine enforce. Weep not for man's frailty--for if the might of Omnipotence has made the elements obedient to the fervency of his daily prayers, he is no puny sufferer tottering, ill at ease, in the universe, but a being of giant energies, architect of his fortunes, master of his eternity. Weep not for the past; for this is duration over which the secret virtue of prayer is powerless, over which the Omnipotence of God is powerless; send no voice of unprofitable wailing back into the depths of time; for prayer can reverse in the future the events of the past. Weep not for your wasted possessions, for the immeasurable future is before you, and the wealth of the universe invites your industry. Nor despair that your present daily lot is lowly, nor succumb to the shallow understanding or ill example of men whose worldly lot is higher. Be not deceived; for what is the past? It is nothing worth. Its value, except as means of wisdom, is, in the nature of things actually nothing. And what is the imposing present? What are the great men and great things that surround you? All that they can do for you is dust, and less than dust to what you can do for yourself. They are like you stretching forward to an infinite hope, the citizens in trust of a future world. They think little of the present; though they seem satisfied, they are not satisfied but repine and endeavour after greater good. They, like you, are born to live when the sun has gone down in darkness and the moon is turned to blood.

My friends, in the remarks that I have just made I have already in part anticipated the third great branch of our subject, which is that *our prayers are written in Heaven.*

III. The great moral doctrines we have attempted to teach would be of limited worth if there were no farther consideration in this series of thought. You are pleased with the acquisition of property; you pray without ceasing to become rich. You lay no tax of conscience on the means. You desire to become rich by dint of virtue or of vice, of force or of fraud. And in virtue of the order of things that prevails in the world as I have stated you come to your ends. Is this all? Is the design of Providence complete? Is there no conclusion to this train of events, thus far conducted?

The wicked has flourished up to his hope. He has ground the faces of the poor. He has the tears of the widow and the curse of the fatherless but they lie light on his habitation; for he has builded his house where these cannot come, in the midst of his broad lands, on a pleasant countryside, sheltered by deep ornamental woods, and the voices of the harp and the viol tinkle in his saloons; the gay and the grave, the rich and the fair swarm to him in crowds and though they salute him and smile often upon him they do not utter one syllable of reproach nor repeat one imprecation of the poor. But far away, too far to be any impediment to his enjoyment, the wretches he has cruelly stripped of their last decent comforts, and the well loved means with which sinking poverty yet strives to bear up and make a respectable appearance in society,--are now, in small accommodated tenements, eating a morsel of bread and uttering in unvisited, unremembered solitude, the name of the oppressor. And have we seen all, my friends, and is poor struggling worth to be rewarded only with worth, and be poor and vile beside, and is vice to go triumphing on to the grave? Aye; to the grave. Hitherto, shalt thou go, and no farther, and here shall thy proud waves be staid. My friends, there is another world. After death there is life. After death in another state, revives your capacity of pleasure and of pain, the evil memory of evil actions; revives yourself, the man within the breast, the gratified petitioner in the exact condition to which his fulfilled desires have, by the inevitable force of things, contracted or expanded his character. There is another world; a world of remuneration; a world to which you and I are going and which it deeply behooves us to survey and scrutinize as faithfully as we can, as it lies before us, "though shadows, clouds and darkness rest upon it." It is plain that *as* we die in this world, we shall be born into that. It is plain, that, it is, if it be anything, a world of spirit; that body, and the pleasures and pains appertaining to body can have no exercise, no mansion there; that it can be the appropriate home only of high thought and noble virtue. Hence it must happen, that if a soul can have access to that ethereal society, fleshed over with bodily appetites, in which no love has grown up of thought and moral beauty, and no sympathy and worship of virtue, but in their place gnawing lusts have coiled themselves with a serpent's trail into the place of every noble affection that God set up in the recesses of the soul when he balanced the parts and modulated the harmony of the whole; and there pampered appetites that grew in the soil of this world, find no aliment for them in heaven, no gaudy vanities of dress, no riotous excitement of song and dances, no filling gluttony of meats and drinks, no unclean enjoyments, finding none of all this, it must happen, that these appetites will turn upon their master, in the shape of direst tormentors; and if the economy of the universe provide no natural issue, whereby these mortal impurities can be purged with fire out of the texture of the soul, they must continue from hour to hour, from age to age, to arm the principles of his nature against the happiness of man.

Of this mysterious eternity, about to open upon us, of the nature of its employments and our relation to it, we know little. But of one thing be certain, that if the analogies of time can teach aught of eternity, if the moral laws taking place in this world, have relation to those of the next, and even the forecasting sagacity of the pagan philosopher taught him that the Laws below were sisters of the Laws above--then the riches of the future are dealt out on a system of compensations. That great class of human beings who in every age turned aside from temptation to pursue the bent of moral nature shall now have *their* interests consulted. They have cast their bread on the waters (for the choice lay often between virtue and their bread), trusting that after many days a solemn retribution of good should be rendered to them in the face of the world. Insult and sorrow, rags and beggary they have borne; they have kept the faith though they dwelled in the dust, and now, the pledge of God that supported them in the trial must be redeemed, and shall be, to the wonder of themselves, through the furthest periods of their undying existence.

Their joy and triumph is that revelation of the gospel which is most emphatically enforced by images borrowed from whatever was most grand and splendid in the imaginations of men; but crowns and thrones of judgment, and purple robes are but poor shadows of that moral magnificence with which in the company of souls disembodied, virtue asserts its majesty, and becomes the home and fountain of unlimited happiness.

Nothing remains but the obligation there is on each of us to make what use we can of this momentous doctrine. Is it to another condition than yours, to some removed mode of life, to the vices of some other class of society that this preaching, with strict propriety, belongs? No, my friends, if you are of the great household of God; if you are distinguishers of good and evil; if you believe in your own eternity; if you are tempted by what you feel to be evil attractions; if you are mortal;--it belongs to you. If you have ever felt a desire for what conscience, God's vicegerent, enthroned within you, condemned; if impelled by that desire, and wilfully deaf to that condemnation, you swerved towards the gratification, and obtained the object, and stifled the monitor--then it is you, and not another; then you have uttered these unseemly prayers; the prayer is granted and is written in heaven. And at this moment, though men are not privy to all the passages of your life and will salute you respectfully, and though it may be your own violated memory has ceased to treasure heedfully the number of your offences--yet every individual transgression has stamped its impress on your character, and moral beings in all the wide tracts of God's dominion and God over all fasten their undeceived eyes on this spectacle of moral ruin. To you therefore it belongs, to every one who now hears me, to look anxiously to his ways; to look less at his outward demeanour, his general plausible action, but to *cleanse his thoughts*. The heart, the heart is pure or impure, and out of it, are the issues of life and of DEATH.

The text is taken from pages 55-62 of *The Complete Sermons of Ralph Waldo Emerson*, Volume I, edited by Albert J. von Frank, published by the University of Missouri Press in 1989, and reprinted with their permission and the permission of the Ralph Waldo Emerson Memorial Association.

# Summer

The day is thine, the night also is thine: thou hast prepared the light, and the sun. Thou hast set all the borders of the earth, thou hast made summer. Psalm LXXIV, 16, 17.

In this grateful season, the most careless eye is caught by the beauty of the external world. The most devoted of the sons of gain cannot help feeling that there is pleasure in the blowing of the southwest wind; that the green tree with its redundant foliage and its fragrant blossoms shows fairer than it did a few weeks since when its arms were naked and its trunk was sapless. The inhabitants of cities pay a high tax for their social advantages, their increased civilization, in their exclusion from the sight of the unlimited glory of the earth. Imprisoned in streets of brick and stone, in tainted air and hot and dusty corners, they only get glimpses of the glorious sun, of the ever changing glory of the clouds, of the firmament and of the face of the green pastoral earth which the great Father of all is now adorning with matchless beauty as one wide garden. Still something of the mighty process of vegetation forces itself on every human eye. The grass springs up between the pavements at our feet and the poplar and the elm send out as vigorous and as graceful branches to shade and to fan the town as in their native forest.

Those who yield themselves to these pleasant influences behold in the activity of vegetation a new expression from moment to moment of the Divine power and goodness. They know that this excellent order did not come of itself, that this organized creation of every new year indicates the presence of God. They see him in the small leaf, in the wide meadow, in the sea and the cloud.

We are confident children, confident in God's goodness. Though we all of us know that the year's subsistence to us depends on the fidelity with which rain and sun shall act on the seed, we never doubt the permanence of the Order. We do not refer our own subsistence, especially in cities, to the rain and the sun and the soil. We do not refer the loaf in our basket, or the meats that smoke on our board to the last harvest. And when we do, we fail often to derive from the changes of nature that lesson which to a pious, to a Christian mind they ought to convey.

My brethren, all nature is a book on which one lesson is written and blessed are the eyes that can read it. On the glorious sky it is writ in characters of fire; on earth it is writ in the majesty of the green ocean; it is writ on the volcanoes of the south, and the icebergs of the polar sea; on the storm, in winter; in summer on every trembling leaf; on man in the motion of the limbs, and the changing expression of the face, in all his dealings, in all his language it is seen and may be read and pondered and practised in all. This lesson is the omnipresence of God--the presence of a love that is tender and boundless. Yet man shuts his eyes to this sovereign goodness, thinks little of the evidence that comes from nature, and looks upon the great system of the world only in parcels as its order happens to affect his petty interest. In the seasons he thinks only whether a rain or sunshine will suit his convenience. In the regions of the world he thinks only of his farm or his town. Let us lift up our eyes to a more generous and thankful view of the earth and the seasons.

Do they not come from Heaven and go like Angels round the globe, scattering hope and pleasant toil and recompense and rest? Each righting the seeming disorders, supplying the defects which the former left; converting its refuse into commodity, and drawing out of the ancient earth new treasures to swell the capital of human comfort. Each fulfils the errand on which it was sent. The faintness and despondence of a spring that never opened into summer; the languor of a constant summer; the satiety of an unceasing harvest; the torpor or the terror of a fourfold winter are not only prevented by the ordination of Providence, but they are not feared; and emotions of an opposite character are called forth as we hail the annual visits of these friendly changes at once too familiar to surprize and too distinct and distant to weary us. It is in these as they come and go, that we may recognize the steps of our heavenly Father. We may accustom our minds to discern his power and benevolence in the profusion and the beauty of his common gifts, as the wheat and the vine. Nor do these seem sufficiently appreciated. We look at the works of human art--a pyramid, a stately church, and do not conceal our pleasure and surprize at the skill and force of men to lift such masses and to create such magnificent forms, which skill after all does but remove, combine, and shape the works of God. For the granite, and the marble, and the hands that hewed them from the quarry, are his work. But after they are builded, and the scaffolding is thrown down, and they stand in strength and beauty, there is more exquisite art goes to the formation of a strawberry than is in the costliest palace that human pride has ever reared. In the constitution of that small fruit is an art that eagle eyed science cannot explore but sits down baffled. It cannot detect how the odour is formed and lodged in these minute vessels, or where the delicate life of the fruit resides.

Our patient science explores as it can, every process, opens its microscopes upon every fibre, and hunts every globule of sap that ascends in the stem but it never has detected the secret it seeks. It cannot restore the vegetable it has dissected and analyzed. Where should we go for an ear of corn if the earth refused her increase? With all our botany how should we transform a seed into an ear, or make from the grain of one stalk the green promise and the full harvest that covers acres with its sheaves? The frequency of occurrence makes it expected that a little kernel properly sowed, will become at harvest time a great number of kernels. Because we have observed the same result on many trials, this multiplication is expected. But explain to me, man of learning! any part of this productiveness. There is no tale of metamorphosis in poetry, no fabulous transformation that children read in the Arabian Tales more unaccountable, none so benevolent as this constant natural process which is going on at this moment in every garden, in every foot of vacant land in three zones of the globe.

Go out into a garden and examine a seed; examine the same plant in the bud and in the fruit, and you must confess the whole process a miracle, a perpetual miracle. Take it at any period, make yourself as familiar with all the facts as you can at each period, and in each explanation there will be some step or appearance to be referred directly to the Great Creator; something not the effect of the sower's deposit, nor of the waterer's hope. It is not the loam, nor the gravel, it is not the furrow of the ploughshare nor the glare of the sun that calls greenness from the dust, it is the present power of Him who said 'Seed-time and harvest shall not fail.' Needs there, my brethren, any other book than this returning summer that reminds us of the first creation, to suggest the Presence of God? Shall we indulge our querulous temper in this earth where nature is fragrant with healthful odours and glowing with every pleasant colour? Man marks with emphatic pleasure or complaint the pleasant and the unpleasant days, as if he forgot the uses of the storm, the masses of vapour it collects and scatters over thirsty soil, and the plants that were hardened or moistened by that rough weather, forgot the ships that were borne homeward by the breeze that chills him, or in short as if he forgot that our Father is in Heaven, and the winds and the seas obey him.

We have been looking at Nature as an exhibition of God's benevolence. It will be felt the more to be so when it is considered that the same results might have been brought about without this beauty. The earth contains abundant materials for the nourishment of the human stomach, but they do not exist there in a state proper for our use. Now the tree, the vegetable may be properly considered as a machine by which the nutritious matter is separated from other elements, is taken up out of chalk, and clay, and manures, and prepared as by a culinary process into grateful forms and delicious flavours for the pleasure of our taste and for our sustenance. The little seed of the apple does not contain the large tree that shall spring from it; it is merely an assimilating engine which has the power to take from the ground whatever particles of water or manure it needs, and turn them to its own substance and give them its own arrangement.

For the nourishment of animal life this process goes on and to such incomputable activity and extent, not in one spot, not in one land, but on the whole surface of the globe. Each soil is finishing its own, and each a different fruit. Not only on the hard soil of New England, the oak, the potato and the corn are swelling their fruit but on the shores of the Red Sea the coffee tree is ripening its berries; on the hills of France and Spain the grape is gathering sweetness. The West Indies are covered with the green canes and the East with spices and the mulberries for the silkworm, the cotton plant is bursting its pod in the warm plantations of the south, and the orange and the fig bloom in the Mediterranean islands.

But all this food might have been prepared as well without this glorious show. To what end this unmeasured magnificence? It is for the soul of man. For his eye the harvest waves, for him the landscape wears this glorious show. For to what end else can it be! Can the wheat admire its own tasselled top? Or the oak in autumn its crimson embroidered foliage, or the rose and the lily their embroidery? If there were no mind in the universe to what purpose this profusion of design? It is for the same reason as the rainbow is beautiful and the sun is bright. It is adapted to give pleasure to us. I cannot behold the cheering beauty of a country landscape at this season without believing that it was intended that I should derive from it this pleasure.

But there is more in nature than beauty; there is more to be seen than the outward eye perceives; there is more to be heard than the pleasant rustle of the corn. There is the language of its everlasting analogies, by which it seems to be the prophet and the monitor of the race of man. The Scripture is always appealing to the tree and the flower and the grass as the emblems of our mortal estate. It was the history of man in the beginning, and it is the history of man now. Man is like the flower of the field. In the morning he is like grass that groweth up; in the evening he is cut down and withereth. There is nothing in external nature but is an emblem, a hieroglyphic of something in us. Youth is the spring, and manhood the summer, and age the autumn, and death the winter of man. My brethren, do you say these things are old and trite? That is their very value and warning; so is the harvest old--the apple that hangs on your tree, six thousand times has shown its white bloom, its green germ, and its ripening yellow since our period of the world begins. And this day as the fruit is as fresh so is its moral as fresh and significant to us as it was to Adam in the garden.

I have spoken of the great system of external nature as exciting in our minds the perception of the benevolence of God by the wonderful contrivance their fruits exhibit; by the food they furnish us, and by the beauty that is added to them; and now, of the admonition they seem intended to convey of our short life.

But there is yet a louder and more solemn admonition which they convey to my mind as they do from year to year their appointed work. They speak to man as a moral being, and reproach his lassitude by their brute fidelity. Here we sit waiting the growing of the grain, with an undoubting reliance. If it is blasted in one field, we are sure it will thrive in another. Yet we know that if one harvest of the earth fails, the race must perish from the face of the earth. We have an expectation always of the proper performance of the vegetable functions that would not be increased if one rose from the dead.

Well now, whilst thus directly we depend on this process, on the punctuality of the sun, on the timely action of saps and seed vessels, and rivers and rains, are we as punctual to our orbit? Are we as trustworthy as the weed at our feet? Yet is that a poor machine--and I, besides the animal machinery that is given me, have been entrusted with a portion of the spirit that governs the material, Creation, that made and directs the machinery.--Are ye not much better than they? Shall we to whom the light of the Almighty has been given, shall we who have been raised in the scale of the creation to the power of self government, not govern ourselves? Shall the flower of the field reprove us and make it clear that it had been better for us to have wanted than to have received intelligence?

My friends, let us accustom ourselves thus to look at the fruits of the earth and the seasons of the year. Let all that we see without, only turn our attention with stricter scrutiny on all that is within us. In the beautiful order of the world, shall man alone, the highly endowed inhabitant, present a spectacle of disorder, the misrule of the passions, and rebellion against the laws of his Maker? Let us learn also the lesson they are appointed to teach of trust in God; that he will provide for us if we do his will; remembering the words of the Lord Jesus, who said--'If God so clothe the grass of the field, which today is and tomorrow is cast into the oven, will he not much more care for you, O ye of little faith!'

The text of "Summer," Sermon # 39, is taken from pages 296-300 of Volume I of *The Complete Sermons of Ralph Waldo Emerson* edited by Albert J. von Frank, published by the University of Missouri Press in 1989 and used with their permission and the permission of the Ralph Waldo Emerson Memorial Association.

# The Genuine Man

Stand therefore having your loins girt about with truth.
Ephesians, VI, 14.

The new man which after God is created in righteousness and true holiness.
Ephesians, IV, 24.

We hear the opinion often expressed that this is an age of rapid improvement. It is thought that juster views of human nature are gaining ground than have yet prevailed. Men are beginning to see with more distinctness what they ought to be, that is, what true greatness is. What was called greatness, they have discovered to be an imposture. We stand on tiptoe looking for a brighter age, whose signs and forerunners have already appeared. If it be so let us rejoice. Certainly the times past have failed and the welfare of men still is only hoped for.

It seems to be left to us to commence the best of all works. Nations long before us have made desolating wars and gained bloody victories. Others have invented useful and elegant arts. Others have reared grand temples and beautiful palaces. Others have bred great kings--terrible to their enemies and to their subjects; have produced ingenious artists, inspired poets, eloquent orators, wise judges, brave soldiers, rich merchants, benevolent benefactors, learned scholars. Let them all have their due praise. To us has been committed by Providence the higher and holier work of forming *men*, true and entire men.

A finished man--who has seen? Men are everywhere, on the land and sea, in mountains and mines; cities and fields swarm with them. They are reckoned by thousands and myriads and millions. Yet where to find one who is that which he should be, that which his Maker designed. There is a plan in us, we have not seen executed out of us. Survey the whole circle of your acquaintance, of your neighborhood, of your town and if you can fix upon one complete man, a man independent of his circumstances, a mind which fills and satisfies your idea of the perfection of human nature--one whom you venerate as a man; whose value to your eye consists entirely in the richness of his own nature, in the ability and dispositions you suppose him to possess, and not because he belongs to a particular family, or fills a certain office or possesses a large estate, or is preceded by a great reputation.

There is nothing for the most part less considered than the essential man. The circumstances are much more attended to. Ordinarily when we speak of great men we mean great circumstances. The man is the least part of himself. We hear the wheels of his carriage. We feel the company that walk with him. We read his name often in the newspapers--but him, the soul of him, the praised, the blamed, the enriched, and accompanied, we know not; what matter and quality and color of character he has by which he is that particular person and no other. (Silsbee, Tazewell, Grundy, Barbour--they are mere names--present no specific idea.) You sit in the same room with him and yet himself you see not. All are sensible that the eminence which men are acquiring in society every day is of an extremely artificial character and can be gotten and given to almost any man. The error lies in supposing we know those people best whose names or faces we see most frequently.

But not only an inferior man is thus often magnified but men of real ability owe to this noise and pomp the largest part of their eclat. It aids and doubles their greatness. Whichever way the great man turns, whatever he saith or doth, he is never considered on his naked merits. His fame wins for him, argues for him, commands for him. Who can resist this influence and feel that the reason of Caesar is really no more weighty than our own? We meet a prosperous person. The imagination is first excited and the judgment a little shaken by the renown of his name. Then he is announced by all sort of cheerful and respectful attentions. Then every word comes loaded with the weight of his professional character. Then there still is another fence of fine plausible manners, and polished speech, and the men are very few who have the firmness of nerve to go behind all these inclosures, and with an undazzled eye penetrate unto and measure and weigh the man himself; and the men are fewer still who can bear the scrutiny. Behind all this splendid barricade of circumstances is often found a poor, shrunken, distorted, almost imperceptible object who, when exposed, is found helpless and unhappy.

Is it not true in your experience, brethren, that thus the man is the least part of himself? Arts and professions, wealth and office, manners and religion are screens which conceal lameness and imperfection of character. The eye is so entertained with the outward parade that rarely does anybody concern himself with the state of the real person that moves under all. The whole world goes after externals and the soul, God's image and likeness, is overlooked. Is it not true that men do not think highly, reverently of their own nature? To some persons it may sound strange that we say people do not think enough of themselves. Does not the Apostle Paul, they say, teach that a man ought not to think highly of himself? Let us draw the distinction between a right and a wrong estimate of oneself.

There are two ways of speaking of self; one, when we speak of a man's low and partial self, as when he is said to be selfish; and the other when we speak of the whole self, that which comprehends a man's whole being, of that self of which Jesus said, What can a man give in exchange for his soul? And in that sense, when you say of a man that he thinks too much of himself, I say, No, the fault is that he does not think of himself at all. He has not got so far as to know himself. He thinks of his dress, he thinks of his money, he thinks of his comely person, and pleasant voice, he thinks of the pretty things he has got to say and do, but the eternal reason which shines within him, the immortal life that dwells at the bottom of his heart he knows not. He is not great enough--not good enough--not man enough to go in and converse with that celestial scene. Very likely he is so utterly unacquainted with himself, has lived so on the outside of his world, that he does not yet believe in its existence.

It seems to me, brethren, as if we wanted nothing so much as a habit of steadily fixing the eye upon this higher self, the habit of distinguishing between our circumstances and ourselves; the practice of rigorous scrutiny into our own daily life to learn how much there is of our own action and how much is not genuine but imitated or mercenary; the advantage of arriving at a precise notion of a genuine man such as all good and great persons have aimed to be, such as Jesus designed to be and to make many become, such in short, as in the language of the Scripture, is "the New Man, created after God in righteousness and true holiness."

And this is my object in the present discourse, to draw the picture of the Genuine Man--I think *very* few such have ever lived.

But it is essential that he should believe in himself because that is the object in view, to raise up a great counterbalance to the engrossing of riches, of popularity, of the love of life in the man and make him feel that all these ought to be his servants and not his masters, that he is as great, nay much greater, than any of these: to make him feel that whereas the consequence of most men now depends on their wealth or their popularity, he is capable of being sought to become a man so rich and so commanding by the simple force of his character, that wealth or poverty would be an unnoticed accident, that his solitary opinion and his support to any cause whatever would be like the acclamation of the world in its behalf.

This as we shall see is the secret of all true greatness, the development of the inward nature, the raising it to its true place, to absolute sovereignty, hearkening to this voice which to most men sounds so faint and insignificant above the thunder of the laws and the customs of mankind. And it is founded and can only be founded in religion. It can only prefer this self because it esteems it to speak the voice of God.

This example of public life is only a glaring instance of the manner in which we are dazzled by circumstances but you and I in the most private condition are quite as apt to make the same mistake. A failure in trade is called ruin though it may only call out the faculties and resources of his character. The death of a parent or relative on whom a family depends is esteemed as irreparable loss. How many women are brought up in the beliefs that an advantageous connection in life is essential to their respectability and comfort and grow up in ignorance of their own resources.

Let me have your attention then (and not that only but your critical judgment. If I speak to any young person engaged in the formation of his character let him compare my account with his own experience) in dwelling on the conspicuous marks of the genuine man.

It is the essence of truth of character that a man should follow his own thought; that he should not be accustomed to adopt his motives or modes of action from any other but should follow the leading of his own mind like a little child.

Vulgar people act from a great variety of motives, sometimes from principle, sometimes from prejudice, sometimes from the expectations other people have of them, sometimes from mean calculation, sometimes from superstition. The genuine man is always consistent for he has but one leader. He acts always in character because he acts always from his character. He is accustomed to pay implicit respect to the dictates of his own reason and to obey them without asking why. He therefore speaks what he thinks. He acts his thought. He acts simply and up to the highest motives he knows of.

The excellence of this character will appear by comparing it with the way of the world. In all our intercourse with men we are obliged to make much allowance for what is said out of complaisance and what is said from self interest. What is meant by "knowledge of the world"? Is it not to be suspicious--not to confide too much in kind words or first impressions?

And sad it is to see how much dissimulation exists. There are some people who never appear to speak from their thought--very well behaved people, too, to whom it never seems to have occurred that they ought to act themselves. They are always plotting. They always have one meaning on their lips and another in their heart; often not so much from a design to deceive, as to make themselves agreeable to their company. It is being agreeable at an immense expense. It cannot deceive any one many times and it cuts up all confidence at the root and undoes the complaisant person. I have seen a person who really never heard with the ear his real intents. He never put off the mask; while every one wondered why one should take so much unnecessary pains he was content to carry that cartload of dishonesty from morning till night, winter and summer for forty years and more.

From such painful folly it is refreshing to come into the pure air and free sunshine of the genuine man. All this imposture seems to him needless and irksome. This duplicity shows that there is no sufficient power of reason within the mind that practises it to counterbalance the temptation of acting from external motives. The person is conscious that his intentions are mean and need concealment. But where the mind has no low ends, and is satisfied of the rectitude of its purpose, it assumes no veil--it needs none, but goes to its object openly, and by the shortest way. He is transparent. His intention shines through all his words and deeds. It was nobly said by an old Roman when the masons offered for a hundred crowns to build him a house such that nobody in the city could look into it: "I will give you twice so much money," he said, "if you will build me a house so that all Rome can see every part of it." It was well said by George Fox, the Quaker, "That which I am in words, I am the same in life." It was to the same purpose that an eminent religious teacher of the last generation, Emanuel Swedenborg, said of his writings that "they would be found another self."

But to come a little closer to this matter, to show more particularly how the genuine man speaks and acts, and what is meant by his following implicitly the leading of his own mind. It was happily said of a great man 'that he was content to stand by, and let reason argue for him.' That is precisely the impression left on your mind whenever you talk with a truth speaker, that it is not he who speaks, so much as reason that speaks through him. You are not dealing with a mere man but with something higher and better than any man--with the voice of Reason, common to him and you and all men. It is as if you conversed with Truth and Justice.

This man has the generosity of spirit to give himself up to the guidance of God and lean upon the laws of nature; he parts with his individuality, leaves all thought of private stake, personal feeling, and in compensation he has in some sort of strength of the whole, as each limb of the human system is able to draw to its aid the whole weight of the body. His heart beats pulse for pulse with the heart of the Universe.

To some this may seem a vague expression. There is this supreme universal reason in your mind which is not yours or mine or any man's but is the Spirit of God in us all. The more it is trusted, the more it proves itself trustworthy.

By the genuine man I understand something more than a man who speaks the literal truth. There are I hope many men who aim to do this, and this, though a commendable, is not the highest virtue, but the genuine man speaks in the spirit of truth. He is one who recognizes his right to examine for himself every opinion, every practice that is received in society and who accepts or rejects it for himself. He is one who though calm and cheerful is in earnest and nothing can make a man calm and cheerful but the belief that he is advancing toward his true ends. Being thus in earnest and examining all things he does what he does and speaks whatever he says with all his heart and soul. And so the effect upon the hearer is that you have his whole being a warrant for every word. So much for speech; not less remarkable is the action of the genuine man.

He is distinguished by the heartiness with which he gives himself to the affairs that engage his attention, following the advice of the Apostle, himself a high example of this sincerity, "Whatsoever ye do, do it heartily, as unto the

Lord, and not as unto men." And this appears first in the choice of his pursuit.

It is plain to all observers that some men have been formed for public life, for the management of general affairs, of a robust fabric of soul that needs the rough discipline of hot contention, of deep stakes, of great antagonists, and a vast theatre. Others as manifestly are born to benefit men by the advancement of science. Others embrace the mechanical arts and find no pleasure like that of exercising their own ingenuity to valuable ends. Others delight in the bustle of commerce. Others have quieter yet scarcely less effectual means of serving their fellowmen in gentle offices of compassion or instruction. But to each is his own mode and the genuine man finds his way to that for which he is fitted. Therein he delights and moves with freedom and joy. You shall see others, and this is the great fault of men that in all public business they do not give themselves to the affairs they undertake, they only half act, they speak much, and do much, and yet do not embark themselves fairly and frankly, for better for worse, in the cause but are ever looking around to see what chance there is for their particular advantage. It is only the means to him of a private end. And you never get a perfect confidence in them. Not so the genuine man. He fairly espouses his cause. He grows in its success, he faints in its failure. It is his own cause and his life is in it. All men understand this difference at a glance. I feel who does his work professionally and who does it with the heart.

I am led in connection with these views of genuineness of character to remark upon the stability that belongs to it. "Be ye steadfast, immoveable"--says Paul, an injunction that cannot be complied with, except by him who possesses truth of character.

By listening to this inward voice, by following this invisible Leader, it is in the power of a man to cast off from himself the responsibility of his words and actions and to make God responsible for him. It is beautiful, it is venerable to see the majesty which belongs to the man who leans directly upon a principle. He has a confidence that it cannot fail him. It is affirmed to him as by oath of God. The conviction that possesses him is equal to the judge. As God liveth it shall be so. Whilst he rests upon it, he has nothing to do with consequences; he is above them, he has nothing to do with the effect of his example; he is following God's finger and cannot go astray. God will take care of the issues. He may walk in the frailty of the flesh with the firm step of an archangel.

Whilst I follow my conscience I know I shall never be ashamed. When I have followed it, I know my conduct is capable of explanation, though I have wholly forgotten the circumstances. Integrity defies the sun to find a flaw in its texture. Scipio burned his African accounts.

Finally in answer to any (if such there be) who shall say, "This quality is good, but is there not something better?" I would add one remark, that the conviction must be produced in our minds that this truth of character is identical with a religious life; that they are one and the same thing; that this voice of your own mind is the voice of God; that the reason why you are bound to reverence it, is because it is the direct revelation of your Maker's Will, not written in books many ages since nor attested by distant miracles but in the flesh and blood, in the faculties and emotions of your constitution; that Jesus Christ came into the world for this express purpose to teach men to prefer the soul to the body. Until this conviction is wrought and acted on a man can never be said to have fairly set out on his journey of improvement, for this alone can teach him how to blend his religion with his daily labor so that every act shall be done with the full consent of his head and his heart and he shall not regard his business as so much interruption or so much injury to his religious life, and leave his faith at home, when he goes to his store. The Sabbath was made for man not man for the Sabbath and Religion is made for man's benefit not for God's.

And yet who knows not that crowds of men are acting on that error, that their religious character is something separate from their daily actions--quite external--like a dress to wear or a chamber to lodge in, and that trade is to get them money, and prayers and sermons are to get them virtue, but either would be hurt by being joined with the other.

If instead of this, he worked with love in his favorite calling; if he saw in every day's labor, that he was thereby growing more skillful and more wise; that he was cooperating with God in his own education so that every dollar he earned was a medal of so much real power, the fruit and the means of so much real goodness; if neither his working hours nor his rest were lost time, but all was helping him onward, would not his heart sing for joy--would not the day be brighter and even the night light about him--would not company be more pleasant and even solitude be sociable and his life reveal a new heaven and a new earth to his purer eyes?

Were it not an unspeakable blessing to the world the appearance of such men in its affairs, who should show us how much radiance may belong to mere character, who should show us that honour may dwell in a small tenement as well as in a state house, and that there is no place that will not shine under the light of virtues. We do not know how rich we are.

What is the practical end of the views we have taken? This, and this only, Be genuine.--Be girt with truth. Aim in all things at all times to be that within which you would appear without. Commune with your own heart that you may learn what it means to be true to yourself and follow that guidance steadily. God would have you introduce another standard of success than that which prevails in the world. When you go home at night, and cast your thoughts on your condition, fix them upon your character: instead of asking whether this day has made you richer, or better known, or what compliments have you received,--you shall ask--Am I more just--am I more useful--more patient--more wise--what have I learned--what new truth has been disclosed to me?

Then you will have an interest in yourselves. You will be watching the wonderful opening and growth of a human character, the birth and growth of an angel that has been born, but never will die--who was designed by his Maker to be a growing benefit to the world, and to find his own happiness in forever enlarging the knowledge, multiplying the powers, and exalting the pleasures of others.

The text is based on the draft reproduced on pages 409-417 of Volume IV of *The Complete Sermons of Ralph Waldo Emerson* edited by Wesley T. Mott and published by the University of Missouri Press. The text is reproduced with their permission and the permission of the Ralph Waldo Emerson Memorial Association.

# Manners

In the Essay we are making in the present course of Lectures to write History from the nature of man and illustrate it by facts instead of selecting primarily a few out of the innumerable facts and thence deducing a rash theory, we must not pass over so important an element as Manners. They deserve a great deal of attention yet are of that subtle and evanescent nature as very much to elude analysis. The manners of nations and of individuals proceed directly from the character of which they are involuntary signs. They make an essential part of our image of an individual. The character, the will, which is the ultimate object of history is ever invisible, inaccessible. It is only inferred from many signs as the language, laws, institutions, trade, customs, which he chooses or creates. Of these signs, Manners are close to the will, are more flexible and obedient to it, and are therefore more significant signs of character than any other.

Manners may be defined [as] the silent and mediate expression of character. History is the record of what men are, is the record of the character of the human race. Human character does evermore publish itself. It will not be concealed. It hates darkness. It rushes into light. The most fugitive deed and word, the mere air of doing a thing, the intimated purpose expresses character. If you act, you show character. If you sit still, you show it. If you sleep, you show it. And this expressiveness of the human being we call his Manners.

Manners are affected by climate, religion, occupation, commerce, age. They are instantly affected by whatsoever affects the man. They are as it were the coat of the man that is worn next to his skin and give more exact knowledge of his form and movement than the outer garments. Manners seem to be always a compound product of circumstances and character. They are the mean between what a man has, and what he is. A man's manners depend somewhat on the constitution of his body, somewhat on the constitution of his mind. They measure the amount of individual energy, because condition is an inert force and the force of the individual character overcomes it in proportion to its intensity. It is a trial of strength to lift weights. Where the personal energy is very little, a perfect conformity will be seen to the place and time; where it is very great, the place and time will be hardly discernible in the manners. A man of slender ability tells in his manners his whole history--you know his business, his residence, his party, his connexion. An able man is a citizen of the world and the spot of earth on which he sleeps does not leave its color on his clothes. His form, his face, his gesture become transparent with the light of his mind. The diversity of these signs of character is infinite. The ancient manners differ from the modern manners; the manners of the cannibals from those of Christendom; those of the Hindoo and Chinese from those of Paris and London; those of the Mohawks and Cherokees from the whites on the coast; those of the country people from those of Boston; and in cities, the manners of the merchant are of one sort, those of the student another, the manners of the rich vary from the manners of the poor; every vocation, every social circle, every family connexion, has its manners; and finally each man has his proper forms of living, speaking, motion, address, which are independent of his will but wholly dependent on his character and condition, and therefore are the sure index of his genius or turn of mind.

That circumstance constitutes their value to the historian and philosopher, that they are the unconscious account which [the] party gives of himself. A man elects his trade; chooses often his residence; and disguises his real will by many capricious choices of associates and enterprises, but his ways of expressing his mind, the habitual movements of his body, and the forms of private or social life into which he falls, he chooses not; he knows them not; he cannot see them, any more than he can see his own face. The least admixture of will in manners vitiates them. All natural manners have their own charm. All assumed manners repel and disgust.

They are very needful to our apprehension of any character. How faintly are we affected by the narrative of the battles of the Saxons or Northmen, but when we learn that their Berserkirs did make themselves downright mad on the eve of battle, did roll in the dirt, foam like dogs, tear off their clothes, and run into the fight,--we begin to understand them. The Spartans would interest us little as the paramount state of Greece, had we not been let into their simple town, witnessed their formidable games, and known something of their mothers, of their marriages, and of their daily public table.

The fame of the wars and of the Art of Athens would be very incomplete but for the many engaging and explanatory anecdotes we have of private life; of the resort to the Olympian games; of the gardens of philosophy; of the poverty of Aristides and Phocion; of the marble brow of Pericles.

This insight into the city, the dwelling house, the bedchamber does us a good office beyond the chronicler. We own our consanguinity with these men of flesh and blood, the distance and time disappear. We find a Roman in us and a Greek, a savage and a lord, who can well enough understand all the differences between men that once seemed mountainous. This information takes off the stiff brocade of state and shows us the hands and feet, the gait and accent of the king or the President. Through the anecdote of the herdsman's wife and her cakes Alfred is a cheerful mortal man to us; through what we have heard of Washington's behaviour at balls and assemblies, through what record Jefferson has made of his heat and harshness when crossed in the council chamber, we know and love him as we could never the author of a hundred proclamations, the object of the homage of both continents.

Men are contradistinguished by their manners as they are not by their actions. How gross and vague is the knowledge we have of a man from hearing of his deed, compared with that we draw from seeing the action done. The same act how unlike in two men. It is a fact of great importance that every individual nature has its own beauty. One who goes with eyes open about the world is struck in every company, at every fireside with the riches of nature, when he hears so many new tones, all musical, sees in each person original manners, which have a proper and peculiar charm, and reads new expressions of face. He feels that Nature has laid for each the foundations of a divine building if the soul will build thereon. There is no face, no form that one cannot in fancy associate with prodigious power of intellect or greatness of soul; and this because there are no necessary barriers to man.

Whilst every man's character writes itself out in his manners, whilst the diversity of manners is as great as that of men, the impression made by all is different, and their law may be stated in general; that, all manners impress us with pleasure and veneration in proportion to the dignity of the Spirit which they betray. Let us proceed under this view to consider certain well-known classes of manners which may give us some insight into the permanent causes of history.

We shall see that in the influence of manners over us, we only pay allegiance to the same spiritual attributes, the attributes of the One Mind, which meets us in Art, in Letters, in Laws, in Trade, in Religion, in social institutions.

What is the foundation of that enduring interest which all men feel in the form of life and manners of the old Greeks and Romans--in all its periods from the heroic age (the state of society described to us in Homer and the Greek tragedians) down to the domestic life of the Athenians and Spartans four or five centuries later; and then in direct sequel the manners of the Romans in the time of the Consuls? A very large part of our youth and especially of such as receive a learned education is devoted exclusively to the language and history of these nations, and mainly of Greece.

This period keeps a permanent interest for us because it describes a perfectly natural state of society and one through which in some sort every man passes. The Greeks and the Romans were but noble savages. Their greatness is the era of the bodily nature; the perfection of the senses; and of the spiritual nature unfolded in subordination to the body. The Christian era is the reverse of this; it is the period of philosophy; the era of the spiritual nature manifested in the subjugation of the body.

Now as long as we are made up of mind and body both these eras must always have a deep interest for us as the two extremes between which the life of man oscillates, the life of the savage and the life of the saint. In the first, existed those human forms which furnished models to the genius of ancient sculpture, not like the forms abounding in the streets of modern cities with faces a confused mass of features, but of incorrupt, sharply defined, and symmetrical features whose eye sockets are so formed that it would be impossible for such eyes to squint and take furtive glances on this side and on that but they must turn the whole head.

The manners of that period are of the same sort, manners of mankind

Ere the base laws of servitude began
When wild in woods the noble savage ran.

The reverence exhibited is for personal qualities; courage, strength, beauty, address, self-command, swiftness, a loud voice, a broad chest. The manners are plain and fierce. Luxury is not known, no elegance. A sparse population and the want of riches makes every man his own valet, cook, butcher, and soldier and the habit of supplying onesself all his wants, educates the body to wonderful performances. Such is the Agamemnon and Diomed of Homer and not far different is the picture which Xenophon gives of himself and his compatriots in the retreat of the Ten Thousand. After the army had crossed the river Teleboas in Armenia there fell much snow and the troops lay miserably on the ground covered with it. But Xenophon arose naked and taking an ax began to split wood, whereupon others rose and did the like. Throughout his army seemed to be boundless liberty of speech; they quarrel for plunder, they wrangle with the generals on each new order, and Xenophon is as sharp-tongued as any and sharper-tongued than most and so gives as good as he gets.

Who does not see that this is a gang of great boys with such a code of honor and such lax discipline as great boys have? The costly charm of the ancient tragedy and indeed of all the old literature is that the persons speak simply; speak as persons who have great good sense but perfect naivete; before yet the reflective habit has become the predominant habit of the mind. Our admiration of the Antique is not admiration of the Old but of the Natural. The Greeks are not reflective but perfect in their senses, perfect in their health; with the finest physical organization in the world. Adults acted with the simplicity and grace of boys. They made vases, tragedies, and statues such as healthy senses should, that is, in good taste. Such things have continued to be made in all ages and are now wherever a healthy physiology exists, but as a class from their superior organization they have surpassed all.

The Roman manners are the continuation of the Greek, continually degraded from their simplicity as the power and opulence of the empire increased. The Fabii, the Lentuli, and Pisones, the great families of Rome were farmers who derived these names from the beans (faba), the lentils (lens-tis), and pulse (pisum) which they cultivated with success on their acres. A naked simplicity of life of which the whole end was Rome, and the whole means was war, makes all their history very easy to read. It was still the period of the corporeal life which a sentence of Seneca will very well illustrate. "The ancient Romans," he says, "kept their youth always standing and taught them nothing that they were to learn sitting."

Now the manners of this period have proved wonderfully attractive to the men of all times. It is, I believe, because they correspond to the sentiments proper to one age of man. They combine the energy of manhood with the engaging unconsciousness of childhood. It is our reverence for childhood. No eye of taste can ever see without pleasure the manners of childhood. The observer finds them not only beautiful, but admirable. The Unconscious is ever the act of God himself. Nobody can reflect upon his unconscious period or any particular word or act in it with regret or contempt. Bard or hero cannot look down upon the word or gesture of a child. It is as great as they. I say I think the attraction of these manners is that they belong to man and are known to every man in virtue of his being once a child, beside that always there are individuals who retain these characteristics. A person of childlike genius and inborn energy is still a Greek, and revives our love of the Muse of Hellas.

A mind in love with Greek genius will meet traits of it in all ages and places. As in old botanical gardens they turn up in the soil every now and then seeds that have lain dormant for ages and as in families they say a feature will sometimes sleep for a hundred years and then reappear in a descendant of the line so I believe this Greek genius is ever reappearing in society and that our attention is struck with traits of it in the schoolhouse and in the fields. Something of the physical perfection of the heroic age and with it a portion of this infantile simplicity is exhibited by the Indian in the woods but without the ardent temperament and without the taste of the Greek. And who does not own the attraction of the romantic manners of the aborigines? We feel especially in regard to them as to the ancients, that they stand in stricter relations with Nature than other persons.

Whoever is still in alliance with eternal nature possesses a portion of her majesty. This is the charm which the red man has for us. We believe that like the moose or the bison he hunts, he belongs to the great order of nature. He is part of the morning and the evening, of the forest and the mountain, and is remembered and provided for as the ravens are. He has not yet eaten of the apple of a selfish knowledge and covered himself with the figleaves of a semi-civilization. This sentiment the Greek and the infant and the Indian alike awaken and what is attractive in the manners of them all, is the sympathy we have with the bodily perfection, and with the expectation they suggest of some more intimate union with nature that has been and shall be accompanied with a greater control over it. The likeness between the wild man and the ancient justifies the remark of Talleyrand, that to go from the American coast one or two thousand miles into the wilderness was like going back one or two thousand years in time; you pass, in both, from the extreme of civilization to the extreme of barbarism. Manners are determined in part by the form and constitution of the body; in part by the habits of life; in part by the genius of the individual.

The countryman, the mountaineer, the backwoodsman, any man whose way of life confines him to the fields and forest derives from his constant intercourse with nature a certain charm in his manners which is very grateful to the lover of beauty. The solitude, the dignity of the objects with which he is conversant, the entire absence of degrading works contributes to this effect. "The countryman," said Cato, "has fewest evil thoughts." And when they chance to be endowed with such vigor of mind as to lead them to animated speech there is tenfold the chance that we shall be melted by some touch of nature than appears when the most thoroughbred mannerist opens his lips. From solitude, from ignorance of artificial society, from the inevitable daily comparing man with beast, village with wilderness, from the inevitable acquaintance with the outward nature of man with his strict dependence on sun, rain, wind, and frost, wood, worm, cow, and bird these men get an education to the Homeric simplicity which all the libraries of the Foreign Reviews and novels does not countervail.

And on what reality does the charm of rustic manners rest? Quite analogously to the last classes, I think the refreshing simplicity of these manners depends upon the fact that what is little and contemptible in man, residing always in his individual as contradistinguished from his universal nature, is overpowered in the countryman by his immediate connexion with nature, so that we catch as it were the tones of her voice and the sparkle of her eye through his passive organs.

Let us now consider another class of manners, the manners of a strong will. Novels, romances, and poems are filled with pictures of the imposing manners of nobles, of kings, of commanders, and of the rich. All these classes of persons usually have somewhat marked and impressive manners which without any ostentation of authority strike the attention and obtain obedience. The circumstances of the poor and of the middle classes in civilized countries do not favor great independence of character. In a crowded population, the small tradesman, the poor laborer distrusts the bare merit of his handiwork and solicits patronage. In crowded employments, and especially in menial service this becomes servility. In some of the learned professions this timidity appears.

Then excessive devotion to single petty employment, especially if of the fingers instead of the hands or arms, or to a minute routine of trade so common in cities are apt to affect unfavorably the mind and the manners. From these influences the rich are exempt; the habit of power makes the exercise of it easy and good-humored. The habit which the man of office, the very rich man, the head of many subalterns and workmen, or the man possessing a practical faculty very much in request acquires,--the habit of command becomes calm and graceful. The manners of the planters in the southern states born among slaves are undoubtedly affected by this circumstance. The manners of a strong will are always most imposing when coupled with external mildness and sweetness, for the imagination is agreeably stimulated by the extreme contrast. It was said of the Duke of Buckingham, the favorite of King James, that his manners were marked with such sweetness and flowing courtesy that he was judged effeminate, but when some courtiers attempted to put affronts upon him, they found his gentleness was only a mask for the most terrible determination that ever lived in man. And it always provokes the fancy to meet some Claverhouse or Napoleon in the lassitude and elegance of a parlor and from the sleeping lion judge of the lion aroused. We are more captivated by masculine resolution under an effeminate show as Caesar said of his soldiers, that "though powdered and perfumed they ran like giants to the battle." In like manner the contrast of plain dress and speech and manners with immense power, makes the eclat of the names of Pitt and Fox and Canning. And when Mr. Canning in 1826 in allusion to his recognition of the Independence of the South American Republics, stretched out his arm towards America and said, "I called a new world into existence to redress the balance of the old," every one must see how much the dignity of the scene is heightened by the simplicity of the rank and manners of the speaker, not a prince or a nobleman but a poor commoner.

The respect which the manners of the rich and the powerful habitually inspire even in virtuous men, must be attributed to two reasons; first, that power, of any kind, educates a strong will, which is always respectable; secondly, because the state of wealth and power is a type of the true state of man--a state without fear, shame, or meanness, a power of beneficence, a power of executing the conceptions of the soul.

There is another theatre of manners where they attain their maximum of importance, inasmuch as this kingdom is built on them, i.e. the court of Fashion. The fashionable body springs directly out of the last, that is, out of the class of Power, but in every civilized state the rich and the vain form themselves into a class more or less strict and exclusive emphatically as the class of good breeding, of good manners. This takes advantage of all the claims which power, wealth, and elegance have for the respect and imitation of the majority and then sublimates these qualities into a still narrower circle which monopolizes the influence and constitutes itself a court without appeal on all questions of manners, customs, and dress. This singular despotism has never been carried to such excess as in England [where] good taste in the arts of life tyrannizes in the brains of the people, where the great number of the wealthy and even of the powerful class did not make wealth or power a sufficient distinction to gratify the love of superiority and so in the very bosom of nobility and property arose the clique of fashion, and a few beauties and beaux thought it bewitching to make the access to their circles difficult or impossible to the grandees of the kingdom and the lawgivers of half the world. This sovereignty is very gratifying for it is easy to see that what they do in the wantonness of their hearts becomes unchangeable law for hundreds and thousands and millions. The practice which they invent or adopt to answer any of the common wants of society; the phrase they make current; the dress which a few fine persons in London, Paris, or Vienna sanction, becomes the usage of class after class in concentric circles from these gay gentlemen and gentlewomen until it travels down to the beggars in the villages of America.

It is very easy to see that throughout all times history is predominated over by an idea to which the popular and admired manners of individuals in each nation are only approximations more or less near--the Idea of the hero; in modern times, the gentleman, or Man of honor, Aristides, Phocion, Pericles in Athens, Epaminondas, Timoleon, Scipeo; St. Louis, Richard I, Saladin, Henry IV, Bayard, Sidney, Milton, Lord Falkland, Clarendon, Chatham, Burke, and Washington seem to have in true and fictitious history filled the eyes and imaginations of men from some common property of heroic manners, or by being persons of that singular force and beauty of spirit that it pervaded every gesture with its grace.

All that is admirable in any manners is the more or less successful adoption of the deportment of the gentleman, that is, of the good and heroic man. The true gentleman seems to have no root whatever in the world, to owe nothing to any family, or party, or property, or nation, but to draw all his life from himself. You cannot persuade yourself that he would act differently if there were no spectators of his conduct. He behaves in that manner he has chosen, following no example and out of no hope of reward or fear of punishment, for he only gratifies his humor for one class of actions, and disrelish of another.

Hoping for nothing from the world and contemning all its principles they mix freely with it and are very able in all its affairs; alike at home in every place and contrive to find their own satisfaction in every place. And this peremptory and cheerful spirit shines in all his manners.

About the air and carriage of these persons is an inexpressible majesty. Every act of theirs is more beautiful than the day to look on. Whatever they do, they seem born for that one thing. Honor is venerable to us because it is no mushroom. It is always ancient virtue. We worship it today because it is not of today. We love it and do it homage because it is not a trap for our love and homage, but is essentially self-dependent, self-derived, and therefore of an old immaculate pedigree coming out of the First Cause even if shown in a young person. It serves those whom society disesteems: it respects those of whose feelings mannerly gentlemen and ladies are careless.

We can find no single trait to characterize the man of honor or the woman of honor who are the fountains of beautiful manners so intimate as this, that they are self-sustained persons whose point of view is always from themselves, never from custom nor from another person. Their hope and their fear is not from without but from the beauty or deformity of the action alone. Hereby they can bring all the splendor of truth, justice, and generosity to shine in corners and upon the smallest dealings. The manners of such a soul make that place where he is, honest and religious. They make that act he does, honest and handsome. From his point of view he refuses to part and the visitor who surprises him in servile occupations or coarse dress and the visitor seeing no foolish fear of him, no fear of what he may think or terror at appearances, but cheerful serenity instead falls at once into his view and prefers being to seeming. The manners of such a man are no painting and gilding but real sunshine. His perfume is no wash of sweet essences, but he is an aromatic substance. "He that governs his thoughts," said Addison, "with the everlasting rules of reason and sense must have something so inexpressibly graceful in his words and actions that every circumstance must become him."

How can one possibly recommend himself to another better than by that dignity of manners and simplicity of expression which brought forward on the stage or related in history inspire almost as much enthusiasm as magnanimous actions. I will moreover observe that a succession of chances may lead a man to make himself conspicuous by some illustrious actions who is nevertheless not gifted with a superior genius or an heroic character but our words, accents, and comportment to those around us are alone capable of constituting that true greatness of mind which defies imitation.

It is easy to see that all the attributes of the gentleman are the attributes of a man under the government of the Reason and not under the government of the senses of the understanding. The man who lives chiefly or altogether to his senses, seems to himself unmoored the moment he has changed his scene and associates. He misses his chair and his hat peg. The man of Reason carries his centre within, and is at home in untrodden wilds. All the gestures of the Reason are graceful and majestic; the uplifted eye of Memory, the regular pace, the perfect repose and simple attitudes of meditation inspire respect; but what we call second thoughts, pieces of prudence and calculation, make us run, start, look askance or behind us, skulk and exceed in voice and manner. Deeply interest the most bashful and awkward man in questions that tax his intellect or touch his heart and his aukwardness vanishes and his manners become graceful. The ambitious youth attaches himself to this or that great man as a satellite, but the man of Reason is he who walks by the light of his own mind and so becomes a fountain of honor round which other stars revolve. The vulgar ambition supplicates marks of honor of all men. The gentleman sees, as has been truly said, that glory is a light which shines from us on others not from others on us.

To glance a moment at the actual history of the world it must be admitted that Christianity and Trade has effected immense amelioration in the external face of society, in the manners of the street and in the manners of private life. Ours is the age of decorum. The grossnesses of ancient manners and of those of the middle age disappear with the rise of the majority to competition of property and of power with the few. There is more purity of speech, moderation of living, and inoffensiveness of deportment. Grossness will not subsist with information and business and the consciousness of claims as fair as our own, on every side of us. But it may be doubted whether in the general levelling, heroic manners still survive; whether the passion of gain and the love or fear of the newly created power of the people has not withdrawn some of that stimulus which the noble minded had felt to live for the enlightening of the world. This however I will not affirm. The ways of glory seem to me to be opened to every man and these gates never shut from everlasting to everlasting.

The text is reprinted from Volume II of *The Early Lectures of Ralph Waldo Emerson,* edited by Stephen E. Whicher, Robert E. Spiller, and Wallace E. Williams, Cambridge, Mass., 1964. Permission to reprint the text was given by the Ralph Waldo Emerson Memorial Association and Harvard University Press.

# Eloquence

It is the doctrine of the popular music-masters, that whoever can speak can sing. So, probably, every man is eloquent once in his life. Our temperaments differ in capacity of heat, or we boil at different degrees. One man is brought to the boiling point by the excitement of conversation in the parlor. The waters, of course, are not very deep. He has a two-inch enthusiasm, a patty-pan ebullition. Another requires the additional caloric of a multitude, and a public debate; a third needs an antagonist, or a hot indignation; a fourth needs a revolution; and a fifth, nothing less than the grandeur of absolute ideas, the splendors and shades of Heaven and Hell.

But because every man is an orator, how long soever he may have been a mute, an assembly of men is so much more susceptible. The eloquence of one stimulates all the rest, some up to the speaking point, and all others to a degree that makes them good receivers and conductors, and they avenge themselves for their enforced silence by increased loquacity on their return to the fireside.

The plight of the phlegmatic brains is better than that of those who prematurely boil, and who impatiently break the silence before their time. Our county conventions often exhibit a small-pot-soon-hot style of eloquence. We are too much reminded of a medical experiment, where a series of patients are taking nitrous-oxide gas. Each patient, in turn, exhibits similar symptoms,--redness in the face, voludexterously addressing the prejudice of the company; no, but a taking sovereign possession of the audience. Him we call an artist, who shall play on an assembly of men as a master on the keys of the piano,--who, seeing the people furious, shall soften and compose them, shall draw them, when he will, to laughter and to tears. Bring him to his audience, and, be they who they may, coarse or refined, pleased or displeased, sulky or savage, with their opinions in the keeping of a confessor, or with their opinions in their banksafes,--he will have them pleased and humored as he chooses; and they shall carry and execute that which he bids them.

This is that despotism which poets have celebrated in the "Pied Piper of

Hamelin," whose music drew like the power of gravitation,--drew soldiers and priests, traders and feasters, women and boys, rats and mice; or that of the minstrel of Meudon, who made the pall-bearers dance around the bier. This is a power of many degrees, and requiring in the orator a great range of faculty and experience, requiring a large composite man, such as Nature rarely organizes, so that, in our experience, we are forced to gather up the figure in fragments, here one talent, and there another.

The audience is a constant metre of the orator. There are many audiences in every public assembly, each one of which rules in turn. If anything comic and coarse is spoken, you shall see the emergence of the boys and rowdies, so loud and vivacious, that you might think the house was filled with them. If new topics are started, graver and higher, these roisters recede; a more chaste and wise attention takes place. You would think the boys slept, and that the men have any degree of profoundness. If the speaker utter a noble sentiment, the attention deepens, a new and highest audience now listens, and the audiences of the fun and of facts and of the understanding are all silenced and awed. There is also something excellent in every audience,--the capacity of virtue. They are ready to be beatified. They know so much more than the orator,--and are so just! There is a tablet there for every line he can inscribe, though he should mount to the highest levels. Humble persons are conscious of new illumination; narrow brows expand with enlarged affections; delicate spirits, long unknown to themselves, masked and muffled in coarsest fortunes, who now hear their own native language for the first time, and leap to hear it. But all these several audiences, each above each, which successively appear to greet the variety of style and topic, are really composed out of the same persons; nay, sometimes the same individual will take active part in them all, in turn.

This range of many powers in the consummate speaker and of many audiences in one assembly leads us to consider the successive stages of oratory.

Perhaps it is the lowest of the qualities of an orator, but it is, on so many occasions, of chief importance,--a certain robust and radiant physical health,--or, shall I say? great volumes of animal heat. When each auditor feels himself to make too large a part of the assembly, and shudders with cold at the thinness of the morning audience, and with fear lest all will heavily fail through one bad speech, mere energy and mellowness are then inestimable. Wisdom and learning would be harsh and unwelcome, compared with a substantial cordial man, made of milk, as we say, who is a house-warmer, with his obvious honesty and good meaning, and a hue-and-cry style of harangue, which inundates the assembly with a flood of animal spirits, and makes all safe and secure, so that any and every sort of good speaking becomes at once practicable. I do not rate this animal eloquence very highly, and yet, as we must be fed and warmed before we can do any work well, even the best, so is this semi-animal exuberance, like a good stove, of the first necessity in a cold house.

Climate has much to do with it,--climate and race. Set a New Englander to describe any accident which happened in his presence. What hesitation and reserve in his narrative! He tells with difficulty some particulars, and gets as fast as he can to the result, and, though he cannot describe, hopes to suggest the whole scene. Now listen to a poor Irishwoman recounting some experience of hers. Her speech flows like a river,--so unconsidered, so humorous, so pathetic, such justice done to all the parts! It is a true transubstantiation,--the fact converted into speech, all warm and colored and alive, as it fell out. Our Southern people are almost all speakers, and have every advantage over the New England people, whose climate is so cold, that, 'tis said, we do not like to open our mouths very wide. But neither can the Southerner in the United States, nor the Irish, compare with the lively inhabitant of the South of Europe. The traveller in Sicily needs no gayer melodramatic exhibition than the table d'hote of his inn will afford him, in the conversation of the joyous guests. They mimic the voice and manner of the person they describe; they crow, squeal, hiss, cackle, bark, and scream like mad, and, were it only by the physical strength exerted in telling the story, keep the table in unbounded excitement. But in every constitution some large degree of animal vigor is necessary as material foundation for the higher qualities of the art.

But eloquence must be attractive, or it is none. The virtue of books is to be readable, and of orators to be interesting, and this is a gift of Nature; as Demosthenes, the most laborious student in that kind, signified his sense of this necessity when he wrote, "Good Fortune," as his motto on his shield. As we know, the power of discourse of certain individuals amounts to fascination, though it may have no lasting effect. Some portion of this sugar must intermingle. The right eloquence needs no bell to call the people together, and no constable to keep them. It draws the children from their play, the old from their armchairs, and the invalid from his warm chamber; it holds the hearer fast, steals away his feet, that he shall not depart,--his memory, that he shall not remember the most pressing affairs,--his belief, that he shall not admit any opposing considerations. The pictures we have of it in semi-barbarous ages, when it has some advantages in the simpler habit of the people, show what it aims at. It is said that the Khans, or storytellers in Ispahan and other cities of the East, attain a controlling power over their audience, keeping them for many hours attentive to the most fanciful and extravagant adventures. The whole world knows pretty well the style of these improvisators, and how fascinating they are, in our translations of the "Arabian Nights." Schehezarade tells these stories to save her life, and the delight of young Europe and your America in them proves that she fairly earned it. And who does not remember in childhood some white or black or yellow Scheherzarade, who, by that talent of telling endless feats of fairies and magicians, and kings and queens, was more dear and wonderful to a circle of children than any orator of England or

America is now? The more indolent and imaginative complexion of the Eastern nations makes them much more impressible by these appeals to the fancy.

These legends are only exaggerations of real occurrences, and every literature contains these high compliments to the art of the orator and the bard, from the Hebrew and the Greek down to the Scottish Glenkindie, who

--"Harpit a fish out o' saut water,
Or water out of a stone,
Or milk out of a maiden's breast
Who bairn had never none."

Homer specially delighted in drawing the same figure. For what is the "Odyssey," but a history of the orator, in the largest style, carried through a series of adventures furnishing brilliant opportunities to his talent? See with what care and pleasure the poet brings him on the stage. Helen is pointing out to Antenor, from a tower, the different Grecian chiefs. "Antenor said: 'Tell me, dear child, who is that man, shorter by a head than Agamemnon, yet he looks broader in his shoulders and breast. His arms lie on the ground but he, like a leader, walks about the bands of the men. He seems to me like a stately ram, who goes as a master of the flock.' Him answered Helen, daughter of Jove: 'This is the wise Ulysses, son of Laertes, who was reared in the state of craggy Ithaca, knowing all wiles and wise counsels.' To her the prudent Antenor replied again: 'O woman, you have spoken truly. For once the wise Ulysses came hither on an embassy, with Menelaus, beloved by Mars. I received them, and entertained them at my house. I became acquainted with the genius and the prudent judgments of both. When they mixed with the assembled Trojans and stood, the broad shoulders of Menelaus rose above the other; but, both sitting, Ulysses was more majestic. When they conversed, and interweaved stories and opinions with all, Menelaus spoke succinctly, few but very sweet words, since he was not talkative, nor superfluous in speech, and was the younger. But when the wise Ulysses arose, and stood, and looked down, fixing his eyes on the ground, and neither moved his sceptre backward nor forward, but held it still, like an awkward person, you would say it was some angry or foolish man; but when he sent his great voice forth out of his breast, and his words fell like the winter snows, not then would any mortal contend with Ulysses; and we, beholding, wondered not afterwards so much at his aspect'". Thus he does not fail to arm Ulysses at first with this power of overcoming all opposition by the blandishments of speech. Plutarch tells us that Thucydides, when Archidamus, king of Sparta, asked him, Which was the best wrestler, Pericles or he? replied, "When I throw him, he says he was never down, and he persuades the very spectators to believe him." Philip of Macedon said of Demosthenes, on hearing the report of one of his orations,

"Had I been there, he would have persuaded me to take up arms against myself"; and Warren Hastings said of Burke's speech on his impeachment, "As I listened to the orator, I felt for more than half an hour as if I were the most culpable being on earth."

In these examples, higher qualities have already entered; but the power of detaining the ear by pleasing speech, and addressing the fancy and imagination, often exists without higher merits. Thus separated, as this fascination of discourse aims only at amusement, though it be decisive in its momentary effect, it is yet a juggle, and of no lasting power. It is heard like a band of music passing through the streets, which converts all the passengers into poets, but is forgotten as soon as it has turned the next corner; and unless this oiled tongue could, in Oriental phrase, lick the sun and moon away, it must take its place with opium and brandy. I know no remedy against it but cotton-wool, or the wax which Ulysses stuffed into the ears of his sailors to pass the Sirens safely.

There are all degrees of power, and the least are interesting, but they must not be confounded. There is the glib tongue and cool self-possession of the salesman in a large shop, which, as is well known, overpower the prudence and resolution of housekeepers of both sexes. There is a petty lawyer's fluency, which is sufficiently impressive to him who is devoid of that talent, though it be, in so many cases, nothing more than a facility of expressing with accuracy and speed what everybody thinks and says more slowly, without new information, or precision of thought,--but the same thing, neither less nor more. It requires no special insight to edit one of our country newspapers. Yet whoever can say off currently, sentence by sentence, matter neither better nor worse than what is there printed, will be very impressive to our easily-pleased population. These talkers are that class who prosper like the celebrated schoolmaster, by being only one lesson ahead of the pupil. Add a little sarcasm, and prompt allusion to passing occurrences, and you have the mischievous member of Congress. A spice of malice, a ruffian touch in his rhetoric, will do him no harm with his audience. These accomplishments are of the same kind, and only a degree higher than the coaxing of the auctioneer, or the vituperative style well described in the street-word "jawing." These kinds of public and private speaking have their use and convenience to the practitioners; but we may say of such collectively, that the habit of oratory is apt to disqualify them for eloquence.

One of our statesmen said, "The curse of this country is eloquent men." And one cannot wonder at the uneasiness sometimes manifested by trained statesmen, with large experience of public affairs, when they observe the disproportionate advantage suddenly given to oratory over the most solid and accumulated public service. In a Senate or other business committee, the solid result depends on a few men with working talent. They know how to deal with the facts before them, to put things into a practical shape, and they value men only as they can forward the work. But some new man comes there, who has no capacity for helping them at all, is insignificant, and nobody in the committee, but has a talent for speaking. In the debate with open doors, this precious person makes a speech, which is printed, and read all over the Union, and he at once becomes famous, and takes the lead in the public mind over all these executive men, who, of course, are full of indignation to find one who has no tact or skill, and knows he has none, put over them by means of this talking power which they despise.

Leaving behind us these pretensions, better or worse, to come a little nearer to the verity, eloquence is attractive as an example of the magic of personal ascendency;--a total and resultant power,--rare, because it requires a rich coincidence of powers, intellect, will, sympathy, organs, and, over all, good fortune in the cause. We have a half-belief that the person is possible who can counterpoise all other persons. We believe that there may be a man who is a match for events,--one who never found his match,--against whom other men being dashed are broken,--one of inexhaustible personal resources, who can give you any odds and beat you. What we really wish for is a mind equal to any exigency. You are safe in your rural district, or in the city, in broad daylight, amidst the police, and under the eyes of a hundred thousand people. But how is it on the Atlantic, in a storm? Do you understand how to infuse your reason into men disabled by terror, and to bring your self off safe then?--how among thieves, or among an infuriated populace, or among cannibals? Face to face with a highwayman who has every temptation and opportunity for violence and plunder, can you bring yourself off safe by your wit, exercised through speech?--a problem easy enough to Caesar, or Napoleon. Whenever a man of that stamp arrives, the highwayman has found a master. What a difference between men in power of face! A man succeeds because he has more power of eye than another, and so coaxes or confounds him. The newspapers, every week, report the adventures of some impudent swindler, who, by steadiness of carriage, duped those who should have known better. Yet any swindlers we have known are novices and bunglers, as is attested by their ill name. A greater power of face would accomplish anything, and, with the rest of their takings, take away the bad name. A greater power of carrying the thing loftily, and with perfect assurance, would confound merchant, banker, judge, men of influence and power, poet, and president, and might head any part, unseat any sovereign, and abrogate any constitution in Europe and America. It was said, that a man has at one step attained vast power, who has renounced his moral sentiment, and settled it with himself that he will no longer stick at anything. It was said of Sir William Pepperel, one of the worthies of New England, that, "put him where you might, he commanded, and saw what he willed come to pass." Julius Caesar said to Metelius, when that tribune interfered to hinder him from entering the Roman treasury, "Young man, it is easier for me to put you to death than to say that I will"; and the youth yielded. In earlier days, he was taken by pirates. What then? He threw himself into their ship; established the most extraordinary intimacies; told them stories; declaimed to them; if they did not applaud his speeches, he threatened them with hanging,--which he performed afterwards,--and, in a short time, was master of all on board. A man this is who cannot be disconcerted, and so can never play his last card, but has a reserve of power when he has hit his mark. With a serene face, he subverts a kingdom. What is told of him is miraculous; it affects men so. The confidence of men in him is lavish, and he changes the face of the world, and histories, poems, and new philosophies arise to account for him. A supreme commander over all his passions and affections; but the secret of his ruling is higher than that. It is the power of Nature running without impediment from the brain and will into the hands. Men and women are his game. Where they are, he cannot be without resource. "Whoso can speak well," said Luther, "Is a man." It was men of this stamp that the Grecian States used to ask of Sparta for generals. They did not send to Lacedaemon for troops, but they said, "Send us a commander;" and Pausanias, or Gylippus, or Brasidas, or Agis, was despatched by the Ephors.

It is easy to illustrate this overpowering personality by these examples of soldiers and kings; but there are men of the most peaceful way of life, and peaceful principle, who are felt, wherever they go, as sensibly as a July sun or a December frost,--men who, if they speak, are heard, though they speak in a whisper,--who, when they act, act effectually, and what they do is imitated: and these examples may be found on very humble platforms, as well as on high ones.

In old countries, a high money-value is set on the services of men who have achieved a personal distinction. He who has points to carry must hire, not a skilful attorney, but a commanding person. A barrister in England is reputed to have made twenty or thirty thousand pounds per annum in representing the claims of railroad companies before committees of the House of Commons. His clients pay not so much for legal as for many accomplishments,--for courage, conduct, and a commanding social position, which enable him to make their claims heard and respected.

I know very well, that among our cool and calculating people, where every man mounts guard over himself, where heats and panics and abandonments are quite out of the system, there is a good deal of skepticism as to extraordinary influence. To talk of an overpowering mind rouses the same jealousy and defiance which one may observe round a table where anybody is recounting the marvelous anecdotes of mesmerism. Each auditor puts a final stroke to the discourse by exclaiming, "Can he mesmerize me?" So each man inquires if any orator can change his convictions.

But does any one suppose himself to be quite impregnable? Does he think that not possibly a man may come to him who shall persuade him out of his most settled determination?--for example, good sedate citizen as he is, to make a fanatic of him? or, if he is penurious, to squander money for some purpose he now least thinks of? or, if he is a prudent, industrious person, to forsake his work, and give days and weeks to a new interest? No, he defies any one, every one. Ah! he is thinking of resistance, and of a different turn from his own. But would if one should come of the same turn of mind as his own, and who sees much farther on his own way than he? A man who has tastes like mine, but in greater power, will rule me any day, and make me love my ruler.

Thus it is not powers of speech that we primarily consider under this word Eloquence, but the power that, being present, gives them their perfection, and, being absent, leaves them a merely superficial value. Eloquence is the appropriate organ of the highest personal energy. Personal ascendency may exist with or without adequate talent for its expression. It is as surely felt as a mountain or a planet; but when it is weaponed with a power of speech, it seems first to become truly human, works actively in all directions, and supplies the imagination with fine materials.

This circumstance enters into every consideration of the power of orators, and is the key to all their effects. In the assembly, you shall find the orator and the audience in perpetual balance, and the predominance of either is indicated by the choice of topic. If the talents for speaking exist, but not the strong personality, then there are good speakers who perfectly receive and express the will of the audience, and the commonest populace is flattered by hearing its low mind returned to it with every ornament which happy talent can add. But if there be personality in the orator, the face of things changes. The audience is thrown into the attitude of pupil, follows like a child its preceptor, and hears what he has to say. It is as if, amidst the king's council at Madrid, Ximenes urged that an advantage might be gained of France, and Mendoza that Flanders might be kept down, and Columbus, being introduced, was interrogated whether his geographical knowledge could aid the cabinet, and he can say nothing to one party or to the other, but he can show how all Europe can be diminished and reduced under the king by annexing to Spain a continent as large as six or seven Europes.

This balance between the orator and the audience is expressed in what is called the pertinence of the speaker. There is always a rivalry between the orator and the occasion, between the demands of the hour and the prepossession of the individual. The emergency which has convened the meeting is usually of more importance than anything the debaters have in their minds, and therefore becomes imperative to them. But if one of them have anything of commanding necessity in his heart, how speedily he will find vent for it, and with the applause of the assembly! This balance is observed in the privatest intercourse. Poor Tom never knew the time when the present occurrence was so trivial that he could tell what was passing in his mind without being checked for unseasonable speech; but let Bacon speak, and wise men would rather listen, though the revolution of kingdoms was on foot. I have heard it reported of an eloquent preacher, whose voice is not yet forgotten in this city, that on occasions of death or tragic disaster, which overspread the congregation with gloom, he ascended the pulpit with more than his usual alacrity, and, turning to his favorite lessons of devout and jubilant thankfulness, "Let us praise the Lord," carried audience, mourners, and mourning along with him, and swept away all the impertinence of private sorrow with his hosannas and songs of praise. Pepys says of Lord Clarendon, with whom "he is mad in love," on his return from a conference, "I did never observe how much easier a man do speak when he knows all the company to be below him, than in him; for, though he spoke indeed excellent well, yet his manner and freedom of doing it, as if he played with it, and was informing only all the rest of the company, was mighty pretty."

This rivalry between the orator and the occasion is inevitable, and the occasion always yields to the eminence of the speaker; for a great man is the greatest of occasions. Of course, the interest of the audience and of the orator conspire. It is well with them only when his influence is complete; then only they are well pleased. Especially, he consults his power by making instead of taking his theme. If he should attempt to instruct the people in that which they already know, he would fail; but, by making them wise in that which he knows, he has the advantage of the assembly every moment. Napoleon's tactics of marching on the angle of an army, and always presenting a superiority of numbers, is the orator's secret also.

The several talents which the orator employs, the splendid weapons which went to the equipment of Demosthenes, of Eschines, of Demades, the natural orator, of Fox, of Pitt, of Patrick Henry, of Adams, of Mirabeau, deserve a special enumeration. We must not quite omit to name the principal pieces.

The orator, as we have seen, must be a substantial personality. Then, first, he must have power of statement,--must have the fact, and know how to tell it. In any knot of men conversing on any subject, the person who knows most about it will have the ear of the company, if he wishes it, and lead the conversation,--no matter what genius or distinction other men there present may have; and in any public assembly, him who has the facts, and can and will state them, people will listen to, though he is otherwise ignorant, though he is hoarse and ungraceful, though he stutters and screams.

In a court of justice, the audience are impartial; they really wish to sift the statements, and know what the truth is. And, in the examination of witnesses, there usually leap out, quite unexpectedly, three or four stubborn words or phrases which are the pith and fate of the business, which sink into the ear of all parties, and stick there, and determine the cause. All the rest is repetition and qualifying; and the court and the county have really come together to arrive at these three or four memorable expressions, which betrayed the mind and meaning of somebody.

In every company, the man with the fact is like the guide you hire to lead your party up a mountain or through a difficult country. He may not compare with any of the party in mind, or breeding, or courage, or possessions, but he is much more important to the present need than any of them. That is what we go to the court-house for,--the statement of the fact, and the elimination of a general fact, the real relation of all the parties; and it is the certainty with which, indifferently in any affair that is well handled, the truth stares us in the face, through all the disguises that are put upon it,--a piece of the well-known human life,--that makes the interest of a court-room to the intelligent spectator.

I remember, long ago, being attracted by the distinction of the counsel, and the local importance of the cause, into the court-room. The prisoner's counsel were the strongest and cunningest lawyers in the Commonwealth. They drove the attorney for the State from corner to corner, taking his reasons from under him, and reducing him to silence, but not to submission. When hard-pressed, he revenged himself, in his turn, on the judge, by requiring the court to define what salvage was. The court, thus pushed, tried words, and said everything it could think of to fill the time, supposing cases, and describing duties of insurers, captains, pilots, and miscellaneous sea-officers that are or might be,--like a schoolmaster puzzled by a hard sum, who reads the context with emphasis. But all this flood not serving the cuttlefish to get away in, the horrible shark of the district-attorney being still there, grimly awaiting with his "The court must define,"--the poor court pleaded its inferiority. The superior court must establish the law for this, and it read away piteously the decisions of the Supreme Court, but read to those who had no pity. The judge was forced at last to rule something, and the lawyers saved their rogue under the fog of a definition. The parts were so well cast and discriminated, that it was an interesting game to watch. The government was well enough represented. It was stupid, but it had a strong will and possession, and stood on that to the last. The judge had a task beyond his preparation, yet his position remained real; he was there to represent a great reality, the justice of states, which we could well enough see battling over his head, and which his trifling talk nowise affected, and did not impede, since he was entirely well-meaning.

The statement of the fact, however, sinks before the statement of the law, which requires immeasurably higher powers, and is a rarest gift, being in all great masters one and the same thing,--in lawyers, nothing technical, but always some piece of common sense, alike interesting to laymen as to clerks. Lord Mansfield's merit is the merit of common sense. It is the same quality we admire in Aristotle, Montaigne, Cervantes, or in Samuel Johnson, or Franklin. Its application to law seems quite accidental. Each of Mansfield's famous decisions contains a level sentence or two, which hit the mark. His sentences are not always finished to the eye, but are finished to the mind. The sentences are involved, but a solid proposition is set forth, a true distinction is drawn. They come from and they go to the sound human understanding; and I read, without surprise, that the black-letter lawyers of the day sneered at his "equitable decisions," as if they were not also learned. This, indeed, is what speech is for, to make the statement; and all that is called eloquence seems to me of little use, for the most part, to those who have it, but inestimable to such as have something to say.

Next to the knowledge of the fact and its law, is method, which constitutes the genius and efficiency of all remarkable men. A crowd of men go up to Faneuil Hall; they are all pretty well acquainted with the object of the meeting; they have all read the facts in the same newspapers. The orator possesses no information which his hearers have not; yet he teaches them to see the thing with his eyes. By the new placing, the circumstances acquire new solidity and worth. Every fact gains consequence by his naming it, and trifles become important. His expressions fix themselves in men's memories, and fly from mouth to mouth. His mind has some new principle of order. Where he looks, all things fly into their places. What will he say next? Let this man speak, and this man only. By applying the habits of a higher style of thought to the common affairs of this world, he introduces beauty and magnificence wherever he goes. Such a power was Burke's, and of this genius we have had some brilliant examples in our own political and legal men.

Imagery. The orator must be, to a certain extent, a poet. We are such imaginative creatures, that nothing so works on the human mind, barbarous or civil, as a trope. Condense some daily experience into a glowing symbol, and an audience is electrified. They feel as if they already possessed some new right and power over a fact, which they can detach, and so completely master in thought. It is a wonderful aid to the memory, which carries away the image, and never loses it. A popular assembly, like the House of Commons, or the French Chamber, or the American Congress, is commanded by these two powers,--first by a fact, then by skill of statement. Put the argument into a concrete shape, into an image, some hard phrase, round and solid as a ball, which they can see and handle and carry home with them, and the cause if half won.

Statement, method, imagery, selection, tenacity of memory, power of dealing with facts, of illuminating them, of sinking them by ridicule or by diversion of the mind, rapid generalization, humor, pathos, are keys which the orator holds; and yet these fine gifts are not eloquence, and do often hinder a man's attainment of it. And if we come to the heart of the mystery, perhaps we should say that the truly eloquent man is a sane man with power to communicate his sanity. If you arm the man with the extraordinary weapons of this art, give him a grasp of facts, learning, quick fancy, sarcasm, splendid allusion, interminable illustration,--all these talents, so potent and charming, have an equal power to ensnare and mislead the audience and the orator. His talents are too much for him, his horses run away with him; and people always perceive whether you drive, or whether the horses take the bits in their teeth and run. But these talents are quite something else when they are subordinated and serve him; and we go to Washington, or to Westminster Hall, or might well go round the world, to see a man who drives, and is not run away with,--a man who, in prosecuting great designs, has an absolute command of the means of representing his ideas, and uses them only to express these; placing facts, placing men; amid the inconceivable levity of human beings, never for an instant warped from his erectness. There is for every man a statement possible of that truth which he is most unwilling to receive,--a statement possible, so broad and so pungent, that he cannot get away from it, but must either bend to it or die of it. Else there would be no such word as eloquence, which means this. The listener cannot hide from himself that something has been shown him and the whole world, which he did not wish to see; and, as he cannot dispose of it, it disposes of him. The history of public men and affairs in America will readily furnish tragic examples of this fatal force.

For the triumphs of the art somewhat more must still be required, namely, a reinforcing of man from events, so as to give the double force of reason and destiny. In transcendent eloquence, there was ever some crisis in affairs, such as could deeply engage the man to the cause he pleads, and draw all this wide power to a point. For the explosions and eruptions, there must be accumulations of heat somewhere, beds of ignited anthracite at the centre. And in cases where profound conviction has been wrought, the eloquent man is he who is no beautiful speaker, but who is inwardly drunk with a certain belief. It agitates and tears him, and perhaps almost bereaves him of the power of articulation. Then it rushes from him as in short, abrupt screams, in torrents of meaning. The possession the subject has of his mind is so entire, that it insures an order of expression which is the order of Nature itself, and so the order of greatest force, and inimitable by any art. And the main distinction between him and other well-graced actors is the conviction, communicated by every word, that his mind is contemplating a whole and inflamed by the contemplation of the whole, and that the words and sentences uttered by him, however admirable, fall from him as unregarded parts of that terrible whole which he sees, and which he means that you shall see. Add to this concentration a certain regnant calmness, which, in all the tumult, never utters a premature syllable, but keeps the secret of its means and method; and the orator stands before the people as a demoniacal power to whose miracles they have no key. This terrible earnestness makes good the ancient superstition of the hunter, that the bullet will hit its mark, which is first dipped in the marksman's blood.

Eloquence must be grounded on the plainest narrative. Afterwards, it may warm itself until it exhales symbols of every kind and color, speaks only through the most poetic forms; but, first and last, it must still be at bottom a biblical statement of fact. The orator is thereby an orator, that he keeps his feet ever on a fact. Thus only is he invincible. No gifts, no graces, no power of wit or learning or illustration will make any amends for want of this. All audiences are just to this point. Fame of voice or of rhetoric will carry people a few times to hear a speaker, but they soon begin to ask, "What is he driving at?" and if this man does not stand for anything, he will be deserted. A good upholder of anything which they believe, a fact-speaker of any kind, they will long follow; but a pause in the speaker's own character is very properly a loss of attraction. The preacher enumerates his classes of men, and I do not find my place therein; I suspect, then, that no man does. Every thing is my cousin, and whilst he speaks things, I feel that he is touching some of my relations, and I am uneasy; but whilst he deals in words, we are released from attention. If you would lift me, you must be on higher ground. If you would liberate me, you must be free. If you would correct my false view of facts,--hold up to me the same facts in the true order of thought, and I cannot go back from the new conviction.

The power of Chatham, of Pericles, of Luther, rested on this strength of character, which, because it did not and could not fear anybody, made nothing of their antagonists, and became sometimes exquisitely provoking and sometimes terrific to these.

We are slenderly furnished with anecdotes of these men, nor can we help ourselves by those heavy books in which their discourses are reported. Some of them were writers, like Burke; but most of them were not, and no record at all adequate to their fame remains. Besides, what is best is lost, the fiery life of the moment. But the conditions for eloquence always exist. It is always dying out of famous places, and appearing in corners. Wherever the polarities meet, wherever the fresh moral sentiment, the instinct of freedom and duty, come in direct opposition to fossil conservatism and the thirst of gain, the spark will pass. The resistance to slavery in this country has been a fruitful nursery of orators. The natural connection by which it drew to itself a train of moral reforms, and the slight yet sufficient party organization it offered, reinforced the city with new blood from the woods and mountains. Wild men, John Baptists, Hermit Peters, John Knoxes, utter the savage sentiment of Nature in the heart of commercial capitals. They send us every year some piece of aboriginal strength, some tough oak-stick of a man who is not to be silenced or insulted or intimidated by a mob, because he is more mob than they,--one who mobs the mob,--some sturdy countryman, on whom neither money, nor politeness, nor hard words, nor eggs, nor blows, nor brickbats, make any impression. He is fit to meet the bar-room wits and bullies; he is a wit and a bully himself, and something more; he is a graduate of the plough, and the stub-hoe, and the bush-whacker; knows all the secrets of swamp and snow-bank, and has nothing to learn of labor or poverty or the rough of farming. His hard head went through in childhood the drill of Calvinism, with text and mortification, so that he stands in the New England assembly a purer bit of New England than any, and flings his sarcasms right and left. He has not only the documents in his pocket to answer all cavils and to prove all his positions, but he has the eternal reason in his head. This man scornfully renounces your civil organizations,--county, or city, or governor, or army,--is his own navy and artillery, judge and jury, legislature and executive. He has learned his lessons in a bitter school. Yet, if the pupil be of a texture to bear it, the best university that can be recommended to a man of ideas is the gauntlet of the mobs.

He who will train himself to mastery in this science of persuasion must lay the emphasis of education, not on popular arts, but on character and insight. Let him see that his speech is not differenced from action; that, when he has spoken, he has not done nothing, nor done wrong, but has cleared his own skirts, has engaged himself to wholesome exertion. Let him look on opposition as opportunity. He cannot be defeated or put down. There is a principle of resurrection in him, an immortality of purpose. Men are averse and hostile, to give value to their suffrages. It is not the people that are in fault for not being convinced, but he that cannot convince them. He should mould them, armed as he is with the reason and love which are also the core of their nature. He is not to neutralize their opposition, but he is to convert them into fiery apostles and publishers of the same wisdom.

The highest platform of eloquence is the moral sentiment. It is what is called affirmative truth, and has the property of invigorating the hearer; and it conveys a hint of our eternity, when he feels himself addressed on grounds which will remain when everything else is taken, and which have no trace of time or place or party. Everything hostile is stricken down in the presence of the sentiments; their majesty is felt by the most obdurate. It is observable, that, as soon as one acts for large masses, the moral element will and must be allowed for, will and must work; and the men least accustomed to appeal to these sentiments invariably recall them when they address nations. Napoleon, even, must accept and use it as he can.

It is only to these simple strokes that the highest power belongs, when a weak human hand touches, point by point, the eternal beams and rafters on which the whole structure of Nature and society is laid. In this tossing sea of delusion, we feel with our feet the adamant; in this dominion of chance, we find a principle of permanence. For I do not accept that definition of Isocrates, that the office of his art is to make the great small and the small great; but I esteem this to be its perfection,--when the orator sees through all masks to the eternal scale of truth, in such sort that he can hold up before the eyes of men the fact of to-day steadily to that standard, thereby making the great great and the small small, which is the true way to astonish and to reform mankind.

All the first orators of the world have been grave men, relying on this reality. One thought the philosophers of Demosthenes' own time found running through all his orations,--this, namely, that "virtue secures its own success." "To stand on one's own feet" Heeren finds the keynote to the discourses of Demosthenes, as of Chatham.

Eloquence, like every other art, rests on laws the most exact and determinate. It is the best speech of the best soul. It may well stand as the exponent of all that is grand and immortal in the mind. If it do not so become an instrument, but inspires to be somewhat of itself, and to glitter for show, it is false and weak. In its right exercise, it is an elastic, unexhausted power,-- who has sounded, who has estimated it?-- expanding with the expansion of our interests and affections. Its great masters, whilst they valued every help to its attainment, and thought no pains too great which contributed in any manner to further it, and, resembling the Arabian warrior of fame, who wore seventeen weapons in his belt, and in personal combat used them all occasionally,--yet undervalued all means, never permitted any talent, neither voice, rhythm, poetic power, anecdote, sarcasm, to appear for show, but were grave men, who preferred their integrity to their talent, and esteemed that object for which they toiled, whether the prosperity of their country or the laws, or a reformation, or liberty of speech or of the press, or letters, or morals, as above the whole world, and themselves also.

This lecture first appeared in *Society and Solitude* published by the Boston firm of Fields and Osgood, 1870. The text is reproduced with the permission of the Ralph Waldo Emerson Memorial Association.

# "The American Scholar"

Mr. President, and Gentlemen,

I greet you on the re-commencement of our literary year. Our anniversary is one of hope, and perhaps, not enough of labor. We do not meet for games of strength or skill, for the recitation of histories, tragedies and odes, like the ancient Greeks; for parliaments of love and poesy, like the Troubadours; nor for the advancement of science, like our cotemporaries in the British and European capitals. Thus far, our holiday has been simply a friendly sign of the survival of the love of letters amongst a people too busy to give to letters any more. As such, it is precious as the sign of an indestructible instinct. Perhaps the time is already come, when it ought to be, and will be something else; when the sluggard intellect of this continent will look from under its iron lids and fill the postponed expectation of the world with something better than the exertions of mechanical skill. Our day of dependence, our long apprenticeship to the learning of other lands, draws to a close. The millions that around us are rushing into life, cannot always be fed on the sere remains of foreign harvests. Events, actions arise, that must be sung, that will sing themselves. Who can doubt that poetry will revive and lead in a new age, as the star in the constellation Harp which now flames in our zenith, astronomers announce, shall one day be the pole-star for a thousand years?

In the light of this hope, I accept the topic which not only usage, but the nature of our association, seem to prescribe to this day,--the AMERICAN SCHOLAR. Year by year, we come up hither to read one more chapter of his biography. Let us inquire what light new days and events have thrown on his character, his duties and his hopes.

It is one of those fables, which out of an unknown antiquity, convey an unlooked-for wisdom, that the gods, in the beginning, divided Man into men, that he might be more helpful to himself; just as the hand was divided into fingers, the better to answer its end.

The old fable covers a doctrine ever new and sublime; that there is One

Man,--present to all particular men only partially, or through one faculty; and that you must take the whole society to find the whole man. Man is not a farmer, or a professor, or an engineer, but he is all. Man is priest, and scholar, and statesm an, and producer, and soldier. In the divided or social state, these functions are parcelled out to individuals, each of whom aims to do his stint of the joint work, whilst each other performs his. The fable implies that the individual to possess himself, must sometimes return from his own labor to embrace all the other laborers. But unfortunately, this original unit, this fountain of power, has been so distributed to multitudes, has been so minutely subdivided and peddled out, that it is spilled into drops, and cannot be gathered. The state of society is one in which the members have suffered amputations from the trunk, and strut about so many walking monsters,--a good finger, a neck, a stomach, an elbow, but never a man.

Man is thus metamorphosed into a thing, into many things. The planter, who is Man sent out into the field to gather food, is seldom cheered by any idea of the true dignity of his ministry. He sees his bushel and his cart, and nothing beyond, and sinks into the farmer, instead of Man on the farm. The tradesman scarcely ever gives an ideal worth to his work, but is ridden by the routine of his craft, and the soul is subject to dollars. The priest becomes a form; the attorney, a statute-book; the mechanic, a machine; the sailor, a rope of a ship.

In this distribution of functions, the scholar is the delegated intellect. In the right state, he is, Man Thinking. In the degenerate state, when the victim of society, he tends to become a mere thinker, or, still worse, the parrot of other men's thinking.

In this view of him, as Man Thinking, the whole theory of his office is contained. Him nature solicits, with all her placid, all her monitory pictures. Him the past instructs. Him the future invites. Is not, indeed, every man a student, and do not all things exist for the student's behoof? And, finally, is not the true scholar the only true master? But, as the old oracle said, "All things have two handles. Beware of the wrong one." In life, too often, the scholar errs with mankind and forfeits his privilege. Let us see him in his school, and consider him in reference to the main influences he receives.

I. The first in time and the first in importance of the influences upon the mind is that of nature. Every day, the sun; and, after sunset, night and her stars. Ever the winds blow; ever the grass grows. Every day, men and women, conversing, beholding and beholden. The scholar must needs stand wistful and admiring before this great spectacle. He must settle its value in his mind. What is nature to him? There is never a beginning, there is never an end to the inexplicable continuity of this web of God, but always circular power returning into itself. Therein it resembles his own spirit, whose beginning, whose ending he never can find--so entire, so boundless. Far, too, as her splendors shine, system on system shooting like rays, upward, downward, without centre, without circumference,--in the mass and in the particle nature hastens to render account of herself to the mind. Classification begins. To the young mind, every thing is individual, stands by itself. By and by, it finds how to join two things, and see in them one nature; then three, then three thousand; and so, tyrannized over by its own unifying instinct, it goes on tying things together, diminishing anomalies, discovering roots running underground, whereby contrary and remote things cohere, and flower out from one stem. It presently learns, that, since the dawn of history, there has been a constant accumulation and classifying of facts. But what is classification but the perceiving that these objects are not chaotic, and are not foreign, but have a law which is also a law of the human mind? The astronomer discovers that geometry, a pure abstraction of the human mind is the measure of planetary motion. The chemist finds proportions and intelligible method throughout matter: and science is nothing but the finding of analogy, identity in the most remote parts. The ambitious soul sits down before each refractory fact; one after another, reduces all strange constitutions, all new powers, to their class and their law, and goes on forever to animate the last fibre of organization, the outskirts of nature, by insight.

Thus to him, to this school-boy under the bending dome of day, is suggested, that he and it proceed from one root; one is leaf and one is flower; relation, sympathy, stirring in every vein. And what is that Root? Is not that the soul of his soul?--A thought too bold--a dream too wild. Yet when this spiritual light shall have revealed the law of more earthly natures,--when he has learned to worship the soul, and to see that the natural philosophy that now is, is only the first gropings of its gigantic hand, he shall look forward to an ever expanding knowledge as to a becoming creator. He shall see that nature is the opposite of the soul, answering to it part for part. One is seal, and one is print. Its beauty is the beauty of his own mind. Its laws are the laws of his own mind. Nature then becomes to him the measure of his attainments. So much of nature as he is ignorant of, so much of his own mind does he not yet possess. And, in fine, the ancient precept, "Know thyself," and the modern precept, "Study nature," become at last one maxim.

II. The next great influence into the spirit of the scholar, is, the mind of the Past,--in whatever form, whether of literature, of art, of institutions, that mind is inscribed. Books are the best type of the influence of the past, and perhaps we shall get at the truth--learn the amount of this influence more conveniently--by considering their value alone.

The theory of books is noble. The scholar of the first age received into him the world around; brooded thereon; gave it the new arrangement of his own mind, and uttered it again. It came into him--life; it went out from him--truth. It came to him--short-lived actions; it went out from him--immortal thoughts. It came to him--business; it went from him--poetry. It was--dead fact; now, it is quick thought. It can stand, and it can go. It now endures, it now flies, it now inspires. Precisely in proportion to the depth of mind from which it issued, so high does it soar, so long does it sing.

Or, I might say, it depends on how far the process had gone, of transmuting life into truth. In proportion to the completeness of the distillation, so will the purity and imperishableness of the product be. But none is quite perfect. As no air-pump can by any means make a perfect vacuum, so neither can any artist entirely exclude the conventional, the local, the perishable from his book, or write a book of pure thought that shall be as efficient, in all respects, to a remote posterity, as to cotemporaries, or rather to the second age. Each age, it is found, must write its own books; or rather, each generation for the next succeeding. The books of an older period will not fit this.

Yet hence arises a grave mischief. The sacredness which attaches to the act of creation,--the act of thought,--is instantly transferred to the record. The poet chanting, was felt to be a divine man. Henceforth the chant is divine also. The writer was a just and wise spirit. Henceforward it is settled, the book is perfect; as love of the hero corrupts into worship of his statue. Instantly, the book becomes noxious. The guide is a tyrant. We sought a brother, and lo, a governor. The sluggish and perverted mind of the multitude, always slow to open to the incursions of Reason, having once so opened, having once received this book, stands upon it, and makes an outcry, if it is disparaged. Colleges are built on it. Books are written on it by thinkers, not by Man Thinking; by men of talent, that is, who start wrong, who set out from accepted dogmas, not from their own sight of principles. Meek young men grow up in libraries, believing it their duty to accept the views which Cicero, which Locke, which Bacon have given, forgetful that Cicero, Locke and Bacon were only young men in libraries when they wrote these books.

Hence, instead of Man Thinking, we have the bookworm. Hence, the book-learned class, who value books, as such; not as related to nature and the human constitution, but as making a sort of Third Estate with the world and the soul. Hence, the restorers of readings, the emendators, the bibliomaniacs of all degrees.

This is bad; this is worse than it seems. Books are the best of things, well used; abused among the worst. What is the right use? What is the one end which all means go to effect? They are for nothing but to inspire. I had better never see a book than to be warped by its attraction clean out of my own orbit, and made a satellite instead of a system. The one thing in the world of value, is, the active soul,--the soul, free, sovereign, active. This every man is entitled to; this every man contains within him, although in almost all men, obstructed, and as yet unborn. The soul active sees absolute truth; and utters truth, or creates. In this action, it is genius; not the privilege of here and there a favorite, but the sound estate of every man. In its essence, it is progressive.

The book, the college, the school of art, the institution of any kind, stop with some past utterance of genius. This is good, say they,--let us hold by this. They pin me down. They look backward and not forward. But genius always looks forward. The eyes of man are set in his forehead, not in his hindhead. Man hopes. Genius creates. To create,--to create,--is the proof of a divine presence. Whatever talents may be, if the man create not, the pure efflux of the Deity is not his:--cinders and smoke, there may be, but not yet flame. There are creative manners, there are creative actions, and creative words; manners, actions, words, that is, indicative of no custom or authority, but springing spontaneous from the mind's own sense of good and fair.

On the other part, instead of being its own seer, let it receive always from another mind its truth, though it were in torrents of light, without periods of solitude, inquest and self-recovery, and a fatal disservice is done. Genius is always sufficiently the enemy of genius by over-influence. The literature of every nation bear me witness. The English dramatic poets have Shakspearized now for two hundred years.

Undoubtedly there is a right way of reading--so it be sternly subordinated. Man Thinking must not be subdued by his instruments. Books are for the scholar's idle times. When he can read God directly, the hour is too precious to be wasted in other men's transcripts of their readings. But when the intervals of darkness come, as come they must,--when the soul seeth not, when the sun is hid, and the stars withdraw their shining--we repair to the lamps which were kindled by their ray to guide our steps to the East again, where the dawn is. We hear that we may speak. The Arabian proverb says, "A fig tree looking on a fig tree, becometh fruitful."

It is remarkable, the character of the pleasure we derive from the best books. They impress us ever with the conviction that one nature wrote and the same reads. We read the verses of one of the great English poets, of Chaucer, of Marvell, of Dryden, with the most modern joy,--with a pleasure, I mean, which is in great part caused by the abstraction of all time from their verses. There is some awe mixed with the joy of our surprise, when this poet, who lived in some past world, two or three hundred years ago, says that which lies close to my own soul, that which I also had well nigh thought and said. But for the evidence thence afforded to the philosophical doctrine of the identity of all minds, we should suppose some pre-established harmony, some foresight of souls that were to be, and some preparation of stores for their future wants, like the fact observed in insects, who lay up food before death for the young grub they shall never see.

I would not be hurried by any love of system, by any exaggeration of instincts, to underrate the Book. We all know, that as the human body can be nourished on any food, though it were boiled grass and the broth of shoes, so the human mind can be fed by any knowledge. And great and heroic men have existed, who had almost no other information than by the printed page. I only would say, that it needs a strong head to bear that diet. One must be an inventor to read well. As the proverb says, "He that would bring home the wealth of the Indies, must carry out the wealth of the Indies." There is then creative reading, as well as creative writing. When the mind is braced by labor and invention, the page of whatever book we read becomes luminous with manifold allusion. Every sentence is doubly significant, and the sense of our author is as broad as the world. We then see, what is always true, that as the seer's hour of vision is short and rare among heavy days and months, so is its record, perchance, the least part of his volume. The discerning will read in his Plato or Shakspeare, only that least part,--only the authentic utterances of the oracle,--and all the rest he rejects, were it never so many times Plato's and Shakspeare's.

Of course, there is a portion of reading quite indispensable to a wise man. History and exact science he must learn by laborious reading. Colleges, in like manner, have their indispensable office,--to teach elements. But they can only highly serve us, when they aim not to drill, but to create; when they gather from far every ray of various genius to their hospitable halls, and by the concentrated fires, set the hearts of their youth on flame. Thought and knowledge are natures in which apparatus and pretension avail nothing. Gowns, and pecuniary foundations, though of towns of gold, can never countervail the least sentence or syllable of wit. Forget this, and our American colleges will recede in their public importance whilst they grow richer every year.

III. There goes in the world a notion that the scholar should be a recluse, a valetudinarian,--as unfit for any handiwork or public labor, as a penknife for an axe. The so-called "practical men" sneer at speculative men, as if, because they speculate or see they could do nothing. I have heard it said that the clergy,--who are always more universally than any other class, the scholars of their day,--are addressed as women: that the rough, spontaneous conversation of men they do not hear, but only a mincing and diluted speech. They are often virtually disfranchised; and, indeed, there are advocates for their celibacy. As far as this is true of the studious classes, it is not just and wise. Action is with the scholar subordinate, but it is essential. Without it, he is not yet man. Without it, thought can never ripen into truth. Whilst the world hangs before the eye as a cloud of beauty, we cannot even see its beauty. Inaction is cowardice, but there can be no scholar without the heroic mind. The preamble of thought, the transition through which it passes from the unconscious to the conscious, is action. Only so much do I know, as I have lived. Instantly we know whose words are loaded with life, and whose not.

The world,--this shadow of the soul, or other me, lies wide around. Its attractions are the keys which unlock my thoughts and make me acquainted with myself. I run eagerly into this resounding tumult. I grasp the hands of those next me, and take my place in the ring to suffer and to work, taught by an instinct that so shall the dumb abyss be vocal with speech. I pierce its order; I dissipate its fear; I dispose of it within the circuit of my expanding life. So much only of life as I know by experience, so much of the wilderness have I vanquished and planted, or so far have I extended my being, my dominion. I do not see how any man can afford, for the sake of his nerves and his nap, to spare any action in which he can partake. It is pearls and rubies to his discourse. Drudgery, calamity, exasperation, want, are instructors in eloquence and wisdom. The true scholar grudges every opportunity of action past by, as a loss of power.

It is the raw material out of which the intellect moulds her splendid products. A strange process too, this, by which experience is converted into thought, as a mulberry leaf is converted into satin. The manufacture goes forward at all hours.

The actions and events of our childhood and youth are now matters of calmest observation. They lie like fair pictures in the air. Not so with our recent actions,--with the business which we now have in hand. On this we are quite unable to speculate. Our affections as yet circulate through it. We no more feel or know it, than we feel the feet, or the hand, or the brain of our body. The new deed is yet a part of life,--remains for a time immersed in our unconscious life. In some contemplative hour, it detaches itself from the life like a ripe fruit, to become a thought of the mind. Instantly, it is raised, transfigured; the corruptible has put on incorruption. Always now it is an object of beauty, however base its origin and neighborhood. Observe, too, the impossibility of antedating this act. In its grub state, it cannot fly, it cannot shine,--it is a dull grub. But suddenly, without observation, the selfsame thing unfurls beautiful wings, and is an angel of wisdom. So is there no fact, no event, in our private history, which shall not, sooner or later, lose its adhesive inert form, and astonish us by soaring from our body into the empyrean. Cradle and infancy, school and playground, the fear of boys, and dogs, and ferules, the love of little maids and berries, and many another fact that once filled the whole sky, are gone already; friend and relative, profession and party, town and country, nation and world, must also soar and sing.

Of course, he who has put forth his total strength in fit actions, has the richest return of wisdom. I will not shut myself out of this globe of action and transplant an oak into a flower pot, there to hunger and pine; nor trust the revenue of some single faculty, and exhaust one vein of thought, much like those Savoyards, who, getting their livelihood by carving shepherds, shepherdesses, and smoking Dutchmen, for all Europe, went out one day to the mountain to find stock, and discovered that they had whittled up the last of their pine trees. Authors we have in numbers, who have written out their vein, and who, moved by a commendable prudence, sail for Greece or Palestine, follow the trapper into the prairie, or ramble round Algiers to replenish their merchantable stock.

If it were only for a vocabulary the scholar would be covetous of action. Life is our dictionary. Years are well spent in country labors; in town--in the insight into trades and manufactures; in frank intercourse with many men and women; in science; in art; to the one end of mastering in all their facts a language, by which to illustrate and embody our perceptions. I learn immediately from any speaker how much he has already lived, through the poverty or the splendor of his speech. Life lies behind us as the quarry from whence we get tiles and copestones for the masonry of to-day. This is the way to learn grammar. Colleges and books only copy the language which the field and the work-yard made.

But the final value of action, like that of books, and better than books, is, that it is a resource. That great principle of Undulation in nature, that shows itself in the inspiring and expiring of the breath; in desire and satiety; in the ebb and flow of the sea, in day and night, in heat and cold, and as yet more deeply ingrained in every atom and every fluid, is known to us under the name of Polarity,--these "fits of easy transmission and reflection," as Newton called them, are the law of nature because they are the law of spirit.

The mind now thinks; now acts; and each fit reproduces the other. When the artist has exhausted his materials, when the fancy no longer paints, when thoughts are no longer apprehended, and books are a weariness,--he has always the resource to live. Character is higher than intellect. Thinking is the function. Living is the functionary. The stream retreats to its source. A great soul will be strong to live, as well as strong to think. Does he lack organ or medium to impart his truths? He can still fall back on this elemental force of living them. This is a total act. Thinking is a partial act. Let the grandeur of justice shine in his affairs. Let the beauty of affection cheer his lowly roof. Those "far from fame" who dwell and act with him, will feel the force of his constitution in the doings and passages of the day better than it can be measured by any public and designed display. Time shall teach him that the scholar loses no hour which the man lives. Herein he unfolds the sacred germ of his instinct, screened from influence. What is lost in seemliness is gained in strength. Not out of those on whom systems of education have exhausted their culture, comes the helpful giant to destroy the old or to build the new, but out of unhandselled savage nature, out of terrible Druids and Berserkirs, come at last Alfred and Shakspear.

I hear therefore with joy whatever is beginning to be said of the dignity and necessity of labor to every citizen. There is virtue yet in the hoe and the spade, for learned as well as for unlearned hands. And labor is every where welcome; always we are invited to work; only be this limitation observed, that a man shall not for the sake of wider activity sacrifice any opinion to the popular judgments and modes of action.

I have now spoken of the education of the scholar by nature, by books, and by action. It remains to say somewhat of his duties.

They are such as become Man Thinking. They may all be comprised in self-trust. The office of the scholar is to cheer, to raise, and to guide men by showing them facts amidst appearances. He plies the slow, unhonored, and unpaid task of observation. Flamsteed and Herschel, in their glazed observatories, may catalogue the stars with the praise of all men, and, the results being splendid and useful, honor is sure. But he, in his private observatory, cataloguing obscure and nebulous stars of the human mind, which as yet no man has thought of as such,--watching days and months, sometimes, for a few facts; correcting still his old records;--must relinquish display and immediate fame. In the long period of his preparation, he must betray often an ignorance and shiftlessness in popular arts, incurring the disdain of the able who shoulder him aside. Long he must stammer in his speech; often forego the living for the dead. Worse yet, he must accept--how often! poverty and solitude. For the ease and pleasure of treading the old road, accepting the fashions, the education, the religion of society, he takes the cross of making his own, and, of course, the self-accusation, the faint heart, the frequent uncertainty and loss of time which are the nettles and tangling vines in the way of the self-relying and self-directed; and the state of virtual hostility in which he seems to stand to society, and especially to educated society. For all this loss and scorn, what offset? He is to find consolation in exercising the highest functions of human nature. He is one who raises himself from private considerations, and breathes and lives on public and illustrious thoughts. He is the world's eye. He is the world's heart. He is to resist the vulgar prosperity that retrogrades ever to barbarism, by preserving and communicating heroic sentiments, noble biographies, melodious verse, and the conclusions of history. Whatsoever oracles the human heart in all emergencies, in all solemn hours has uttered as its commentary on the world of actions,--these he shall receive and impart. And whatsoever new verdict Reason from her inviolable seat pronounces on the passing men and events of to-day,--this he shall hear and promulgate.

These being his functions, it becomes him to feel all confidence in himself, and to defer never to the popular cry. He and he only knows the world. The world of any moment is the merest appearance. Some great decorum, some fetish of a government, some ephemeral trade, or war, or man, is cried up by half mankind and cried down by the other half, as if all depended on this particular up or down. The odds are that the whole question is not worth the poorest thought which the scholar has lost in listening to the controversy. Let him not quit his belief that a popgun is a popgun, though the ancient and honorable of the earth affirm it to be the crack of doom. In silence, in steadiness, in severe abstraction, let him hold by himself; add observation to observation, patient of neglect, patient of reproach; and bide his own time,--happy enough if he can satisfy himself alone that this day he has seen something truly. Success treads on every right step. For the instinct is sure that prompts him to tell his brother what he thinks. He then learns that in going down into the secrets of is own mind, he has descended into the secrets of all minds. He learns that he who has mastered any law in his private thoughts, is master to that extent of all men whose language he speaks, and of all into whose language his own can be translated. The poet in utter solitude remembering his spontaneous thoughts and recording them, is found to have recorded that which men in crowded cities find true for them also. The orator distrusts at first the fitness of his frank confessions,--his want of knowledge of the persons he addresses,--until he finds that he is the complement of his hearers;--that they drink his words because he fulfils for them their own nature; the deeper he dives into his privatest secretest presentiment,--to his wonder he finds, this is the most acceptable, most public, and universally true. The people delight in it; the better part of every man feels, This is my music: this is myself.

In self-trust, all the virtues are comprehended. Free should the scholar be, free and brave. Free even to the definition of freedom, "without any hindrance that does not arise out of his own constitution." Brave; for fear is a thing which a scholar by his very function puts behind him. Fear always springs from ignorance. It is a shame to him if his tranquility, amid dangerous times, arise from the presumption that like children and women, his is a protected class; or if he seek a temporary peace by the diversion of his thoughts from politics or vexed questions, hiding his head like an ostrich in the flowering bushes, peeping into microscopes, and turning rhymes, as a boy whistles to keep his courage up. So is the danger a danger still: so is the fear worse. Manlike let him turn and face it. Let him look into its eye and search its nature, inspect its origin,--see the whelping of this lion,--which lies no great way back; he will then find in himself a perfect comprehension of its nature and extent; he will have made his hands meet on the other side, and can henceforth defy it, and pass on superior. The world is his who can se through its pretension. What deafness, what stone-blind custom, what overgrown error you behold, is there only by sufferance,--by your sufferance. See it to be a lie, and you have already dealt it its mortal blow.

Yes, we are the cowed,--we the trustless. It is a mischievous notion that we are come late into nature; that the world was finished a long time ago. As the world was plastic and fluid in the hands of God, so it is ever to so much of his attributes as we bring to it. To ignorance and sin, it is flint. They adapt themselves to it as they may; but in proportion as a man has anything in him divine, the firmament flows before him, and takes his signet and form. Not he is great who can alter matter, but he who can alter my state of mind. They are the kings of the world who give the color of their present thought to all nature and all art, and persuade men by the cheerful serenity of their carrying the matter, that this thing which they do, is the apple which the ages have desired to pluck, now at last ripe, and inviting nations to the harvest. The great man makes the great thing. Wherever Macdonald sits, there is the head of the table. Linnaeus makes botany the most alluring of studies and wins it from the farmer and the herb-woman. Davy, chemistry: and Cuvier, fossils. The day is always his, who works in it with serenity and great aims. The unstable estimates of men crowd to him whose mind is filled with a truth, as the heaped waves of the Atlantic follow the moon.

For this self-trust, the reason is deeper than can be fathomed,--darker than can be enlightened. I might not carry with me the feeling of my audience in stating my own belief. But I have already shown the ground of my hope, in adverting to the doctrine that man is one. I believe man has been wronged: he has wronged himself. He has almost lost the light that can lead him back to his prerogatives. Men are become of no account. Men in history, men in the world of to-day are bugs, are spawn, and are called "the mass" and "the herd." In a century, in a millennium, one or two men; that is to say--one or two approximations to the right state of every man. All the rest behold in the hero or the poet their own green and crude being--ripened; yes, and are content to be less, so that may attain to its full stature. What a testimony--full of grandeur, full of pity, is borne to the demands of his own nature, by the poor clansman, the poor partisan, who rejoices in the glory of his chief. The poor and the low find some amends to their immense moral capacity, for their acquiescence in a political and social inferiority. They are content to be brushed like flies from the path of a great person, so that justice shall be done by him to that common nature which it is the dearest desire of all to see enlarged and glorified. They sun themselves in the great man's light, and feel it to be their own element. They cast the dignity of man from their downtrod selves upon the shoulders of a hero, and will perish to add one drop of blood to make that great heart beat, those giant sinews combat and conquer. He lives for us, and we live in him.

Men such as they are, very naturally seek money or power; and power because it is as good as money,--the "spoils," so called, "of office." And why not? for they aspire to the highest, and this, in their sleep-walking, they dream is highest. Wake them, and they shall quit the false good and leap to the true, and leave governments to clerks and desks. This revolution is to be wrought by the gradual domestication of the idea of Culture. The main enterprise of the world for splendor, for extent, is the upbuilding of a man. Here are the materials strown along the ground. The private life of one man shall be a more illustrious monarchy,--more formidable to its enemy, more sweet and serene in its influence to its friend, than any kingdom in history. For a man, rightly viewed, comprehendeth the particular natures of all men. Each philosopher, each bard, each actor, has only done for me, as by a delegate, what one day I can do for myself. The books which once we valued more than the apple of the eye, we have quite exhausted. What is that but saying that we have come up with the point of view which the universal mind took through the eyes of that one scribe; we have been that man, and have passed on. First, one; then, another; we drain all cisterns, and waxing greater by all these supplies, we crave a better and more abundant food. The man has never lived that can feed us ever. The human mind cannot be enshrined in a person who shall set a barrier on any one side to this unbounded, unboundable empire. It is one central fire which flaming now out of the lips of Etna, lightens the capes of Sicily; and now out of the throat of Vesuvius, illuminates the towers and vineyards of Naples. It is one light which beams out of a thousand stars. It is one soul which animates all men.

But I have dwelt perhaps tediously upon this abstraction of the Scholar. I ought not to delay longer to add what I have to say, of nearer reference to the time and to this country.

Historically, there is thought to be a difference in the ideas which predominate over successive epochs, and there are data for marking the genius of the Classic, of the Romantic, and now of the Reflective or Philosophical age. With the views I have intimated of the oneness or the identity of the mind through all individuals, I do not much dwell on these differences. In fact, I believe each individual passes through all three. The boy is a Greek; the youth, romantic; the adult, reflective. I deny not, however, that a revolution in the leading idea may be distinctly enough traced.

Our age is bewailed as the age of Introversion. Must that needs be evil? We, it seems, are critical. We are embarrassed with second thoughts. We cannot enjoy any thing for hankering to know whereof the pleasure consists. We are lined with eyes. We see with our feet. The time is infected with Hamlet's unhappiness,--

"Sicklied o'er with the pale cast of thought."

Is it so bad then? Sight is the last thing to be pitied. Would we be blind? Do we fear lest we should outsee nature and God, and drink truth dry? I look upon the discontent of the literary class as a mere announcement of the fact that they find themselves not in the state of mind of their fathers, and regret the coming state as untried; as a boy dreads the water before he has learned that he can swim. If there is any period one would desire to be born in,--is it not the age of Revolution; when the old and the new stand side by side, and admit of being compared; when the energies of all men are searched by fear and by hope; when the historic glories of the old, can be compensated by the rich possibilities of the new era? This time, like all times, is a very good one, if we but know what to do with it.

I read with joy some of the auspicious signs of the coming days as they glimmer already through poetry and art, through philosophy and science, through church and state.

One of these signs is the fact that the same movement which effected the elevation of what was called the lowest class in the state, assumed in literature a very marked and as benign an aspect. Instead of the sublime and beautiful, the near, the low, the common, was explored and poetized. That which had been negligently trodden under foot by those who were harnessing and provisioning themselves for long journeys into far countries, is suddenly found to be richer than all foreign parts. The literature of the poor, the feelings of the child, the philosophy of the street, the meaning of household life, are the topics of the time. It is a great stride. It is a sign--is it not? of new vigor, when the extremities are made active, when currents of warm life run into the hands and the feet. I ask not for the great, the remote, the romantic; what is doing in Italy or Arabia; what is Greek art, or Provencal Minstrelsy; I embrace the common, I explore and sit at the feet of the familiar, the low. Give me insight into to-day, and you may have the antique and future worlds. What would we really know the meaning of? The meal in the firkin; the milk in the pan; the ballad in the street; the news of the boat; the glance of the eye; the form and the gait of the body;--show me the ultimate reason of these matters;--show me the sublime presence of the highest spiritual cause lurking, as always it does lurk, in these suburbs and extremities of nature; let me see every trifle bristling with the polarity that ranges it instantly on an eternal law; and the shop, the plough, and the leger, referred to the like cause by which light undulates and poets sing;--and the world lies no longer a dull miscellany and lumber room, but has form and order; there is no trifle; there is no puzzle; but one design unites and animates the farthest pinnacle and the lowest trench.

This idea has inspired the genius of Goldsmith, Burns, Cowper, and, in a newer time, of Goethe, Wordsworth, and Carlyle. This idea they have differently followed and with various success. In contrast with their writing, the style of Pope, of Johnson, of Gibbon, looks cold and pedantic. This writing is blood-warm. Man is surprised to find that things near are not less beautiful and wondrous than things remote. The near explains the far. The drop is a small ocean. A man is related to all nature. This perception of the worth of the vulgar, is fruitful in discoveries. Goethe, in this very thing the most modern of the moderns, has shown us, as none ever did, the genius of the ancients.

There is one man of genius who has done much for this philosophy of life, whose literary value has never yet been rightly estimated;--I mean Emanuel Swedenborg. The most imaginative of men, yet writing with the precision of a mathematician, he endeavored to engraft a purely philosophical Ethics on the popular Christianity of his time. Such an attempt, of course, must have difficulty which no genius could surmount. But he saw and showed the connexion between nature and the affections of the soul. He pierced the emblematic or spiritual character of the visible, audible, tangible world. Especially did his shade-loving muse hover over and interpret the lower parts of nature; he showed the mysterious bond that allies moral evil to the foul material forms, and has given in epical parables a theory of insanity, of beasts, of unclean and fearful things.

Another sign of our times, also marked by an analogous political movement is, the new importance given to the single person. Every thing that tends to insulate the individual,--to surround him with barriers of natural respect, so that each man shall feel the world is his, and man shall treat with man as a sovereign state with a sovereign state;--tends to true union as well as greatness. "I learned," said the melancholy Pestalozzi, "that no man in God's wide earth is either willing or able to help any other man." Help must come from the bosom alone. The scholar is that man who must take up into himself all the ability of the time, all the contributions of the past, all the hopes of the future. He must be an university of knowledges. If there be one lesson more than another which should pierce his ear, it is, The world is nothing; the man is all; in yourself is the law of all nature, and you know not yet how a globule of sap ascends; in yourself slumbers the whole of Reason; it is for you to know all, it is for you to dare all. Mr. President and Gentlemen, this confidence in the unsearched might of man, belongs by all motives, by all prophecy, by all preparation, to the American Scholar. We have listened too long to the courtly muses of Europe. The spirit of the American freeman is already suspected to be timid, imitative, tame. Public and private avarice make the air we breathe thick and fat. The scholar is decent, indolent, complaisant. See already the tragic consequence. The mind of this country taught to aim at low objects, eats upon itself. There is no work for any but the decorous and the complaisant. Young men of the fairest promise, who begin life upon our shores, inflated by the mountain winds, shined upon by all the stars of God, find the earth below not in unison with these,--but are hindered from action by the disgust which the principles on which business is managed inspire, and turn drudges, or die of disgust,--some of them suicides. What is the remedy? They did not yet see, and thousands of young men as hopeful now crowding to the barriers for the career, do not yet see, that if the single man plant himself indomitably on his instincts, and there abide, the huge world will come round to him. Patience--patience;--with the shades of all the good and great for company; and for solace, the perspective of your own infinite life; and for work, the study and the communication of principles, the making those instincts prevalent, the conversion of the world. Is it not the chief disgrace in the world, not to be an unit;--not to be reckoned one character;--not to yield that peculiar fruit which each man was created to bear, but to be reckoned in the gross, in the hundred, or the thousand, of the party, the section, to which we belong; and our opinion predicted geographically, as the north, or the south. Not so, brothers and friends,--please God, ours shall not be so. We will walk on our own feet; we will work with our own hands; we will speak our own minds. The study of letters shall be no longer a name for pity, for doubt, and for sensual indulgence. The dread of man and the love of man shall be a wall of defence and a wreath of joy around all. A nation of men will for the first time exist, because each believes himself inspired by the Divine Soul which also inspires all men.

The speech was originally printed in a pamphlet by James Monroe and Company in 1837. The text published here is based on the original and was printed in Volume I of the *Collected Works of Ralph Waldo Emerson* edited by Robert E. Spiller and Alfred R. Ferguson, published by Harvard University Press in 1971 and used by their permission and the permission of the Ralph Waldo Emerson Memorial Association.

# "The Young American"

Gentlemen:

It is remarkable, that our people have their intellectual culture from one country, and their duties from another. Our books are European. We are born within the fame and sphere of Shakspeare and Milton, of Bacon, Dryden and Pope; our college text-books are the writings of Butler, Locke, Paley, Blackstone, and Stewart; and our domestic reading has been Clarendon and Hume, Addison and Johnson, Young and Cowper, Edgeworth and Scott, Southey, Coleridge and Wordsworth, and the Edinburgh and Quarterly Reviews. We are sent to a feudal school to learn democracy. A gulf yawns for the young American between his education and his work. We are like the all-accomplished banker's daughter, who, when her education was finished, and her father had become a bankrupt, and she was asked what she could do for him in his sickness and misfortunes,--could she make a shirt, mix bread, scald milk pans? No, but she could waltz, and cut rice-paper, and paint velvet, and transfer drawings, and make satin stitch, and play on the clavichord, and sing German songs, and act charades, and arrange tableaux, and a great many other equally useful and indispensable performances. It has seemed verily so with the education of our young men; the system of thought was the growth of monarchical institutions, whilst those that were flourishing around them were not consecrated to their imagination nor interpreted to their understanding.

This false state of things is newly in a way to be corrected. America is beginning to assert itself to the senses and to the imagination of her children, and Europe is receding in the same degree. This their reaction on education gives a new importance to the internal improvements and to the politics of the country.

There is no American citizen who has not been stimulated to reflection by the facilities now in progress of construction for travel and the transportation of goods in the United States. The alleged effect to augment disproportionately the size of cities, is in a rapid course of fulfilment in this metropolis of New England.

The growth of Boston, never slow, has been so accelerated since the railroads have been opened which join it to Providence, to Albany, and to Portland, that the extreme depression of general trade has not concealed it from the most careless eye. The narrow peninsula, which a few years ago easily held its thirty or forty thousand people, with many pastures and waste lands, not to mention the large private gardens in the midst of the town, has been found too strait when forty are swelled to a hundred thousand. The waste lands have been fenced in and builded over, the private gardens one after the other have become streets. Boston proper consisted of seven hundred and twenty acres of land. Acre after acre has been since won from the sea, and in a short time the antiquary will find it difficult to trace the peninsular topography. Within the last year, the news papers tell us, from twelve to fifteen hundred buildings of all sorts have been erected, many of them of a rich and durable character. And because each of the new avenues of iron road ramifies like the bough of a tree, the growth of the city proceeds at a geometrical rate. Already a new road is shooting northwest towards the Connecticut and Montreal; and every great line of road that is completed makes cross sections from road to road more practicable, so that the land will presently be mapped in a network of iron.

This rage for road building is beneficent for America, where vast distance is so main a consideration in our domestic politics and trade, inasmuch as the great political promise of the invention is to hold the Union staunch, whose days seemed already numbered by the mere inconvenience of transporting representatives, judges, and officers, across such tedious distances of land and water. Not only is distance annihilated, but when, as now, the locomotive and the steamboat, like enormous shuttles, shoot every day across the thousand various threads of national descent and employment, and bind them fast in one web, an hourly assimilation goes forward, and there is no danger that local peculiarities and hostilities should be preserved.

The new power is hardly less noticeable in its relation to the immigrant population, chiefly to the people of Ireland, as having given employment to hundreds of thousands of the natives of that country, who are continually arriving in every vessel from Great Britain.

In an uneven country the railroad is a fine object in the making. It has introduced a multitude of picturesque traits into our pastoral scenery. The tunneling of mountains, the bridging of streams, the bold mole carried out into a broad silent meadow, silent and unvisited by any but its own neighbors since the planting of the region; the encounter at short distances along the track of gangs of laborers; the energy with which they strain at their tasks; the cries of the overseer or boss; the character of the work itself, which so violates and revolutionizes the primal and immemorial forms of nature; the village of shanties, at the edge of beautiful lakes until now the undisturbed haunt of the wild duck, and in the most sequestered nooks of the forest, around which the wives and children of the Irish are seen; the number of foreigners, men and women, whom now the woodsman encounters singly in the forest paths; the blowing of rocks, explosions all day, with the occasional alarm of frightful accident, and the indefinite promise of what the new channel of trade may do and undo for the rural towns, keep the senses and imagination active; and the varied aspects of the enterprise make it the topic of all companies, in cars and boats, and by firesides.

This picture is a little saddened, when too nearly seen, by the wrongs that are done in the contracts that are made with the laborers. Our hospitality to the poor Irishman has not much merit in it. We pay the poor fellow very ill. To work from dark to dark for sixty, or even fifty cents a day, is but pitiful wages for a married man. It is a pittance when paid in cash; but when, as generally happens, through the extreme wants of the one party, met by the shrewdness of the other, he draws his pay in clothes and food, and in other articles of necessity, his case is still worse; he buys everything at disadvantage, and has no adviser or protector. Besides, the labor done is excessive, and the sight of it reminds one of negro-driving. Good farmers and sturdy laborers say that they have never seen so much work got out of a man in a day. Poor fellows! Hear their stories of their exodus from the old country, and their landing in the new, and their fortunes appear as little under their own control as the leaves of the forest around them. As soon as the ship that brought them is anchored, one is whirled off to Albany, one to Ohio, one digs at the levee at New Orleans, and one beside the waterwheels at Lowell, some fetch and carry on the wharves of New York and Boston, some in the woods of Maine. They have too little money, and too little knowledge, to allow them the exercise of much more election of whither to go, or what to do, than the leaf that is blown into this dike or that brook to perish.

And yet their plight is not so grievous as it seems. The escape from the squalid despair of their condition at home, into the unlimited opportunities of their existence here, must be reckoned a gain. The Irish father and mother are very ill paid, and are victims of fraud and private oppression; but their children are instantly received into the schools of the country; they grow up in perfect communication and equality with the native children, and owe to their parents a vigor of constitution which promises them at least an even chance in the competitions of the new generation. Whether it is this confidence that puts a drop of sweetness in their cup, or whether the buoyant spirits natural to the race, it is certain that they seem to have almost a monopoly of the vivacity and good nature in our towns, and contrast broadly, in that particular, with the native people. In the village where I reside, through which a railroad is being built, the charitable ladies, who, moved by the report of the wrongs and distresses of the newly arrived laborers, explored the shanties, with offers of relief, were surprised to find the most civil reception, and the most bounding sportfulness from the oldest to the youngest. Perhaps they may thank these dull shovels as safe vents for peccant humors; and this grim day's work of fifteen or sixteen hours, though deplored by all the humanity of the neighborhood, is a better police than the sheriff and his deputies.

1. But I have abstained too long from speaking of that which led me to this topic,--its importance in creating an American sentiment. An unlooked for consequence of the railroad, is the increased acquaintance it has given the American people with the boundless resources of their own soil. If this invention has reduced England to a third of its size, by bringing people so much nearer, in this country it has given a new celerity to time, or anticipated by fifty years the planting of tracts of land, the choice of water-privileges, the working of mines, and other natural advantages. Railroad iron is a magician's rod, in its power to evoke the sleeping energies of land and water.

The railroad is but one arrow in our quiver, though it has great value as a sort of yard-stick, and surveyor's line. The bountiful continent is ours, state on state, and territory on territory, to the waves of the Pacific sea;

"Our garden is the immeasurable earth,
The heaven's blue pillars are Medea's house,"

and new duties, new motives await and cheer us. The task of planting, of surveying, of building upon this immense tract, requires an education and a sentiment commensurate thereto. A consciousness of this fact, is beginning to take the place of the purely trading spirit and education which sprang up whilst all the population lived on the fringe of sea-coast. And even on the coast, prudent men have begun to see that every American should be educated with a view to the values of land. The arts of engineering and of architecture are studied; scientific agriculture is an object of growing attention; the mineral riches are explored; limestone, coal, slate, and iron; and the value of timber-lands is enhanced.

Columbus alleged as a reason for seeking a continent in the West, that the harmony of nature required a great tract of land in the western hemisphere, to balance the known extent of land in the eastern; and it now appears that we must estimate the native values of this broad region to redress the balance of our own judgment, and appreciate the advantages opened to the human race in this country, which is our fortunate home. The land is the appointed remedy for whatever is false and fantastic in our culture. The great continent we inhabit is to be physic and food for our mind, as well as our body. The land, with its tranquillizing, sanative influences, is to repair the errors of a scholastic and traditional education, and bring us into just relations with men and things.

This habit of living in the presence of these invitations of natural wealth is not inoperative; and this habit, combined with the moral sentiment which, in the recent years, has interrogated every institution, and usage, and law, has, very naturally, given a strong direction to the wishes and aims of active young men to withdraw from cities, and cultivate the soil. This inclination has appeared in the most unlooked for quarters, in men supposed to be absorbed in business, and in those connected with the liberal professions. And since the walks of trade were crowded, whilst that of agriculture cannot easily be, inasmuch as the farmer who is not wanted by others, can yet grow his own bread, whilst the manufacturer or the trader who is not wanted, cannot,--this seemed a happy tendency. For, beside all the moral benefit which we may expect from the farmer's profession, when a man enters it from moral causes, this promised the conquering of the soil, plenty, and beyond this, the adorning of the whole continent with every advantage and ornament which labor, ingenuity, and affection for a man's home, could suggest. This great savage country should be furrowed by the plough, and combed by the harrow; these rough Alleganies should know their master; these foaming torrents should be bestridden by proud arches of stone; these wild prairies should be loaded with wheat; the swamps with rice; the hill-tops should pasture innumerable sheep and cattle; the interminable forests should become graceful parks, for use and for delight.

In this country, where land is cheap, and the disposition of the people pacific, every thing invites to the arts of agriculture, of gardening, and domestic architecture. Public gardens, on the scale of such plantations in Europe and Asia, are now unknown to us. There is no feature of the old countries that more agreeably and newly strikes an American, than the beautiful gardens of Europe; such as the Boboli in Florence, the Villa Borghese in Rome, the Villa d'Este in Tivoli, the gardens at Munich, and at Frankfort on the Maine: works easily imitated here, and which might well make the land dear to the citizen, and inflame patriotism. It is the fine art which is left for us, now that sculpture, and painting, and religious and civil architecture have become effete, and have passed into second childhood. We have twenty degrees of latitude wherein to choose a seat, and the new modes of travelling enlarge the opportunity of selection, by making it easy to cultivate very distant tracts, and yet remain in strict intercourse with the centres of trade and population. And the whole force of all the arts goes to facilitate the decoration of lands and dwellings. A garden has this advantage, that it makes it indifferent where you live. A well-laid garden makes the face of the country about you of no account; low or high, grand or mean, you have made a beautiful abode worthy of man. If the landscape is pleasing, the garden shows it,--if tame, it excludes it. A little grove, which any farmer can find, or cause to grow near his house, will, in a few years, so fill the eye and mind of the inhabitant, as to make cataracts and chains of mountains quite unnecessary to his scenery; and he is so contented with his alleys, woodlands, orchards, and river, that Niagara, and the Notch of the White Hills, and Nantasket Beach, are superfluities. And yet the selection of a fit houselot has the same advantage over an indifferent one, as the selection to a given employment of a man who has a genius for that work. In the last case, all the culture of years will never make the most painstaking apprentice his equal: no more will gardening give the advantage of a happy site to a house in a hole or on a pinnacle. "God Almighty first planted a garden," says Lord Bacon, "and it is the purest of human pleasures. It is the greatest refreshment to the spirits of man, without which, buildings and palaces are but gross handyworks; and a man shall ever see that when ages grow to civility and elegancy, men come to build stately, sooner than to garden finely, as if gardening were the greater perfection." Bacon has followed up this sentiment in his two Essays on Buildings, and on Gardens, with many pleasing details on the decoration of lands; and Aubrey has given us an engaging account of the manner in which Bacon finished his own manor at Gorhambury. In America, we have hitherto little to boast in this kind. The cities continually drain the country of the best part of its population: the flower of the youth, of both sexes, goes into the towns, and the country is cultivated by a so much inferior class. The land,--travel a whole day together,--looks poverty-stricken, and the buildings plain and poor. In Europe, where society has an aristocratic structure, the land is full of men of the best stock, and the best culture, whose interest and pride it is to remain half the year on their estates, and to fill them with every convenience and ornament. Of course these make model farms, and model architecture, and are a constant education to the eye of the surrounding population. Whatever events in progress shall go to disgust men with cities, and infuse into them the passion for country-life, and country-pleasures, will render a prodigious service to the whole face of this continent, and will further the most poetic of all the occupations of real life, the bringing out by art the native but hidden graces of the landscape.

I look on such improvements, also, as directly tending to endear the land to the inhabitant, and give him whatever is valuable in local attachment. Any relation to the land, the habit of tilling it, or mining it, or even hunting on it, generates the feeling of patriotism. He who keeps shop on it, or he who merely uses it as a support to his desk and ledger, or to his manufactory, values it very little. The vast majority of the people of this country live by the land, and carry its quality in their manners and opinions. We in the Atlantic states, by position, have been commercial, and have, as I said, imbibed easily an European culture. Luckily for us, now that steam has narrowed the Atlantic to a strait, the nervous, rocky West is intruding a new and continental element into the national mind, and we shall yet have an American genius. How much better when the whole land is a garden, and the people have grown up in the bowers of a paradise. Without looking, then, to those extraordinary social influences which are now acting in precisely this direction, but only at what is inevitably doing around us, I think we must regard the land as a commanding and increasing power on the American citizen, the sanative and Americanizing influence, which promises to disclose new virtues for ages to come.

2. In the second place, the uprise and culmination of the new and anti-feudal power of Commerce, is the political fact of most significance to the American at this hour.

We cannot look on the freedom of this country, in connexion with its youth, without a presentiment that here shall laws and institutions exist on some scale of proportion to the majesty of nature. To men legislating for the vast area betwixt the two oceans, betwixt the snows and the tropics, somewhat of the gravity and grandeur of nature will infuse itself into the code. A heterogeneous population crowding on all ships from all corners of the world to the great gates of North America, namely, Boston, New York, and New Orleans, and thence proceeding inward to the prairie and the mountains, and quickly contributing their private thought to the public opinion, their toll to the treasury, and their vote to the election, it cannot be doubted that the legislation of this country should become more catholic and cosmopolitan than that of any other. It seems so easy for America to inspire and express the most expansive and humane spirit; newborn, free, healthful, strong, the land of the laborer, of the democrat, of the philanthropist, of the believer, of the saint, she should speak for the human race. America is the country of the Future. From Washington, its capital city, proverbially 'the city of magnificent distances,' through all its cities, states, and territories, it is a country of beginnings, of projects, of vast designs, and expectations. It has no past: all has an onward and prospective look. And herein is it fitted to receive more readily every generous feature which the wisdom or the fortune of man has yet to impress.

Gentlemen, there is a sublime and friendly Destiny by which the human race is guided,--the race never dying, the individual never spared,--to results affecting masses and ages. Men are narrow and selfish, but the Genius, or Destiny, is not narrow, but beneficent. It is not discovered in their calculated and voluntary activity, but in what befalls, with or without their design. Only what is inevitable interests us, and it turns out that love and good are inevitable, and in the course of things. That Genius has infused itself into nature. It indicates itself by a small excess of good, a small balance in brute facts always favorable to the side of reason. All the facts in any part of nature shall be tabulated, and the results shall indicate the same security and benefit; so slight as to be hardly observable, and yet it is there. The sphere is found flattened at the poles, and swelled at the equator; a form flowing necessarily from the fluid state, yet the form, the mathematician assures us, required to prevent the great protuberances of the continent, or even of lesser mountains cast up at any time by earthquakes, from continually deranging the axis of the earth. The census of the population is found to keep an invariable equality in the sexes, with a trifling predominance in favor of the male, as if to counterbalance the necessarily increased exposure of male life in war, navigation, and other accidents. Remark the unceasing effort throughout nature at somewhat better than the actual creatures: amelioration in nature, which alone permits and authorizes amelioration in mankind. The population of the world is a conditional population; these are not the best, but the best that could live in the existing state of soils, of gases, animals, and morals: the best that could yet live; there shall be a better, please God. This Genius, or Destiny, is of the sternest administration, though rumors exist of its secret tenderness. It may be styled a cruel kindness, serving the whole even to the ruin of the member; a terrible communist, reserving all profits to the community, without dividend to individuals. Its law is, you shall have every thing as a member, nothing to yourself. For Nature is the noblest engineer, yet uses a grinding economy, working up all that is wasted today into tomorrow's creation;--not a superfluous grain of sand, for all the ostentation she makes of expense and public works. It is because Nature thus saves and uses, laboring for the general, that we poor particulars are so crushed and straitened, and find it so hard to live. She flung us out in her plenty, but we cannot shed a hair, or a paring of a nail, but instantly she snatches at the shred, and appropriates it to the general stock. Our condition is like that of the poor wolves: if one of the flock wound himself, or so much as limp, the rest eat him up incontinently.

That serene Power interposes an irresistible check upon the caprices and officiousness of our wills. His charity is not our charity. One of his agents is our will, but that which expresses itself in our will, is stronger than our will. We are very forward to help it, but it will not be accelerated. It resists our meddling, eleemosynary contrivances. We devise sumptuary laws and relief laws, but the principle of population is always reducing wages to the lowest pittance on which human life can be sustained. We legislate against forestalling and monopoly; we would have a common granary for the poor; but the selfishness which stores and hoards the corn for high prices, is the preventive of famine; and the law of self-preservation is surer policy than any legislation can be. We concoct eleemosynary systems, and it turns out that our charity increases pauperism. We inflate our paper currency, we repair commerce with unlimited credit, and are presently visited with unlimited bankruptcy.

It is easy to see that we of the existing generation are conspiring with a beneficence, which, in its working for coming generations, sacrifices the passing one, which infatuates the most selfish men to act against their private interest for the public welfare. We build railroads, we know not for what or for whom; but one thing is very certain, that we who build will receive the very smallest share of benefit therefrom. Immense benefit will accrue; they are essential to the country, but that will be felt not until we are no longer countrymen. We do the like in all matters:--

"Man's heart the Almighty to the Future set

By secret and inviolable springs."

We plant trees, we build stone houses, we redeem the waste, we make long prospective laws, we found colleges, hospitals, but for many and remote generations. We should be very much mortified to learn that the little benefit we chanced in our own persons to receive was the utmost they would yield.

The history of commerce, which of course includes the history of the world, is the record of this beneficent tendency. The patriarchal form of government readily becomes despotic, as each person may see in his own family. Fathers wish to be the fathers of the minds of their children, as well as of their bodies, and behold with great impatience a new character and way of thinking presuming to show itself in their own son or daughter. This feeling, which all their love and pride in the powers of their children cannot subdue, becomes petulance and tyranny when the head of the clan, the emperor of an empire, deals with the same difference of opinion in his subjects. Difference of opinion is the one crime which kings never forgive. An empire is an immense egotism. "I am the State," said the French Louis. When a French ambassador mentioned to Paul of Russia, that a man of consequence in St. Petersburgh was interesting himself in some matter, the Czar vehemently interrupted him with these words,--"There is no man of consequence in this empire, but he with whom I am actually speaking; and so long only as I am speaking to him, is he of any consequence." And the emperor Nicholas is reported to have said to his council, "Gentlemen, the age is embarrassed with new opinions. Rely on me, gentlemen, I shall oppose an iron will to the progress of liberal opinions." It is very easy to see that this patriarchal or family management gets to be rather troublesome to all but the papa; the sceptre comes to be a crowbar. And this very unpleasant egotism, Feudalism or the power of Aristocracy opposes, and finally destroys. The king is compelled to call in the aid of his brothers and cousins, and remote relations, to help him keep his overgrown house in order; and this club of noblemen always come at last to have a will of their own; they combine to brave the sovereign, and call in the aid of the people. Each chief attaches as many followers by kindness, and maintenance, and gifts, as he can; and as long as war lasts, the nobles, who must be soldiers, rule very well. But when peace comes, the nobles prove very whimsical and uncomfortable masters; their frolics turn out to be very insulting and degrading to the commoner. Feudalism grew to be a bandit and brigand.

Meantime Trade (or the merchant and manufacturer) had begun to appear: Trade, a plant which always grows wherever there is peace, as soon as there is peace, and as long as there is peace. The luxury and necessity of the noble fostered it. And as quickly as men go to foreign parts, in ships or caravans, a new order of things springs up; new ideas awake in their minds. New command takes place, new servants and new masters. Their information, their wealth, their correspondence, have made them quite other men than left their native shore. They are nobles now, and by another patent than the king's. Feudalism had been good, had broken the power of the kings, and had some very good traits of its own; but it had grown mischievous, it was time for it to die, and, as they say of dying people, all its faults came out. Trade was the strong man that broke it down, and raised a new and unknown power in its place. It is a new agent in the world, and one of great function; it is a very intellectual force. This displaces physical strength, and installs computation, combination, information, science, in its room. It calls out all force of a certain kind that slumbered in the former dynasties. It is now in the midst of its career. Feudalism is not ended yet. Our governments still partake largely of that element. Trade goes to make the governments insignificant, and to bring every kind of faculty of every individual that can in any manner serve any person, on sale. Instead of a huge Army and Navy, and Executive Departments, it tends to convert Government into a bureau of intelligence, an Intelligence-Office, where every man may find what he wishes to buy, and expose what he has to sell, not only produce and manufactures, but art, skill, and intellectual and moral values. This is the good and this the evil of trade, that it goes to put everything into market, talent, beauty, virtue, and man himself.

By this means, however, it has done its work. It has its faults, and will come to an end, as the others do. We rail at Trade, and the philosopher and lover of man have much harm to say of it; but the historian of the world will see that Trade was the principle of Liberty; that Trade planted America and destroyed Feudalism; that it makes peace and keeps peace, and it will abolish slavery. We complain of its grievous oppression of the poor, and of its building up a new aristocracy on the ruins of the aristocracy it destroyed. But there is this immense difference, that the aristocracy of trade has no permanence, is not entailed, was the result of toil and talent, the result of merit of some kind, and is continually falling, like the waves of the sea, before new claims of the same sort. Trade is an instrument in the hands of that friendly Power which works for us in our own despite. We design it thus and thus; but it turns out otherwise and far better. This beneficent tendency, omnipotent without violence, exists and works. Every line of history inspires a confidence that we shall not go far wrong; that things mend. That is it. That is the moral of all we learn, that it warrants Hope, HOPE, the prolific mother of reforms. Our part is plainly not to throw ourselves across the track, not to block improvement, and sit till we are stone, but to watch the uprise of successive mornings, and to conspire with the new works of new days. Government has been a fossil; it should be a plant. I conceive that the office of statute law should be to express, and not to impede the mind of mankind. New thoughts, new things. Trade was one instrument, but Trade is also but for a time, and must give way to somewhat broader and better, whose signs are already dawning in the sky.

3. I pass in the third place to speak of the signs of that which is the sequel of trade.

It is in consequence of the revolution in the state of society wrought by trade, that Government in our times is beginning to wear so clumsy and cumbrous an appearance. We have already seen our way to shorter methods. The time is full of good signs. Some of them shall ripen to fruit. All this beneficent socialism is a friendly omen, and the swelling cry of voices for the education of the people, indicates that Government has other offices than those of banker and executioner. Witness the new movements in the civilized world, the Communism of France, Germany, and Switzerland; the Trades' Unions; the English League against the Corn Laws; and the whole Industrial Statistics, so called. In Paris, the blouse, the badge of the operative, has begun to make its appearance in the saloons. Witness too the spectacle of three Communities which have within a very short time sprung up within this Commonwealth, besides several others undertaken by citizens of Massachusetts within the territory of other States. These proceeded from a variety of motives, from an impatience of many usages in common life, from a wish for greater freedom than the manners and opinions of society permitted, but in great part from a feeling that the true offices of the State, the State had let fall to the ground; that in the scramble of parties for the public purse, the main duties of government were omitted,--the duty to instruct the ignorant, to supply the poor with work and with good guidance. These communists preferred the agricultural life as the most favorable condition for human culture; but they thought that the farm, as we manage it, did not satisfy the right ambition of man. The farmer, after sacrificing pleasure, taste, freedom, thought, love, to his work, turns out often a bankrupt, like the merchant. This result might well seem astounding. All this drudgery, from cockcrowing to starlight, for all these years, to end in mortgages and the auctioneer's flag, and removing from bad to worse. It is time to have the thing looked into, and with a sifting criticism ascertained who is the fool. It seemed a great deal worse because the farmer is living in the same town with men who pretend to know exactly what he wants. On one side, is agricultural chemistry, coolly exposing the nonsense of our spendthrift agriculture and ruinous expense of manures, and offering, by means of a teaspoonful of artificial guano, to turn a sandbank into corn; and, on the other, the farmer, not only eager for the information, but with bad crops and in debt and bankruptcy, for want of it. Here are Etzlers and countless mechanical projectors, who, with the Fourierists, undoubtingly affirm that the smallest union would make every man rich;--and, on the other side, is this multitude of poor men and women seeking work, and who cannot find enough to pay their board. The science is confident, and surely the poverty is real. If any means could be found to bring these two together!

This was one design of the projectors of the Associations which are now making their first feeble experiments. They were founded in love, and in labor. They proposed, as you know, that all men should take a part in the manual toil, and proposed to amend the condition of men by substituting harmonious, for hostile industry. It was a noble thought of Fourier, which gives a favorable idea of his system, to distinguish in his Phalanx a class as the Sacred Band, by whom whatever duties were disagreeable, and likely to be omitted, were to be assumed.

At least, an economical success seemed certain for the enterprise, and that agricultural association must, sooner or later, fix the price of bread, and drive single farmers into association, in self-defence; as the great commercial and manufacturing companies had already done. The Community is only the continuation of the same movement which made the joint-stock companies for manufactures, mining, insurance, banking, and so forth. It has turned out cheaper to make calico by companies; and it is proposed to plant corn, and to bake bread by companies, and knowing men affirm it will be tried until it is done.

Undoubtedly, abundant mistakes will be made by these first adventurers, which will draw ridicule on their schemes. I think, for example, that they exaggerate the importance of a favorite project of theirs, that of paying talent and labor at one rate, paying all sorts of service at one rate, say ten cents the hour. They have paid it so; but not an instant would a dime remain a dime. In one hand it became an eagle as it fell, and in another hand a copper cent. For, obviously, the whole value of the dime is in knowing what to do with it. One man buys with it a land-title of an Indian, and makes his posterity princes; or buys corn enough to feed the world; or pen, ink, and paper, or a painter's brush, by which he can communicate himself to the human race as if he were fire; and the other buys plums and gooseberries. Money is of no value: it cannot spend itself. All depends on the skill of the spender. Whether, too, the objection almost universally felt by such women in the community as were mothers, to an associate life, to a common table, and a common nursery, &c., setting a higher value on the private family with poverty, than on an association with wealth, will not prove insuperable, remains to be determined.

But the Communities aimed at a much greater success in securing to all their members an equal, and very thorough education. And, on the whole, one may say, that aims so generous, and so forced on them by the times, will not be relinquished, even if these attempts fail, but will be prosecuted by like-minded men in all society, until they succeed.

This is the value of the Communities; not what they have done, but the revolution which they indicate as on the way. Yes, Government must educate the poor man. Look across the country from any hill-side around us, and the landscape seems to crave Government. The actual differences of men must be acknowledged, and met with love and wisdom. These rising grounds which command the champaign below, seem to ask for lords, true lords, land-lords, who understand the land and its uses, and the applicabilities of men, and whose government would be what it should, namely, mediation between want and supply. How gladly would each citizen pay a commission for the support and continuation of such good guidance. Goethe said, 'no man should be rich but those who understand it:' and certainly the poor are prone to think that very few of the rich understand how to use their advantage to any good purpose; they have not originality, nor even grace in their expenditure. But if this is true of wealth, it is much more true of power; none should be a governor who has not a talent for governing. Now many people have a native skill for carving out business for many hands; a genius for the disposition of affairs; and are never happier than when difficult practical questions which embarrass other men, are to be solved: all lies in light before them: they are in their element. Could any means be contrived to appoint only these! There really seems a progress towards such a state of things, in which this work shall be done by these natural workmen: and this, not certainly through any increased discretion shown by the citizens at elections, but by the gradual contempt into which official government falls, and the increasing disposition of private adventurers to assume its fallen functions. Thus the costly Post Office is likely to go into disuse before the private transportation shop of Harnden and his competitors. The currency threatens to fall entirely into private hands. Justice is continually administered more and more by private reference, and not by litigation. We have feudal governments in a commercial age. It would be but an easy extension of our commercial system, to pay a private emperor a fee for services, as we pay an architect, or engineer, or a lawyer for advice. If any man has a talent for righting wrong, for administering difficult affairs, for counselling poor farmers how to turn their estates to good husbandry, for combining a hundred private enterprises to a general benefit, let him in the county-town, or in Court-street, put up his sign-board, Mr. Smith, Governor, Mr. Johnson, Working king.

How can our young men complain of the poverty of things in New England, and not feel that poverty as a demand on their charity to make New England rich? Where is he who seeing a thousand men useless and unhappy, and making the whole region look forlorn by their inaction, and conscious himself of possessing the faculty they want, does not hear his call to go and be their king?

We must have kings, and we must have nobles. Nature is always providing such in every society,--only let us have the real instead of the titular. Let us have our leading and our inspiration from the best. The actual differences in personal power are not to be disputed. In every society some men are born to rule, and some to advise. Let the powers be well directed, directed by love, and they would everywhere be greeted with joy and honor. The chief is the chief all the world over, only not his cap and his plume. It is only their dislike of the pretender, which makes men sometimes unjust to the true and finished man. If society were transparent, the noble would everywhere be gladly received and accredited, and would not be asked for his day's work, but would be felt as benefit, inasmuch as he was noble. That were his duty and stint,--to keep himself pure and purifying, the leaven of his nation. I think I see place and duties for a nobleman in every society; but it is not to drink wine and ride in a fine coach, but to guide and adorn life for the multitude by forethought, by elegant studies, by perseverance, self-devotion, and the remembrance of the humble old friend, by making his life secretly beautiful.

I call upon you, young men, to obey your heart, and be the nobility of this land. In every age of the world, there has been a leading nation, one of a more generous sentiment, whose eminent citizens were willing to stand for the interests of general justice and humanity, at the risk of being called, by the men of the moment, chimerical and fantastic. Which should be that nation but these States? Which should lead that movement, if not New England? Who should lead the leaders, but the Young American? The people, and the world, is now suffering from the want of religion and honor in its public mind. In America, out of doors all seems a market; in doors, an air-tight stove of conventionalism. Every body who comes into our houses savors of these precious habits; the men of the market, the women of the custom. I find no expression in our state papers or legislative debate, in our lyceums or churches, specially in our newspapers, of a high national feeling, no lofty counsels that rightfully stir the blood. I speak of those organs which can be presumed to speak a popular sense. They recommend only conventional virtues, whatever will earn and preserve property; always the capitalist; the college, the church, the hospital, the theatre, the hotel, the road, the ship, of the capitalist,--whatever goes to secure, adorn, enlarge these, is good; what jeopardizes any of these, is damnable. The 'opposition' papers, so-called, are on the same side. They attack the great capitalist, but with the aim to make a capitalist of the poor man. The opposition is between the ins and the outs; between those who have money, and those who wish to have money. But who announces to us in journal, or in pulpit, or in the street, the secret of heroism,

> Man alone
> Can perform the
> impossible?

I take pleasure in adding the succeeding lines from the ode of the German poet:

> He distinguishes,
> Chooses, and judges,
> He can impart to the
> Moment duration.

Noble be man,
Helpful and good!
Since that alone
Distinguishes him
From all the beings
Which we know.

Hail to the unknown
Higher powers
Whom we divine!
His pattern teach us
Faith in them!

I shall not need to go into an enumeration of our national defects and vices which require this Order of Censors in the state, I might not set down our most proclaimed offences as the worst. It is not often the worst trait that occasions the loudest outcry. Men complain of their suffering, and not of the crime. I fear little from the bad effect of Repudiation; I do not fear that it will spread. Stealing is a suicidal business; you cannot repudiate but once. But the bold face and tardy repentance permitted to this local mischief, reveal a public mind so preoccupied with the love of gain, that the common sentiment of indignation at fraud does not act with its natural force. The more need of a withdrawal from the crowd, and a resort to the fountain of right, by the brave. The timidity of our public opinion, is our disease, or, shall I say, the publicness of opinion, the absence of private opinion. Good-nature is plentiful, but we want justice, with heart of steel, to fight down the proud. The private mind has the access to the totality of goodness and truth, that it may be a balance to a corrupt society; and to stand for the private verdict against popular clamor, is the office of the noble. If a humane measure is propounded in behalf of the slave, or of the Irishman, or the Catholic, or for the succor of the poor, that sentiment, that project, will have the homage of the hero. That is his nobility, his oath of knighthood, to succor the helpless and oppressed; always to throw himself on the side of weakness, of youth, of hope, on the liberal, on the expansive side, never on the defensive, the conserving, the timorous, the lock and bolt system. More than our good will we may not be able to give. We have our own affairs, our own genius, which chains us to our proper work. We cannot give our life to the cause of the debtor, of the slave, or the pauper, as another is doing, but to one thing we are bound, not to blaspheme the sentiment and the work of that man, not to throw stumbling blocks in the way of the abolitionist, the philanthropist, as the organs of influence and opinion are swift to do. It is for us to confide in the beneficent Supreme Power, and not to rely on our money, and on the state because it is the guard of money. At this moment, the terror of old people and of vicious people, is lest the

Union of these States be destroyed. As if the Union had any other real basis than the good pleasure of a majority of the citizens to be united. But the wise and just man will always feel that he stands on his own feet; that he imparts strength to the state, not receives security from it; and that if all went down, he and such as he would quite easily combine in a new and better constitution. Every great and memorable community has consisted of formidable individuals, each of whom, like the Roman or the Spartan, lent his own spirit to the state and so made it great. Yet only by the supernatural is a man strong: only by confiding in the Divinity which stirs in us. Nothing is so weak as an egotist. Nothing is mightier than we, when we are vehicles of a truth before which the state and the individual are alike ephemeral.

Gentlemen, the development of our American internal resources, the extension to the utmost of the commercial system, and the appearance of new moral causes which are to modify the state, are giving an aspect of greatness to the Future, which the imagination fears to open. One thing is plain for all men of common sense and common conscience, that here, here in America, is the home of man. After all the deductions which are to be made for our pitiful and most unworthy politics, which stake every gravest national question on the silly die, whether James or whether Jonathan shall sit in the chair and hold the purse, after all the deduction is made for our frivolities and insanities, there still remains an organic simplicity and liberty, which, when it loses its balance redresses itself presently, which offers opportunity to the human mind not known in any other region.

It is true, the public mind wants self-respect. We are full of vanity, of which the most signal proof is our sensitiveness to foreign and especially English censure. One cause of this is our immense reading, and that reading chiefly confined to the productions of the English press. But a more misplaced sensibility than this tenderness to fame on the subject of our country and civil institutions, I cannot recall. Could we not defend and apologize for the sun and rain. Here are we, men of English blood, planted now for five, six, or seven generations on this immense tract in the temperate zone, and so planted at such a conjuncture of time and events, that we have left behind us whatever old and odious establishments the mind of men had outgrown. The unsupportable burdens under which Europe staggers, and almost every month mutters 'A Revolution! a Revolution!' we have escaped from as by one bound. No thanks to us; but in the blessed course of events it did happen that this country was not open to the Puritans until they had felt the burden of the feudal system, and until the commercial era in modern Europe had dawned, so that without knowing what they did, they left the whole curse behind, and put the storms of the Atlantic between them and this antiquity. And the felling of the forest, and the settling in so far of the area of this continent, was accomplished under the free spirit of trading communities with a complete success. Not by our right hand, or foresight, or skill, was it done, but by the simple acceptance of the plainest road ever shown men to walk in. It was the human race, under Divine leading, going forth to receive and inhabit their patrimony. And now, if any Englishman, or Frenchman, or Spaniard, or Russian, or German, can find any food for merriment in the spectacle,make him welcome to shake his sides. There never was a people that could better afford to be the subject of a little fun, than we. An honest man may, perhaps, wonder how, with so much to call forth congratulation, our lively visiters should be so merry and critical. Perhaps they have great need of a little holiday and diversion from their domestic cares, like other house-keepers who have a heavy time of it at home, and need all the refreshment they can get from kicking up their feet a little now that they have got away on a frolic.

It is also true, that, to imaginative persons in this country, there is somewhat bare and bald in our short history, and unsettled wilderness. They ask, who would live in a new country, that can live in an old? Europe is to our boys and girls, what novels and romances are; and it is not strange they should burn to see the picturesque extremes of an antiquated country. But it is one thing to visit the pyramids, and another to wish to live there. Would they like tithes to the clergy, and sevenths to the government, and horse-guards, and licensed press, and grief when a child is born, and threatening, starved weavers, and a pauperism now constituting one-thirteenth of the population? Instead of the open future expanding here before the eye of every boy to vastness, would they like the closing in of the future to a narrow slit of sky, and that fast contracting to be no future? One thing, for instance, the beauties of aristocracy, we commend to the study of the travelling American. The English, the most conservative people this side of India, are not sensible of the restraint, but an American would seriously resent it. The aristocracy, incorporated by law and education, degrades life for the unprivileged classes. It is a questionable compensation to the embittered feeling of a proud commoner, the reflection that the worthless lord who, by the magic of title, paralyzes his arm, and plucks from him half the graces and rights of a man, is himself also an aspirant excluded with the same ruthlessness from higher circles, since there is no end to the wheels within wheels of this spiral heaven. Something may be pardoned to the spirit of loyalty when it becomes fantastic; and something to the imagination, for the baldest life is symbolic. Phillip II of Spain rated his ambassador for neglecting business of great importance in Italy, whilst he debated some point of honor with the French ambassador; "You have left a business of importance for a ceremony." The ambassador replied, "How? for a ceremony? your majesty's self is but a ceremony." In the East, where the religious sentiment comes in to the support of the aristocracy, and in the Romish church also, there is a grain of sweetness in the tyranny; but in England, the fact seems to me intolerable, what is commonly affirmed, that such is the transcendent honor accorded to wealth and birth, that no man of letters, be his eminence what it may, is received into the best society, except as a lion and a show. It seems to me, that with the lights which are now gleaming in the eyes of all men, residence in that country becomes degradation to any man not employed to revolutionize it. The English have many virtues, many advantages, and the proudest history of the world; but they need all, and more than all the resources of the past to indemnify a heroic gentleman in that country for the mortifications prepared for him by the system of society, and which seem to impose the alternative to resist or to avoid it. That there are mitigations and practical alleviations to this rigor, is not an excuse for the rule. Commanding worth, and personal power must sit crowned in all companies, nor will extraordinary persons be slighted or affronted in any company of civilized men. But the system is an invasion of the sentiment of justice and the native rights of men, which, however decorated, must lessen the value of English citizenship. It is for Englishmen to consider, not for us: we only say, let us live in America, too thankful for our want of feudal institutions. Our houses and towns are like mosses and lichens, so slight and new; but youth is a fault of which we shall daily mend. And really at last all lands are alike. Ours, too, is as old as the Flood, and wants no ornament or privilege which nature could bestow. Here stars, here woods, here hills, here animals, here men abound, and the vast tendencies concur of a new order. If only the men are well employed in conspiring with the designs of the Spirit who led us hither, and is leading us still, we shall quickly enough advance out of all hearing of other's censures, out of all regrets of our own, into a new and more excellent social state than history has recorded.

The text is taken from *The Dial*, Volume 4, April 1844, pages 484-507, and is reprinted with the permission of the Ralph Waldo Emerson Memorial Association.

# Robert Burns

Mr. President and Gentlemen--I do not know by what untoward accident it has chanced--and I forbear to inquire--that, in this accomplished circle, it should fall to me, the worse Scotsman of all, to receive your commands, and at the latest hour, too, to respond to the sentiment just offered, and which indeed makes the occasion. But I am told there is no appeal, and I must trust to the inspiration of the theme to make a fitness which does not otherwise exist.

Yes, sir, I heartily feel the singular claims of the occasion. At the first announcement, from I know not whence, that the 25th of January was the hundredth anniversary of the birth of Robert Burns, a sudden consent warmed the great English race, in all its kingdoms, colonies, and states, all over the world, to keep the festival.

I can only explain this singular unanimity in a race which rarely acts together, but rather after their watchword, each for himself--by the fact that Robert Burns, the poet of the middle class, represents in the mind of men today that great uprising of the middle class against the armed and privileged minorities--that uprising which worked politically in the American and French Revolutions, and which, not in governments so much as in education and in social order, has changed the face of the world.

In order for this destiny, his birth, breeding, and fortune were low. His organic sentiment was absolute independence, and resting, as it should, on a life of labour. No man existed who could look down on him. They that looked into his eyes saw that they might look down the sky as easily. His muse and teaching was common sense, joyful, aggressive, irresistible.

Not Latimer, not Luther, struck more telling blows against false theology than did this brave singer. The "Confession of Augsburg," the "Declaration of Independence," the French "Rights of Man," and the "Marseillaise" are not more weighty documents in the history of freedom than the songs of Burns. His satire has lost none of its edge. His musical arrows yet sing through the air.

He is so substantially a reformer, that I find his grand plain sense in close chain with the greatest masters--Rabelais, Shakespeare in comedy, Cervantes, Butler, and Burns. If I should add another name, I find it only in a living countryman of Burns. He is an exceptional genius. The people who care nothing for literature and poetry care for Burns. It was indifferent--they thought who saw him--whether he wrote verse or not; he could have done anything else as well.

Yet how true a poet is he! and the poet, too, of poor men, of grey hodden, and the guernsey coat, and the blouse. He has given voice to all the experiences of common life; he has endeared the farm-house and cottage, patches and poverty, beans and barley; ale, the poor man's wine; hardship, the fear of debt, the dear society of weans and wife, of brothers and sisters, proud of each other, knowing so few, and finding amends for want and obscurity in books and thought. What a love of nature, and, shall I say it? of middle-class nature. Not great like Goethe in the stars, or like Byron on the ocean, or Moore in the luxurious East, but in the lonely landscape which the poor see around them, bleak leagues of pasture and stubble, ice, and sleet, and rain, and snow-choked brooks; birds, hares, field-mice, thistles and heather, which he daily knew. How many "Bonnie Doons," and "John Anderson, my joes," and "Auld Langsynes," all round the earth have his verses been applied to! And his love songs still woo and melt the youths and maids; the farm-work, the country holiday, the fishing coble, are still his debtors to-day. And as he was thus the poet of poor, anxious, cheerful, working humanity, so he had the language of low life. He grew up in a rural district, speaking a patois unintelligible to all but natives, and he has made that lowland Scotch a Doric dialect of fame. It is the only example in history of a language made classic by the genius of a single man. But more than this, he had that secret of genius, to draw from the bottom of society the strength of its speech, and astonish the ears of the polite with these artless words, better than art, and filtered of all offense through his beauty. It seemed odious to Luther that the devil should have all the best tunes; he would bring them into the churches; and Burns knew how to take from fairs and gypsies, blacksmiths and drovers, the speech of the market and street, and clothe it with melody. But I am detaining you too long. The memory of Burns--I am afraid heaven and earth have taken too good care of it, to leave us anything to say. The west winds are murmuring it. Open the windows behind you, and hearken for the incoming tide what the waves say of it. The doves perching always on the eaves of the stone chapel opposite may know something of it. Every name in broad Scotland keeps his fame bright. The memory of Burns--every man's and boy's, and girl's head carries snatches of his songs, and can say them by heart, and, what is strangest of all, never learned them from a book, but from mouth to mouth. The wind whispers them, the birds whistle them, the corn, barley, and bulrushes hoarsely rustle them; nay, the music-boxes at Geneva are framed and toothed to play them; the hand organs of the Savoyards in all cities repeat them, and the chimes of bells ring them in the spires. They are the property and the solace of mankind.

This speech first appeared in pages 355-359 of volume 6 of *The Collected Works of Ralph Waldo Emerson*, edited by James F. Cabot, published at Boston in 1883 by Houghton, Mifflin. The text is reprinted with the permission of the Ralph Waldo Emerson Memorial Association.

# Speech to the Manchester Athenaeum

Mr. Chairman and Gentlemen: It is pleasant to me to meet this great and brilliant company, and doubly pleasant to see the faces of so many distinguished persons on this platform. But I have known all these persons already. When I was at home, they were as near to me as they are to you. The arguments of the League and its leader are known to all the friends of free trade. The gayeties and genius, the political, the social, the parietal wit of "Punch" go duly every fortnight to every boy and girl in Boston and New York. Sir, when I came to sea, I found the "History of Europe" on the ship's cabin table, the property of the captain;--a sort of programme or play-bill to tell the seafaring New Englander what he shall find on his landing here. And as for Dombey, sir, there is no land where paper exists to print on, where it is not found; no man who can read, that does not read it, and, if he cannot, he finds some charitable pair of eyes that can, and hears it.

But these things are not for me to say; these compliments, though true, would better come from one who felt and understood these merits more. I am not here to exchange civilities with you, but rather to speak of that which I am sure interests these gentlemen more than their own praises; of that which is good in holidays and working-days, the same in one century and in another century. That which lures a solitary American in the woods with the wish to see England, is the moral peculiarity of the Saxon race,--its commanding sense of right and wrong,--the love and devotion to that,--this is the imperial trait, which arms them with the sceptre of the globe. It is this which lies at the foundation of that aristocratic character, which certainly wanders into strange vagaries, so that its origin is often lost sight of, but which, if it should lose this, would find itself paralyzed; and in trade, and in the mechanic's shop, gives that honesty in performance, that thoroughness and solidity of work, which is a national characteristic. This conscience is one element, and the other is that loyal adhesion, that habit of friendship, that homage of man to man, running through all classes,--the electing of worthy persons to a certain fraternity, to acts of kindness and warm and staunch support, from year to year, from youth to age,--which is alike lovely and honorable to those who render and those who receive it;--which stands in strong contrast with the superficial attachments of other races, their excessive courtesy, and short-lived connection.

You will think me very pedantic, gentlemen, but holiday though it be, I have not the smallest interest in any holiday, except as it celebrates real and not pretended joys; and I think it just, in this time of gloom and commercial disaster, of affliction and begary in these districts, that, on these very accounts I speak of, you should not fail to keep your literary anniversary. I seem to hear you say, that, for all that is come and gone yet, we will not reduce by one chaplet or one oak leaf the braveries of our annual feast. For I must tell you, I was given to understand in my childhood, that the British island from which my forefathers came, was no lotus-garden, no paradise of serene sky and roses and music and merriment all the year round, no, but a cold foggy mournful country, where nothing grew well in the open air, but robust men and virtuous women, and these of a wonderful fibre and endurance; that their best parts were slowly revealed; their virtues did not come out until they quarrelled: they did not strike twelve the first time; good lovers, good haters, and you could know little about them till you had seen them long, and little good of them till you had seen them in action; that in prosperity they were moody and dumpish, but in adversity they were grand. Is it not true, sir, that the wise ancients did not praise the ship parting with flying colors from the port, but only that brave sailer which came back with torn sheets and battered sides, stript of her banners, but having ridden out the storm? And so, gentlemen, I feel in regard to this aged England, with the possessions, honors and trophies, and also with the infirmities of a thousand years gathering around her, irretrievably committed as she now is to many old customs which cannot be suddenly changed; pressed upon by the transitions of trade, and new and all incalculable modes, fabrics, arts, machines, and competing populations,--I see her not dispirited, not weak, but well remembering that she has seen dark days before;--indeed with a kind of instinct that she sees a little better in a cloudy day, and that in storm of battle and calamity, she has a secret vigor and a pulse like a cannon. I see her in her old age, not decrepit, but young, and still daring to believe in her power of endurance and expansion. Seeing this, I say, All hail! mother of nations, mother of heroes with strength still equal to the time; still wise to entertain and swift to execute the policy which the mind and heart of mankind requires in the present hour, and thus only hospitable to the foreigner, and truly a home to the thoughtful and generous who are born in the soil. So be it! so let it be! If it be not so, if the courage of England goes with the chances of a commercial crisis, I will go back to the capes of Massachusetts, and my own Indian stream, and say to my countrymen, the old race are all gone, and the elasticity and hope of mankind must henceforth remain on the Alleghany ranges, or nowhere.

Emerson reprinted this speech in *English Traits* published by Phillips, Sampson and Company of Boston in 1856. This text is printed with the permission of the Ralph Waldo Emerson Memorial Association.

# The Fugitive Slave Law

I do not often speak to public questions;--they are odious and hurtful, and it seems like meddling or leaving your work. I have my own spirits in prison;--spirits in deeper prisons, whom no man visits if I do not. And then I see what havoc it makes with any good mind, a dissipated philanthropy. The one thing not to be forgiven to intellectual persons is, not to know their own task, or to take their ideas from others. From this want of manly rest in their own and rash acceptance of other people's watchwords come the imbecility and fatigue of their conversation. For they cannot affirm these from any original experience, and of course not with the natural movement and total strength of their nature and talent, but only from their memory, only from their cramped position of standing for their teacher. They say what they would have you believe, but what they do not quite know.

My own habitual view is to the well-being of students or scholars. And it is only when the public event affects them, that it very seriously touches me. And what I have to say is to them. For every man speaks mainly to a class whom he works with and more or less fully represents. It is to these I am beforehand related and engaged, in this audience or out of it--to them and not to others. And yet, when I say the class of scholars or students,--that is a class which comprises in some sort all mankind, comprises every man in the best hours of his life; and in these days not only virtually but actually. For who are the readers and thinkers of 1854? Owing to the silent revolution which the newspaper has wrought, this class has come in this country to take in all classes. Look into the morning trains which, from every suburb, carry the business men into the city to their shops, counting-rooms, work-yards and warehouses. With them enters the car--the newsboy, that humble priest of politics, finance, philosophy, and religion. He unfolds his magical sheets,--twopence a head his bread of knowledge costs--and instantly the entire rectangular assembly, fresh from their breakfast, are bending as one man to their second breakfast. There is, no doubt, chaff enough in what he brings;

but there is fact, thought, and wisdom in the crude mass, from all regions of the world.

I have lived all my life without suffering any known inconvenience from American Slavery. I never saw it; I never heard the whip; I never felt the check on my free speech and action, until, the other day, when Mr. Webster, by his personal influence, brought the Fugitive Slave Law on the country. I say Mr. Webster, for though the Bill was not his, it is yet notorious that he was the life and soul of it, that he gave it all he had: it cost him his life, and under the shadow of his great name inferior men sheltered themselves, threw their ballots for it and made the law. I say inferior men. There were all sorts of what are called brilliant men, accomplished men, men of high station, a President of the United States, Senators, men of eloquent speech, but men without self-respect, without character, and it was strange to see that office, age, fame, talent, even a repute for honesty, all count for nothing. They had no opinions, they had no memory for what they had been saying like the Lord's Prayer all their lifetime; they were only looking to what their great Captain did: if he jumped, they jumped, if he stood on his head, they did. In ordinary, the supposed sense of their district and State is their guide, and that holds them to the part of liberty and justice. But it is always a little difficult to decipher what this public sense is; and when a great man comes who knots up into himself the opinions and wishes of the people, it is so much easier to follow him as an exponent of this. He too is responsible; they will not be. It will always suffice to say,--"I followed him."

I saw plainly that the great show their legitimate power in nothing more than in their power to misguide us. I saw that a great man, deservedly admired for his powers and their general right direction, was able,--fault of the total want of stamina in public men,--when he failed, to break them all with him, to carry parties with him.

In what I have to say of Mr. Webster I do not confound him with vulgar politicians before or since. There is always base ambition enough, men who calculate on the immense ignorance of the masses; that is their quarry and farm: they use the constituencies at home only for their shoes. And, of course, they can drive out from the contest any honorable man. The low can best win the low, and all men like to be made much of. There are those too who have power and inspiration only to do ill. Their talent or their faculty deserts them when they undertake anything right. Mr. Webster had a natural ascendancy of aspect and carriage which distinguished him over all his contemporaries. His countenance, his figure, and his manners were all in so grand a style, that he was, without effort, as superior to his most eminent rivals as they were to the humblest; so that his arrival in any place was an event which drew crowds of people, who went to satisfy their eyes, and could not see him enough. I think they looked at him as the representative of the American Continent. He was there in his Adamitic capacity, as if he alone of all men did not disappoint the eye and the ear, but was a fit figure in the landscape.

I remember his appearance at Bunker's Hill. There was the Monument, and here was Webster. He knew well that a little more or less of rhetoric signified nothing: he was only to say plain and equal things,--grand things if he had them, and, if he had them not, only to abstain from saying unfit things,--and the whole occasion was answered by his presence. It was a place for behavior more than for speech, and Mr. Webster walked through his part with entire success. His excellent organization, the perfection of his elocution and all that thereto belongs,--voice, accent, intonation, attitude, manner,--we shall not soon find again. Then he was so thoroughly simple and wise in his rhetoric, he saw through his matter, hugged his fact so close, went to the principle or essential, and never indulged in a weak flourish, though he knew perfectly well how to make such exordiums, episodes and perorations as might give perspective to his harangues without in the least embarrassing his march or confounding his transitions. In his statement things lay in daylight; we saw them in order as they were. Though he knew very well how to present his own personal claims, yet in his argument he was intellectual,--stated his fact pure of all personality, so that his splendid wrath, when his eyes became lamps, was the wrath of the fact and the cause he stood for.

His power, like that of all great masters, was not in excellent parts, but was total. He had a great and everywhere equal propriety. He worked with that closeness of adhesion to the matter in hand which a joiner or a chemist uses, and the same quiet and sure feeling of right to his place that an oak or a mountain have to theirs. After all his talents have been described, there remains that perfect propriety which animated all the details of the action or speech with the character of the whole, so that his beauties of detail are endless. He seemed born for the bar, born for the senate, and took very naturally a leading part in large private and in public affairs; for his head distributed things in their right places, and what he saw so well he compelled other people to see also. Great is the privilege of eloquence. What gratitude does every man feel to him who speaks well for the right,--who translates truth into language entirely plain and clear!

The history of this country has given a disastrous importance to the defects of this great man's mind. Whether evil influences and the corruption of politics, or whether original infirmity, it was the misfortune of his country that with this large understanding he had not what is better than intellect, and the source of its health. It is a law of our nature that great thoughts come from the heart. If his moral sensibility had been proportioned to the force of his understanding, what limits could have been set to his genius and beneficent power? But he wanted that deep source of inspiration. Hence a sterility of thought, the want of generalization in his speeches, and the curious fact that, with a general ability which impresses all the world, there is not a single general remark, not an observation on life and manners, not an aphorism that can pass into literature from his writings.

Four years ago tonight, on one of those high critical moments in history when great issues are determined, when the powers of right and wrong are mustered for conflict, and it lies with one man to give a casting vote,--Mr. Webster, most unexpectedly, threw his whole weight on the side of Slavery, and caused by his personal and official authority the passage of the Fugitive Slave Bill.

It is remarked of the Americans that they value dexterity too much, and honor too little; that they think they praise a man more by saying that he is "smart" than by saying that he is right. Whether the defect be national or not, it is the defect and calamity of Mr. Webster; and it is so far true of his countrymen, namely, that the appeal is sure to be made to his physical and mental ability when his character is assailed. His speeches on the seventh of March, and at Albany, at Buffalo, at Syracuse and Boston are cited in justification. And Mr. Webster's literary editor believes that it was his wish to rest his fame on the speech of the seventh of March. Now, though I have my own opinions on this seventh of March discourse and those others, and think them very transparent and very open to criticism,--yet the secondary merits of a speech, namely, its logic, its illustrations, its points, etc., are not here in question. Nobody doubts that Daniel Webster could make a good speech. Nobody doubts that there were good and plausible things to be said on the part of the South. But this is not a question of ingenuity, not a question of syllogisms, but of sides. How came he there?

There are always texts and thoughts and arguments. But it is the genius and temper of the man which decides whether he will stand for right or for might. Who doubts the power of any fluent debater to defend either of our political parties, or any client in our courts? There was the same law in England for Jeffries and Talbot and Yorke to read slavery out of, and for Lord Mansfield to read freedom. And in this country one sees that there is always margin enough in the statute for a liberal judge to read one way and a servile judge another.

But the question which History will ask is broader. In the final hour, when he was forced by the peremptory necessity of the closing armies to take a side, did he take the part of great principles, the side of humanity and justice, or the side of abuse and oppression and chaos?

Mr. Webster decided for Slavery, and that, when the aspect of the institution was no longer doubtful, no longer feeble and apologetic and proposing soon to end itself, but when it was strong, aggressive, and threatening an illimitable increase. He listened to State reasons and hopes, and left, with much complacency we are told, the testament of his speech to the astonished State of Massachusetts, vera pro gratis; a ghastly result of all those years of experience in affairs, this, that there was nothing better for the foremost American man to tell his countrymen than that Slavery was now at that strength that they must beat down their conscience and become kidnappers for it.

This was like the doleful speech falsely ascribed to the patriot Brutus: "Virtue, I have followed thee through life, and I find thee but a shadow." Here was a question of an immoral law; a question agitated for ages, and settled always in the same way by every great jurist, that an immoral law cannot be valid. Cicero, Grotius, Coke, Blackstone, Burlamaqui, Vattel, Burke, Jefferson, do all affirm this, and I cite them, not that they can give evidence to what is indisputable, but because, though lawyers and practical statesmen, the habit of their profession did not hide from them that this truth was the foundation of States.

Here was the question, Are you for man and for the good of man; or are you for the hurt and harm of man? It was the question whether man shall be treated as leather? whether the Negro shall be, as the Indians were in Spanish America, a piece of money? Whether this system, which is a kind of mill or factory for converting men into monkeys, shall be upheld and enlarged? And Mr. Webster and the country went for the application to these poor men of quadruped law.

People were expecting a totally different course from Mr. Webster. If any man had in that hour possessed the weight with the country which he had acquired, he could have brought the whole country to its senses. But not a moment's pause was allowed. Angry parties went from bad to worse, and the decision of Webster was accompanied with everything offensive to freedom and good morals. There was something like an attempt to debauch the moral sentiment of the clergy and of the youth. Burke said he "would pardon something to the spirit of liberty." But by Mr. Webster the opposition to the law was sharply called treason, and prosecuted so. He told the people at Boston "they must conquer their prejudices;" that "agitation of the subject of Slavery must be suppressed." He did as immoral men usually do, made very low bows to the Christian Church, and went through all the Sunday decorums; but when allusion was made to the question of duty and the sanctions of morality, he very frankly said, at Albany, "Some higher law, something existing somewhere between here and the third heaven,--I do not know where." And if the reporters say true, this wretched atheism found some laughter in the company.

I said I had never in my life up to this time suffered from the Slave Institution. Slavery in Virginia or Carolina was like Slavery in Africa or the Feejees, for me. There was an old fugitive law, but it had become, or was fast becoming, a dead letter, and, by the genius and laws of Massachusetts, inoperative. The new Bill made it operative, required me to hunt slaves, and it found citizens in Massachusetts willing to act as judges and captors. Moreover, it discloses the secret of the new times, that Slavery was no longer mendicant, but was become aggressive and dangerous.

The way in which the country was dragged to consent to this, and the disastrous defection (on the miserable cry of Union) of the men of letters, of the colleges, of educated men, nay, of some preachers of religion,--was the darkest passage in the history. It showed that our prosperity had hurt us, and that we could not be shocked by crime. It showed that the old religion and the sense of the right had faded and gone out; that while we reckoned ourselves a highly cultivated nation, our bellies had run away with our brains, and the principles of culture and progress did not exist.

For I suppose that liberty is an accurate index, in men and nations, of general progress. The theory of personal liberty must always appeal to the most refined communities and to the men of the rarest perception and of delicate moral sense. For there are rights which rest on the finest sense of justice, and, with every degree of civility, it will be more truly felt and defined. A barbarous tribe of good stock will, by means of their best heads, secure substantial liberty. But where there is any weakness in a race, and it becomes in a degree a matter of concession and protection from their stronger neighbors, the incompatibility and offensiveness of the wrong will of course be most evident to the most cultivated. For it is,--is it not?--the essence of courtesy, of politeness, of religion, of love, to prefer another, to postpone oneself, to protect another from oneself. That is the distinction of the gentleman, to defend the weak and redress the injured, as it is of the savage and the brutal to usurp and use others.

In Massachusetts, as we all know, there has always existed a predominant conservative spirit. We have more money and value of every kind than other people, and wish to keep them. The plea on which freedom was resisted was Union. I went to certain serious men, who had a little more reason than the rest, and inquired why they took this part? They answered that they had no confidence in their strength to resist the Democratic party; that they saw plainly that all was going to the utmost verge of license; each was vying with his neighbor to lead the party, by proposing the worst measure, and they threw themselves on the extreme conservatism, as a drag on the wheel: that they knew Cuba would be had, and Mexico would be had, and they stood stiffly on conservatism, and as near to monarchy as they could, only to moderate the velocity with which the car was running down the precipice. In short, their theory was despair; the Whig wisdom was only reprieve, a waiting to be last devoured. They side with Carolina, or with Arkansas, only to make a show of Whig strength, wherewith to resist a little longer this general ruin.

I have a respect for conservatism. I know how deeply founded it is in our nature, and how idle are all attempts to shake ourselves free from it. We are all conservatives, half Whig, half Democrat, in our essences: and might as well try to jump out of our skins as to escape from our Whiggery. There are two forces in Nature, by whose antagonism we exist; the power of Fate,

Fortune, the laws of the world, the order of things, or however else we choose to phrase it, the material necessities on the other: May and Must. In vulgar politics the Whig goes for what has been, for the old necessities,--the Musts. The reformer goes for the Better, for the ideal good, for the Mays. But each of these parties must of necessity take in, in some measure, the principles of the other. Each wishes to cover the whole ground; to hold fast and to advance. Only, one lays the emphasis on keeping, and the other on advancing. I too think the musts are a safe company to follow, and even agreeable. But if we are Whigs, let us be Whigs of nature and science, and so for all the necessities. Let us know that, over and above all the musts of poverty and appetite, is the instinct of man to rise, and the instinct to love and help his brother.

Now, Gentlemen, I think we have in this hour instruction again in the simplest lesson. Events roll, millions of men are engaged, and the result is the enforcing of some of those first commandments which we heard in the nursery. We never get beyond our first lesson, for, really, the world exists, as I understand it, to teach the science of liberty, which begins with liberty from fear.

The events of this month are teaching one thing plain and clear, the worthlessness of good tools to bad workmen; that official papers are of no use; resolutions of public meetings, platforms of conventions, no, nor laws, nor constitutions, any more. These are all declaratory of the will of the moment, and are passed with more levity and on grounds far less honorable than ordinary business transactions of the street.

You relied on the constitution. It has not the word slave in it; and very good argument has shows that it would not warrant the crimes that are done under it; that, with provisions so vague for an object not named, and which could not be availed of to claim a barrel of sugar or a barrel of corn, the robbing of a man and of all his posterity is effected. You relied on the Supreme Court. The law was right, excellent law for the lambs. But what if unhappily the judges were chosen from the wolves, and give to all the law a wolfish interpretation? You relied on the Missouri Compromise. That is ridden over. You relied on State sovereignty in the Free States to protect their citizens. They are driven with contempt out of the courts and out of the territory of the Slave States,--if they are so happy as to get out with their lives,--and now you relied on these dismal guaranties infamously made in 1850; and, before the body of Webster is yet crumbled, it is found that they have crumbled. This eternal monument of his fame and of the Union is rotten in four years. They are no guaranty to the Free States. They are a guaranty to the Slave States that, as they have hitherto met with no repulse, they shall meet with none.

I fear there is no reliance to be put on any kind or form of covenant, no, not on sacred forms, none on churches, none on bibles. For one would have said that a Christian would not keep slaves;--but the Christians keep slaves. Of course they will not dare to read the Bible? Won't they? They quote the Bible, quote Paul, quote Christ, to justify slavery. If slavery is good, then is lying, theft, arson, homicide, each and all good, and to be maintained by Union societies.

These things show that no forms, neither constitutions, nor laws, nor covenants, nor churches, nor bibles, are of any use in themselves. The Devil nestles comfortably into them all. There is no help but in the head and heart and hamstrings of a man. Covenants are of no use without honest men to keep them; laws of none; but with loyal citizens to obey them. To interpret Christ it needs Christ in the heart. The teachings of the Spirit can be apprehended only by the same spirit that gave them forth. To make good the cause of Freedom, you must draw off from all foolish trust in others. You must be citadels and warriors yourselves, declarations of Independence, the charter, the battle and the victory. Cromwell said, "We can only resist the superior training of the King's soldiers, by enlisting godly men." And no man has a right to hope that the laws of New York will defend him from the contamination of slaves another day until he has made up his mind that he will not owe his protection to the laws of New York, but to this own sense and spirit. Then he protects New York. He only who is able to stand alone is qualified for society. And that I understand to be the end for which a soul exists in this world,--to be himself the counterbalance of all falsehood and all wrong. "The army of unright is encamped from pole to pole, but the road of victory is known to the just." Everything may be taken away; he may be poor, he may be houseless, yet he will know out of his arms to make a pillow, and out of his breast a bolster. Why have the minority no influence? Because they have not a real minority of one.

I conceive that thus to detach a man and make him feel that he is to owe all to himself, is the way to make him strong and rich; and here the optimist must find, if anywhere, the benefit of Slavery. We have many teachers; we are in this world for culture, to be instructed in realities, in the laws of moral and intelligent nature; and our education is not conducted by toys and luxuries, but by austere and rugged masters, by poverty, solitude, passions, War, Slavery; to know that Paradise is under the shadow of swords; that divine sentiments which are always soliciting us are breathed into us from on high, and are an offset to a Universe of suffering and crime; that self-reliance, the height and perfection of man, is reliance on God. The insight of the religious sentiment will disclose to him unexpected aids in the nature of things. The Persian Saadi said, "Beware of hurting the orphan. When the orphan sets a-crying, the throne of the Almighty is rocked from side to side."

Whenever a man has come to this mind, that there is no Church for him but his believing prayer; no Constitution but his dealing well and justly with his neighbor; no liberty but his invincible will to do right,--then certain aids and allies will promptly appear: for the constitution of the Universe is on his side.

It is of no use to vote down gravitation of morals. What is useful will last, whilst that which is hurtful to the world will sink beneath all the opposing forces which it must exasperate. The terror which the Marseillaise struck into oppression, it thunders again today,--

"Tout est soldat pour vous combattre."

Everything turns soldier to fight you down. The end for which man was made is not crime in any form, and a man cannot steal without incurring the penalties of the thief, though all the legislatures vote that it is virtuous, and though there be a general conspiracy among scholars and official persons to hold him up, and to say, "Nothing is good but stealing." A man who commits a crime defeats the end of his existence. He was created for benefit, and he exists for harm; and as well-doing makes power and wisdom, ill-doing takes them away. A man who steals another man's labor steals away his own faculties; his integrity, his humanity is flowing away from him. The habit of oppression cuts out the moral eyes, and, though the intellect goes on simulating the moral as before, its sanity is gradually destroyed. It takes away the presentiments.

I suppose in general this is allowed, that if you have a nice question of right and wrong, you would not go with it to Louis Napoleon, or to a political hack, or to a slave-driver. The habit of mind of traders in power would not be esteemed favorable to delicate moral perception. American slavery affords no exception to this rule. No excess of good nature or of tenderness in individuals has been able to give a new character to the system, to tear down the whipping-house. The plea in the mouth of a slave-holder that the negro is an inferior race sounds very oddly in my ear. "The masters of slaves seem generally anxious to prove that they are not of a race superior in any noble quality to the meanest of their bondmen." And indeed when the Southerner points to the anatomy of the negro, and talks of chimpanzee,--I recall Montesquieu's remark, "It will not do to say that negroes are men, lest it should turn out that whites are not."

Slavery is disheartening; but Nature is not so helpless but it can rid itself at last of every wrong. But the spasms of Nature are centuries and ages, and will tax the faith of short-lived men. Slowly, slowly the Avenger comes, but comes surely. The proverbs of the nations affirm these delays, but affirm the arrival. They say, "God may consent, but not forever." The delay of the Divine Justice--this was the meaning and soul of the Greek Tragedy; this the soul of their religion. "There has come, too, one to whom lurking warfare is dear, Retribution, with a soul full of wiles; a violator of hospitality; guileful without the guilt of guile; limping, late in her arrival." They said of the happiness of the unjust, that "at its close it begets itself an offspring and does not die childless, and instead of good fortune, there sprouts forth for posterity ever-ravening calamity:'--

> "For evil word shall evil word be said,
> For murder-stroke a murder-stroke be paid.
> Who smites must smart."

These delays, you see them now in the temper of the times. The national spirit in this country is so drowsy, preoccupied with interest, deaf to principle. The Anglo-Saxon race is proud and strong and selfish. They believe only in Anglo-Saxons. In 1825 Greece found America deaf, Poland found America deaf, Italy and Hungary found her deaf. England maintains trade, not liberty; stands against Greece; against Hungary; against Schleswig-Holstein; against the French Republic whilst it was a republic.

To faint hearts the times offer no invitation, and torpor exists here throughout the active classes on the subject of domestic slavery and its appalling aggressions. Yes, that is the stern edict of Providence, that liberty shall be no hasty fruit, but that event on event, population on population, age on age, shall cast itself into the opposite scale, and not until liberty has slowly accumulated weight enough to countervail and preponderate against all this, can the sufficient recoil come. All the great cities, all the refined circles, all the statesmen, Guizot, Palmerston, Webster, Calhoun, are sure to be found befriending liberty with their words, and crushing it with their votes. Liberty is never cheap. It is made difficult, because freedom is the accomplishment and perfectness of man. He is a finished man; earning and bestowing good; equal to the world; at home in Nature and dignifying that; the sun does not see anything nobler, and has nothing to teach him. Therefore mountains of difficulty must be surmounted, stern trials met, wiles of seduction, dangers, healed by a quarantine of calamities to measure his strength before he dare say, I am free.

Whilst the inconsistency of slavery with the principles on which the world is built guarantees its downfall, I own that the patience it requires is almost too sublime for mortals, and seems to demand of us more than mere hoping. And when one sees how fast the rot spreads,--it is growing serious,--I think we demand of superior men that they be superior in this,--that the mind and the virtue shall give their verdict in their day, and accelerate so far the progress of civilization. Possession is sure to throw its stupid strength for existing power, and appetite and ambition will go for that. Let the aid of virtue, intelligence and education be cast where they rightfully belong. They are organically ours. Let them be loyal to their own. I wish to see the instructed class here know their own flag, and not fire on their comrades. We should not forgive the clergy for taking on every issue the immoral side; nor the Bench, if it put itself on the side of the culprit; nor the Government, if it sustain the mob against the laws.

It is a potent support and ally to a brave man standing single, or with a few, for the right, and out-voted and ostracized, to know that better men in other parts of the country appreciate the service and will rightly report him to his own and the next age. Without this assurance, he will sooner sink. He may well say, 'If my countrymen do not care to be defended, I too will decline the controversy, from which I only reap invectives and hatred.' Yet the livers of liberty may with reason tax the coldness and indifferentism of scholars and literary men. They are lovers of liberty in Greece and Rome and in the English Commonwealth, but they are lukewarm lovers of the liberty of America in 1854. The universities are not, as in Hobbes's time, "the core of rebellion," no, but the seat of inertness. They have forgotten their allegiance to the Muse, and grown worldly and political. I listened, lately, on one of those occasions when the university chooses one of its distinguished sons returning from the political arena, believing that senators and statesmen would be glad to throw off the harness and to dip again in the Castalian pools. But if audiences forget themselves, statesmen do not. The low bows to all the crockery gods of the day were duly made:--only in one part of the discourse the orator allowed to transpire, rather against his will, a little sober sense. It was this: "I am, as you see, a man virtuously inclined, and only corrupted by my profession of politics. I should prefer the right side. You, gentlemen of these literary and scientific schools, and the important class you represent, have the power to make your verdict clear and prevailing. Had you done so, you would have found me its glad organ and champion. Abstractly, I should have preferred that side. But you have not done it. You have not spoken out. You have failed to arm me. I can only deal with masses as I find them. Abstractions are not for me. I go then for such parties and opinions as have provided me with a working apparatus. I give you my word, not without regret, that I was first for you; and though I am now to deny and condemn you, you see it is not my will but the party necessity." Having made this manifesto and professed his adoration for liberty in the time of his grandfathers, he proceeded with his work of denouncing freedom and freemen at the present day, much in the tone and spirit in which Lord Bacon prosecuted his benefactor Essex. He denounced every name and aspect under which liberty and progress dare show themselves in this age and country, but with a lingering conscience which qualified each sentence with a recommendation to mercy.

But I put it to every noble and generous spirit, to every poetic, every heroic, every religious heart, that not so is our learning, our education, our poetry, our worship to be declared. Liberty is aggressive, Liberty is the Crusade of all brave and conscientious men, the Epic Poetry, the new religion, the chivalry of all gentlemen. This is the oppressed Lady whom true knights on their oath and honor must rescue and save.

Now at last we are disenchanted and shall have no more false hopes. I respect the Anti-Slavery Society. It is the Cassandra that has foretold all that has befallen, fact for fact, years ago; foretold all, and no man laid it to heart. It seemed, as the Turks say, "Fate makes that a man should not believe his own eyes." But the Fugitive Law did much to unglue the eyes of men, and now the Nebraska Bill leaves us staring. The Anti-Slavery Society will add many members this year. The Whig Party will join it; the Democrats will join it. The population of the free states will join it. I doubt not, at last, the slave states will join it. But be that sooner or later, and whoever comes or stays away, I hope we have reached the end of our unbelief, have come to a belief that there is a divine Providence in the world, which will not save us but through our own cooperation.

The formal title for this speech is "Address on the Anniversary of Webster's 'Seventh of March Speech'." It was read before a meeting of the American Anti-Slavery Society, at the Tablernacle in New York City on March 7, 1854. I have used a more familiar title to convey the substance of the speech.

The text of the speech is in vol. 11, pages 217-244 of *The Complete Works of Ralph Waldo Emerson*, 12 vols. Edward W. Emerson, ed. (Boston: Houghton Mifflin Co., 1903-1904), and is reprinted with the permission of the Ralph Waldo Emerson Memorial Association.

# Chronology of Major Speeches

**1833 November 5:** "The Uses of Natural History." Introductory Lecture read before the Natural History Society, Masonic Temple, Boston, Mass.
**1834 January 6:** "On the Relation of Man to the Globe," Part of the Franklin Lectures, Boston, Mass.
**1834 January 17:** "Water," Read to the Mechanic's Institution, Athenaeum, Boston, Mass.
**1834 March 19 and 26:** "Italy," Two Lectures on Italy, New Bedford Unitarian Congregation and Repeated to the Concord Lyceum on May 14 and November 26.
**1834 May 7:** "The Naturalist," Address to the Boston Natural History Society at Their Fourth Annual Meeting.
**1835 January 29:** "The Study and Uses of Biography." Introductory Lecture for the Biography Series, Society for the Diffusion of Useful Knowledge, Masonic Temple, Boston, Mass.
**1835 February 5:** "Michel Angelo Buonaroti."
**1835 February 12:** "Martin Luther."
**1835 February 19:** "John Milton."
**1835 February 26:** "George Fox."
**1835 March 5:** "Edmund Burke," Concluding Lecture in the Biography Series.
**1835 August 20:** "On the Best Mode of Inspiring a Correct Taste in English Literature." Address at the Sixth Annual Meeting of the American Institute of Instruction, Boston, Mass.
**1835 September 12:** "Historical Discourse." Read Before the Assembled Citizens of Concord, Second Centennial Celebration.
**1835 November 5:** "Introductory Lecture," First in a Series of Lectures on English Literature, Society for the Diffusion of Useful Knowledge, Masonic Temple, Boston, Mass.
**1835 November 12:** "Permanent Traits of the English National Genius."

**1835 November 19:** "The Age of Fable."
**1835 November 26:** "Chaucer."
**1835 December 10:** "Shakspear." [First Lecture]
**1835 December 17:** "Shakspear." [Second Lecture]
**1835 December 24:** "Lord Bacon."
**1835 December 31:** "Ben Jonson, Herrick, Herbert, Wotton."
**1836 January 7:** "Ethical Writers."
**1836 January 14:** "Modern Aspects of Letters." Concluding Lecture in the English Literature Series.
**1836 December 8:** "Introductory Lecture," First in a Series of Lectures on the Philosophy of History, Masonic Temple, Boston, Mass.
**1836 December 22:** "Humanity of Science."
**1836 December 29:** "Art."
**1837 January 5:** "Literature."
**1837 January 12:** "Politics."
**1837 January 19:** "Religion."
**1837 January 26:** "Society."
**1837 February 2:** "Trades and Professions."
**1837 February 9:** "Manners."
**1837 February 16:** "Ethics."
**1837 February 23:** "The Present Age."
**1837 March 2:** "The Individual," Concluding Lecture in the Philosophy of History Series.
**1837 June 10:** "An Address Delivered at the Opening of the Greene Street School," Providence, R. I.
**1837 August 31:** "The American Scholar, an Oration," Phi Beta Kappa Society, Cambridge, Mass.
**1837 December 6:** "Introductory Lecture," Beginning a Course of Lectures on Human Culture, Masonic Temple, Boston, Mass.
**1837 December 13:** "Doctrine of the Hands."
**1837 December 20:** "The Head."
**1837 December 27:** "The Eye and the Ear."
**1838 January 3:** "The Heart."
**1838 January 10:** "Being and Seeming."
**1838 January 17:** "Prudence."
**1838 January 24:** "Heroism."
**1838 January 31:** "Holiness."
**1838 February 5:** "General Views," Concluding Lecture in the Human Culture Series.
**1838 March 12:** "War," American Peace Society, Odeon Hall, Boston, Mass.
**1838 July 15:** " An Address," Senior Class in Divinity College, Cambridge, Mass.

**1838 July 24:** "Literary Ethics," Literary Societies of Dartmouth College, Hanover, N. H.
**1838 December 5:** "Doctrine of the Soul." Introductory Lecture for the Series on "Human Life," Masonic Temple, Boston, Mass.
**1838 December 12:** "Home."
**1838 December 19**: "The School."
**1838 December 26**: "Love."
**1839 January 9**: "Genius."
**1839 January 16:** "The Protest."
**1839 January 23:** "Tragedy."
**1839 January 30:** "Comedy."
**1839 February 6:** "Duty."
**1839 February 20:** "Demonology." Concluding Lecture in the Human Life Series.
**1839 December 4:** "Introductory Lecture." Beginning the Course Entitled, The Present Age, Masonic Temple, Boston, Mass.
**1839 December 11**: "Literature." [First Lecture]
**1839 December 18:** "Literature." [Second Lecture]
**1840 January 1:** "Politics."
**1840 January 8:** "Private Life."
**1840 January 15:** "Reforms."
**1840 January 15:** "Address to the People of East Lexington on the Dedication of Their Church," East Lexington, Mass.
**1840 January 22:** "Religion."
**1840 January 29:** "Ethics."
**1840 February 5:** "Education."
**1840 February 12:** "Tendencies." Conclusion of Present Age Series.
**1840 March 10**: "Philosophy of History," Introduction to a Course of Lectures presented at the New York Merchantile Library.
**1840 March 13:** "The Character of the Present Age," New York Merchantile Library.
**1840 March 15:** "The Literature of the Present Age," New York Merchantile Library.
**1841 January 25:** "Man the Reformer," Mechanics' Apprentices Library Association, Masonic Temple, Boston, Mass.
**1841 August 11:** " The Method of Nature," Society of the Adelphi, Waterville College, Maine.
**1841 December 2:** "Introductory Lecture" Beginning a Course of Lectures on The Times, Masonic Temple, Boston, Mass.
**1841 December 9:** "The Conservative."
**1841 December 16:** "The Poet."
**1841 December 23:** "The Transcendentalist."
**1841 December 30:** "Manners."

**1842 January 6:** "Character."
**1842 January 13:** "Relation of Man to Nature."
**1842 January 20:** "Prospects," Concluding Lecture in the Series.
**1842 March 3:** "The Times." Introductory Lecture for the Course Read at the Society Library, New York, N.Y.
**1842 March 5:** "The Poet."
**1842 March 7:** "The Conservative."
**1842 March 9:** "The Transcendentalist."
**1842 March 12:** "Manners."
**1842 March 14:** "Prospects," Concluding Lecture in the Society Library Series.
**1843 January 23:** "New England," Introductory Lecture in the Series Given in Philadelphia, Penn.
**1843 January 25:** "Trade of New England."
**1843 January 28:** "New England."
**1843 January 30:** "Recent Literary and Spiritual Influences."
**1843 February 1:** "Tendencies," Concluding Lecture in the New England Series.
**1843 February 7:** "Origins of New England Character," Introductory lecture for a series on New England, Berean Society, Universalist Church, New York, N.Y.
**1843 February 9:** "Trade," Berean Society New York, N.Y.
**1843 February 11:** "Genius of the Anglo Saxon Race," Society Library, New York, N.Y.
**1843 February 14:** "Genius and Character of New England People," Franklin Society, Brooklyn, N.Y.
**1843 February 15:** "Trade," Society Library, New York, N.Y.
1843 February 17: "Manners and Customs of New England," Society Library, New York, N.Y.
**1843 February 20:** "Recent Literature and Spiritual Influences," Society Library, New York, N.Y.
**1843 February 22:** "Results and Tendencies," Concluding Lecture in the New England Series, Society Library, New York, N.Y.
**1843 February 28:** "Domestic Life," Mercantile Library Association, Broadway Tabernacle, New York, N.Y.
**1843 March 1**: "New England," Mercantile Association, Newark, N. J.
**1843 March 7**: "Politics, " Mercantile Library Association, Broadway Tabernacle, New York, N.Y.
**1843 July 4**: "Address," Temperance Society, Harvard University, Cambridge, Mass.
**1844 February 7:** "The Young American," Mercantile Library Association, Odeon Theatre, Boston, Mass.
**1844 March 10:** "An Address," Congregation of the Second Church,

Boston, Mass.

**1844 August 1:** "An Address on Emancipation in the British West Indies," Anti-Slavery Society, Concord, Mass.

**1845 July 22:** "Discourse at Middlebury College," Middlebury, Vt.

**1845 December 11:** "Introductory Lecture," Beginning a Seven Lecture Course on Representative Men, Boston Lyceum, Odeon Theatre, Boston, Mass.

**1847 February 10:** "Eloquence," Mercantile Library Association, Tremont Temple, Boston, Mass.

**1847 November 2:** "The Uses of Great Men," Athenaeum, Manchester, England.

**1847 November 4:** "Swedenborg: the Mystic," Athenaeum, Manchester, England.

**1847 November 8:** "Eloquence," Mechanics' Institution, Liverpool, England.

**1847 November 9:** "Montaigne: The Sceptic," Athenaeum, Manchester, England.

**1847 November 11:** "Shakespeare: The Poet," Athenaeum, Manchester, England.

**1847 November 15:** "Domestic Life," Mechanics' Institution, Liverpool, England.

**1847 November 16:** " Napoleon: The Man of Action," Athenaeum, Manchester, England.

**1847 November 18**: "Address," Given to Acknowledge his Warm Reception by the Athenaeum, Manchester, England.

**1847 November 20:** "Goethe: The Man of Letters," Mechanics' Institution, Liverpool, England.

**1847 November 22:** " Books," Mechanics' Institution, Manchester, England.

**1847 November 29:** "The Superlative in Manners and Literature," Mechanics' Institution, Manchester, England.

**1847 December 8:** "Domestic Life," Mechanics' Institution, Nottingham, England.

**1847 December 9:** "Shakespeare," Derby Literary and Scientific Society, Derby, England.

**1847 December 10:** "Shakespeare," Mechanics' Institution, Nottingham, England.

**1848 February 11:** "Natural Aristocracy," Edinburgh Philosophical Institution, Edinburgh, Scotland.

**1848 June 6:** "Powers and Laws of Thought," Portman Square Literary and Scientific Institution, London, England.

**1848 June 8:** "Relation of Intellect to Natural Science," Portman Square Literary and Scientific Institution, London, England.

**1848 June 10:** "Tendencies and Duties of Men of Thought," Portman Square Literary and Scientific Institution, London, England.

**1848 June 13:** "Politics and Socialism," Portman Square Literary and Scientific Institution, London, England.

**1848 June 15:** "Poetry and Eloquence," Portman Square Literary and Scientific Institution , London, England.

**1848 June 17:** "Natural Aristocracy," Portman Square Literary and Scientific Institution, London, England.

**1848 December 27:** " England," Mercantile Library Association, Tremont Temple, Boston, Mass.

**1850 May 16:** "England," Cleveland Library Association.

**1850 May 20:** "Natural Aristocracy," Cincinnati Literary Club.

**1850 May 22:** "Eloquence." Read before Cincinnati Literary Club.

**1850 May 24:** "The Spirit of the Times," Cincinnati Literary Club.

**1850 May 27:** "England," Cincinnati Literary Club.

**1850 May 28:** "Books," Cincinnati Literary Club.

**1850 May 30:** "The Natural History of Intellect," Private Lecture, Cincinnati.

**1850 May 31:** "Identity of Thought with Nature," Private Lecture, Cincinnati.

**1851 March 21:** "The Conduct of Life," Introductory Lecture and Five Others Given at Pittsburgh, Pa.

**1851 May 3:** "Address to the Citizens of Concord," Statement on Fugitive Slave Law, Concord, Mass.

**1852 May 11:** "Welcoming Address to Kossuth," Concord, Mass.

**1853 January 10:** "The Anglo-Saxon," Springfield, Illinois.

**1853 February 27:** " The Anglo-American," Philadelphia, Pa.

**1854 January 3:** New lectures in a course in Philadelphia: "Norseman, and English Influence in Modern Civilization," "Poetry and English Poetry," and "France, or Urbanity."

**1854 March 7:** "Address on the Anniversary of Webster's 'Seventh of March' Speech," American Anti-Slavery Society, Tabernacle, New York, N.Y.

**1854 August 15:** "Address to the Adelphi Union of Williamstown College."

**1855 January 25:** "Slavery," Tremont Temple, Boston, Mass.

**1855 September 20:** "Address at the Women's Rights Convention," Boston, Mass.

**1855 September 29:** "Address at the Consecration of Sleepy Hollow Cemetery," Concord, Mass.

**1856 September 10:** "Address at the Kansas Relief Meeting," Cambridge, Mass.

**1858 September 29:** "The Man with the Hoe." Address to Open the

Exhibition of the Middlesex Agricultural Society.

**1858 December 14:** " Success," Hartford, Connecticut.

**1859 January 25:** "Robert Burns." An Address Read at the Celebration of the Centenary of Robert Burns.

**1859 May 22:** "The Superlative or Mental Temperance," Music Hall, Boston, Mass.

**1859 October 2:** "Beauty in Art" Music Hall, Boston, Mass.

**1859 November 8**: "Courage," Music Hall, Boston, Mass.

**1859 November 18:** Speech at a meeting to raise money for the family of John Brown, Tremont Temple, Boston, Mass.

**1860 January 6:** "John Brown," Memorial Address, Salem, Mass.

**1860 March 18:** "Moral Sense," Music Hall, Boston, Mass.

**1860 June 17:** "Theordore Parker," Memorial Address, Music Hall, Boston, Mass.

**1860 November 20:** "Classes of Men," Music Hall, Boston, Mass.

**1861 January 24:** Attempted speech at the Annual Meeting of the Massachusetts Anti-Slavery Society, Tremont Temple, Boston, Mass.

**1861 April 9:** First lecture in course on "Life and Letters" given at the Melodeon, Boston, Mass.

**1862 October 12:** "Address on the Proclamation Emancipation," Boston, Mass.

**1863 July 22:** "Discourse Before the Literary Societies of Dartmouth College," Hanover, N.H.

**1863 December 1**: "The Fortune of the Republic," Boston, Mass.

1864 August 9: "Discourse Before the Literary Societies of Middlebury College," Middlebury, Vt.

**1864 November 27:** First Lecture in the Course American Life, Melodeon, Boston, Mass. Followed by: "Education"; "Social Aims"; "Resources"; "Table-Talk"; "Books"; and "Character."

**1865 April 19:** "Address at Memorial Service for Abraham Lincoln, Concord, Mass.

**1865 July 21:** "Commemoration Speech for Harvard Men who Died in the War," Harvard University, Cambridge, Mass.

**1865 July 31:** "Address before the Adelphi Union," Williams College, Williamstown, Mass.

**1866 April 14:** First of Six Lectures on the "Philosophy of the People" Chickering's Hall, Boston, Mass.

**1867 April 19:** "Address at the Dedication of the Soldier's Monument," Concord, Mass.

**1867 May 12:** "Rule of Life," Radical Association in Horticultural Hall, Boston, Mass.

**1867 May 30:** "Remarks at the Organization of the Free Religious Association," Horticultural Hall, Boston, Mass.

**1867 August 21**: "Welcoming Speech to the Chinese Embassy" at Dinner in Their Honor, Boston, Mass.

**1869 March 1:** "Mary Moody Emerson." Speech Memorializing Her Before the Woman's Club, Boston, Mass.

**1869 May 26:** "Address," New England Woman Suffrage Association, Boston, Mass.

**1869 September 14:** "Address at the Centennial Anniversary of Alexander Humboldt's Birth," Meeting of the Boston Society of Natural History.

**1870 April 26:** The Beginning of a Course of Sixteen Lectures at Harvard University on The Natural History of the Intellect.

**1870 December 22:** Speech Before the New England Society, Delmonico's, New York City.

**1870 December 23:** "Discourse on the Anniversary of the Landing of the Pilgrims at Plymouth," New England Society, Steinway Hall, New York, N.Y.

**1871 April 23:** "Immortality," The First of a Series of Five Lectures, Unitarian Association of San Francisco, California. The other four: "Society in America"; "Resources"; "Greatness"; and "Chivalry."

**1871 May 18:** "Hospitality," Oakland, California.

**1871 August 15:** "Walter Scott," Massachusetts Historical Society on the Centennial Anniversary of his birth.

**1871 November 27:** "Nature and Art," Chicago, Illinois.

**1872 January 4:** "Inspiration," Peabody Institute, Baltimore, Maryland.

**1872 January 7:** "Books and Reading," Howard University, Washington, D.C.

**1872 January 15:** "Attractive Homes." YMCA, New Brunswick, New Jersey.

**1872 April-May:** A Series of Six Informal Afternoon Conversations Presented at Mechanics' Hall, Boston, Mass.

**1872 August 2:** "Speech of Welcome," Dinner to Honor Visiting Japanese Envoys, Boston, Mass.

**1872 October 15:** Speech at Dinner Honoring James Anthony Froude, New York, N.Y.

**1873 October 1:** "Address," At the Opening of the Monroe Public Library, Concord, Mass.

**1875 April 19:** "Address at the Unveiling of the Statue of the Minute-Man at Concord Bridge," Concord, Mass.

**1876 June 28:** "Oration to the Senior Class of the University of Virginia," Charlottesville, Va.

**1876 November 8**: "Commemorative Speech at the Latin School Association," On the Centennial Anniversary of the Reopening of the School Following the Evacuation of British Troops, Boston, Mass.

**1877 April 20:** "Boston," Old South Church, Boston, Mass.

**1880 February 4:** "Historic Notes of Life and Letters in Massachusetts," Read on the Occasion of Emerson's One Hundredth Lecture before the Concord Lyceum.

**1881 February 10:** "Carlyle," Given to the Massachusetts Historical Society. Emerson's last appearance before an audience.

# Selected Bibliography

## MANUSCRIPTS AND ARCHIVAL MATERIAL

The Manuscript Department at Houghton Library, Harvard University has over 11,000 items including the manuscripts for his sermons, lectures, journals, and poems. It also contains family papers. All of these papers have been carefully catalogued. Much of this material has been published and is available to scholars in expertly edited editions. The Houghton also has the papers of many of Emerson's friends such as Margaret Fuller Ossoli and James Freeman Clarke.

## BOOKS AND MAJOR ESSAYS ABOUT EMERSON

Allen, Gay Wilson. *Waldo Emerson*. New York: Viking, 1981.

Antczak, Frederick J. "Ralph Waldo Emerson as Democratic Educator: Man Thinking." In *Thought and Character. The Rhetoric of Democratic Education*. Ames: Iowa State University Press, 1985.

Bishop, Johnathan. *Emerson on the Soul*. Cambridge, Mass.: Harvard University Press, 1964.

Bode, Carl. *The American Lyceum: Town Meeting of the Mind*. Carbondale: Southern Illinois University Press, 1968.

Buell, Lawrence. *Literary Transcendentalism: Style and Vision in the American Renaissance*. Ithaca: Cornell University Press, 1973.

Burke, Kenneth. "I, Eye, Ay: Emerson's Early Essay on 'Nature'." In *Language as Symbolic Action*, 186-200. Berkeley: University of California Press, 1966.

Cameron, Kenneth. *A Commentary on Emerson's Early Lectures (1833-1836). With an Index-Concordance*. Hartford, Conn: Transcendental Books, 1961.

Chapman, John Jay. "Emerson." In *Emerson and Other Essays*, 3-110. New York: Scribner's, 1898.

Charvat, William. *Emerson's American Lecture Engagements: A Chronological List*. New York: 1961.

Firkins, Oscar W. *Ralph Waldo Emerson*. Boston: Houghton Mifflin, 1915.

Gougeon, Len. *Virtue's Hero. Emerson, Antislavery, and Reform*. Athens: University of Georgia Press, 1990.

Hopkins, Vivian C. *Spires of Form: A Study of Emerson's Aesthetic Theory*. Cambridge, Mass.: Harvard University Press, 1951.

Howe, Daniel Walker. *The Unitarian Conscience: Harvard Moral Philosophy 1805-1861*. Cambridge, Mass.: Harvard University Press, 1970.

Konvitz, Milton R., ed. *The Recognition of Ralph Waldo Emerson*. Ann Arbor: University of Michigan Press, 1972.

Lowell, James Russell. "Emerson the Lecturer" In *My Study Windows*. Boston: 1871. 375-84.

Matthiessen, F.O. *American Renaissance: Art and Expression in the Age of Emerson and Whitman*. New York: Oxford University Press, 1941.

McAleer, John. *Ralph Waldo Emerson: Days of Encounter*. Boston: Little, Brown, 1984.

Mead, David. *Yankee Eloquence in the Middle West: The Ohio Lyceum. 1850-1880.* East Lansing: Michigan State University Press, 1951.

Mott, Wesley T. *"The Strains of Eloquence". Emerson and His Sermons*. University Park: Pennsylvania State University Press, 1989.

Mumford, Lewis. "The Golden Day." In *The Golden Day*. New York: Boni and Liveright, 1926. 85-153.

Paul, Sherman. *Emerson's Angle of Vision: Man and Nature in American Experience*. Cambridge, Mass: Harvard University Press, 1952.

Perry, Bliss. "Emerson's Most Famous Speech." in *The Praise of Folly and Other Papers*. Boston: Houghton Mifflin, 1923. 81-113.

Porte, Joel. *Representative Man: Ralph Waldo Emerson in His Time*. New York: Oxford University Press, 1979.

Roberson, Susan L. *Emerson in His Sermons*. Columbia: University of Missouri Press, 1995.

Rusk, Ralph. *The Life of Ralph Waldo Emerson*. New York: Charles Scribner's Sons, 1949.

Scudder, Townsend. *The Lonely Wayfaring Man: Emerson and Some Englishmen*. New York: 1936.

Sealts, Merton M., Jr. *Emerson on the Scholar*. Columbia: University of Missouri Press, 1992.

Toulouse, Teresa. *The Art of Prophesying: New England Sermons and the Shaping of Belief*. Athens: University of Georgia Press, 1987.

Whicher, Stephen E. *Freedom and Fate: An Inner Life of Ralph Waldo Emerson*. Philadelphia: University of Pennsylvania Press, 1953.

## ARTICLES ABOUT EMERSON

Adams, Richard P. "Emerson and the Organic Metaphor." *PMLA* 69 (1954): 117-30.

Allen, Gay Wilson. "Emerson's Audiences: American and British." *Ariel* 7 (76): 87-108.

Baumgartner, A. M. "The Lyceum is my Pulpit: Homiletics in Emerson's Early Lectures." *American Literature* 34 (1963): 478-86.

Beltz, Linda. "Emerson's Lectures in Indianapolis." *Indiana Magazine of History* 60 (1964): 269-80.

Bercovitch, Sacvan. "The Philosophical Background to the Fable of Emerson's 'American Scholar'" *Journal of the History of Ideas* 28 (1967): 123-28.

Buell, Lawrence. "Reading Emerson for the Structures: The Coherence of the Essays." *Quarterly Journal of Speech 58* (1972): 581-69.
Buell, Lawrence. "The Unitarian Movement and the "Art of Preaching in Nineteenth Century America." *American Quarterly* 24 (1972): 167-190.
Burke, Kenneth. "Acceptance and Rejection." *Southern Review* 2 (Winter 1937): 600-32.
Cayton, Mary K. "The Making of an American Prophet: Emerson, his Audiences, and the Rise of the Culture Industry in Nineteenth Century America." *American Historical Review* 92 (1987): 597-620.
Commanger, Henry S. "Tempest in a Boston Tea Cup." *New England Quarterly* 6 (1933): 651-675.
Cronin, Morton. "Some Notes on Emerson's Prose Diction." *American Speech* 29 (1954): 105-13.
Foerster, Norman. "Emerson on the Organic Principle in Art." *PMLA* 41 (1926): 193-208.
Hastings, Louise. "Emerson in Cincinnati." *New England Quarterly* 11 (1938): 443-469.
Hillbruner, Anthony. "Emerson: Democratic Egalitarian." *Central States Speech Journal* 10 (1959): 25-30.
Johnston, Carol. "Underlying Structure of the Divinity School Address: Emerson as Jeremiah." *Studies in the American Renaissance* 1980: 41-49.
LaRosa, Ralph C. "Bacon and the 'Organic Method' of Emerson's Early Lectures." *English Language Notes* 8 (1970): 107-14.
LaRosa, Ralph C. "Invention and Imitation in Emerson's Early Lectures." *American Literature* 44 (Mar 1972): 13-30.
Lee, Roland F. "Emerson through Kierkegaard. Toward a Definition of Emerson's Theory of Communication." *ELH* 24 (1957): 229-48.
Liebman, Sheldon W. "The Development of Emerson's Theory of Rhetoric, 1821-1836." *American Literature* 41 (1969): 178-206.
Miller, Perry. "From Edwards to Emerson." *New England Quarterly* 13 (1940): 589-618.
Moody, Marjory M. "The Evolution of Emerson as an Abolitionists." *American Literature* 17 (1945): 1-21.
Moss, Sidney P. "Analogy: The Heart of Emerson's Style." *ESQ*, no. 39 (1965): 21-24.
Mott, Wesley T. "Emerson and Antinomianism: The Legacy of the Sermons." *American Literature* 50 (1978): 369-97.
Packer, Barbara. "Uriel's Clouds: Emerson's Rhetoric." *Georgia Review* 31: 322-42.
Ray, Roberta K. "The Role of the Orator in the Philosophy of Ralph Waldo Emerson." *Speech Monographs* 41 (1974): 215-225.
Roberson, Susan. "The Private Voice behind the Public Text: Two Emerson Sermons." *ESQ* 32 (1986): 173-181.
Scudder, Townsend. "Emerson's British Lecture Tour, 1847-1848." *American Literature* 7 (1935): 15-36 and 166-180.
Scudder, Townsend. "Emerson in London and the London Lectures." *American Literature* 12 (1936): 22-36.
Sealts, Merton M., Jr. "Emerson on the Scholar, 1833-1837," *PMLA* 85 (1970): 185-95.

Sloan, John H. "'The Miraculous Uplifting':Emerson's Relationship with his Audience." *Quarterly Journal of Speech* 52 (1966) 10-15.

Smith, Henry Nash. "Emerson's Problem of Vocation: A Note on 'The American Scholar'" *New England Quarterly* 12 (1939): 52-67.

Tacey, William S. "Emerson on Eloquence." *Today's Speech* 6 (1958): 22-27.

Thorp, Willard. "Emerson on Tour." *Quarterly Journal of Speech* 16 (1930): 19-34.

Williams, Paul 0. "Emerson in Alton, Illinois." *ESQ* 47 (1967): 98.

## EMERSON'S OWN WRITINGS

*The Collected Works of Ralph Waldo Emerson.* Ed. Robert E. Spiller and Alfred R. Ferguson. Vol. 1. *Nature, Addresses, and Lectures.* Cambridge, Mass.: Harvard University Press, 1971.

Vol. 2. *Essays. First Series.* Ed. Joseph Slater, Cambridge, Mass.: Harvard University Press, 1979.

Vol. 3. *Essays. Second Series.* Ed. Joseph Slater, Cambridge, Mass.: Harvard University Press, 1983.

Vol. 4. *Representative Men.* Ed. Joseph Slater, and Wallace E. Williams, Cambridge, Mass.: Harvard University Press, 1987.

*The Complete Sermons of Ralph Waldo Emerson.* Ed. Albert J. von Frank, et al. 4 vols. Columbia, Mo.: University of Missouri Press, 1989.

*The Complete Works of Ralph Waldo Emerson.* With a Biographical Introduction and Notes, by Edward Waldo Emerson, Centenary Edition. Boston and New York: Houghton Mifflin Co., 1903-1904. 12 vols.

*The Correspondence of Emerson and Carlyle.* Ed. Joseph Slater. New York: Columbia University Press, 1964.

*The Early Lectures of Ralph Waldo Emerson.* Ed. Stephen E. Whicher, Robert E. Spiller, and Wallace E. Williams. 3 vols., Cambridge: Harvard University Press, 1959, 1964, 1972.

*The Journals and Miscellaneous Notebooks of Ralph Waldo Emerson*, Ed. by William H. Gilman, et al. 16 vols., Cambridge: Harvard University Press, 1960-1982.

*The Letters of Ralph Waldo Emerson.* Ed. Ralph L. Rusk. 6 vols., New York: Columbia University Press, 1939.

*The Letters of Ralph Waldo Emerson.* Ed. Eleanor M. Tilton. Vol. 8, New York: Columbia University Press, 1991.

*Young Emerson Speaks.* Ed. Arthur C. McGiffert, Jr. Boston: Houghton Mifflin Co., 1938.

## BIBLIOGRAPHIES AND REFERENCE WORKS

Barton, William B., Jr. *A Calendar of the Complete Edition of the Sermons of Ralph Waldo Emerson.* Memphis, Tenn., 1977.

Cameron, Kenneth Walter. *Index-Concordance to Emerson's Sermons, with Homiletical Papers.* Hartford, Conn., 1963.

Charvat, William. *Emerson's American Lecture Engagements: A Chronological List.* New York, 1961.

Myerson, Joel. *Ralph Waldo Emerson: A Descriptive Bibliography.* Pittsburgh, Pa., 1982.

Scudder, Townsend, III. "A Chronological List of Emerson's Lectures on his British Lecture Tour of 1847-48." *PMLA* 51 (March,1936): 243-248.

# Index

## About the Author

LLOYD ROHLER, Associate Professor of Speech Communication, University of North Carolina, has written at length about American orators and oratory. His recent book-length studies include *Great Speeches for Criticism and Analysis* (1992).

**Great American Orators**

Patrick Henry, The Orator
*David A. McCants*

Anna Howard Shaw: Suffrage Orator and Social Reformer
*Wil A. Linkugel and Martha Solomon*

William Jennings Bryan: Orator of Small-Town America
*Donald K. Springen*

Robert M. La Follette, Sr.: The Voice of Conscience
*Carl R. Burgchardt*

Ronald Reagan: The Great Communicator
*Kurt Ritter and David Henry*

Clarence Darrow: The Creation of an American Myth
*Richard J. Jensen*

"Do Everything" Reform: The Oratory of Frances E. Willard
*Richard W. Leeman*

Abraham Lincoln the Orator: Penetrating the Lincoln Legend
*Lois J. Einhorn*

Mark Twain: Protagonist for the Popular Culture
*Marlene Boyd Vallin*

Delightful Conviction: Jonathan Edwards and the Rhetoric of Conversion
*Stephen R. Yarbrough and John C. Adams*

Harry S. Truman: Presidential Rhetoric
*Halford R. Ryan*

Dwight D. Eisenhower: Strategic Communcator
*Martin J. Medhurst*

www.ingramcontent.com/pod-product-compliance
Lightning Source LLC
Chambersburg PA
CBHW060529310726
48982CB00002B/476